Joseph Joy Dean

Devotions To The Sacred Heart Of Jesus

Containing Exercises For Confession, Communion, And The Holy Mass, With Numerous Other Prayers & Reflections Suited To The Devotion, 3rd Ed.

Joseph Joy Dean

Devotions To The Sacred Heart Of Jesus
Containing Exercises For Confession, Communion, And The Holy Mass, With Numerous Other Prayers & Reflections Suited To The Devotion, 3rd Ed.

ISBN/EAN: 9783337349455

Printed in Europe, USA, Canada, Australia, Japan

Cover: Foto ©Lupo / pixelio.de

More available books at **www.hansebooks.com**

DEVOTIONS

TO THE

SACRED HEART OF JESUS;

CONTAINING

EXERCISES FOR CONFESSION, COMMUNION,

AND THE

HOLY MASS,

WITH

NUMEROUS OTHER PRAYERS & REFLECTIONS

SUITED TO THE DEVOTION.

TRANSLATED FROM THE FRENCH, AND

REVISED, BY THE REV. JOSEPH JOY DEAN.

President of St. Bridget's Seminary, Blancherstown.

(REPRINTED FROM THE THIRD EDITION.)

LONDON:
R. WASHBOURNE, 18A. PATERNOSTER ROW.

PREFACE
TO THE THIRD EDITION.

——:o:——

It would indeed be superfluous to indulge in prefatory matter, illustrative of a Work which sufficiently explains itself; or to extol the merits of a Book, whose best eulogium is the fact, that it contains all which its Title—a Title so sacred—imparts.

It has been already submitted to the judgment of the Public. The very quick sale of the two former impressions, and an anxious enquiry for another Edition, are sufficient proofs of the approbation with which the Work has been received. A sincere desire on the part of the Translator, to meet the wishes of the Public, and also to assist thereby in the extension of this widely-spreading Devotion, has been the chief inducement to the publication of this present Edition.

The Work, it will be easily perceived, has been much improved and enlarged, not only by the addition of Reflections and other Exercises, (translated for the first time from the French,) well calculated to excite the devotion and enliven the piety of the sincere Christian, but also by the introduction of the PROPER MASS for the Festival of the Sacred Heart, the LITTLE OFFICE of the Sacred Heart, the NOVENA, and several other appropriate and necessary Devotions; altogether rendering it the most complete work of its kind ever yet published.

FIRST PART.

ON

THE DEVOTION
TO THE
SACRED HEART OF JESUS.

CHAPTER I.

Of the Origin and Progress of this Devotion.

THE devotion to the Sacred Heart of Jesus, of great antiquity in the Church, has been renewed in these latter times by the Blessed Mother Marguerite Marie Alacoque, a Religious of the Visitation, who died, aged forty, in the odour of sanctity, in the monastery of Parai-le-Monial, in Charolais, in the year 1690. The life of this great servant of God was embellished with every christian virtue; the Lord replenished her soul with a profusion of his heavenly grace, and chose her in order to revive the devotion to his Sacred Heart. Thus she expresses herself on this subject:—" Whilst prostrate before the blessed Sacrament, during the octave of the feast, I received from my Saviour extraordinary marks of his love; animated with a desire of making some return, and of repaying love with love, he disclosed to me his most Sacred Heart, saying, 'Behold this Heart, which has loved man to such excess, that it has exhausted and consumed itself to testify to him its love: you cannot give me a stronger proof of yours, than by carrying into effect what I have so often required to be done. From the greater number I receive ingratitude, contempt, irreverence, sacrilege, and indifference, which they manifest in this Sacrament of love; but what is still more afflicting is, that I receive these insults from hearts which are peculiarly consecrated to my service. Therefore I require of thee, that the first Friday after the octave of the feast of the Blessed Sacrament be particularly dedicated to honour my Heart, in making reparation to it, by an act of atonement, and going to Communion on that day, in order to repair the indignities which the Blessed Sacrament may have received during the time it has been exposed on the altars; and I promise thee, that my Heart shall be dilated, to impart abundantly the influence of its divine love, to those who shall render this honour, or cause it to be rendered, to my Heart.'"

This revelation corresponds with that which

Saint Gertrude had received four hundred years before, as we read in her life, when God communicated to her, that he had particularly reserved for *these latter ages* the devotion to his Sacred Heart, in order to awaken the faithful from their torpor, and excite them to his love.

The progress of this devotion was obvious and rapid.—After the death of Father La Colombiere, of the society of Jesus, a man as well known for his piety as his works, the journal of his spiritual retreats was published, in which is contained the revelation which we have just now quoted; and this was the first means which the Lord employed, not only to give publicity to this revelation, but also to increase the devotion to his Sacred Heart. Several other works appeared soon after on the same subject, and many new editions were published. Thus the devotion to the Sacred Heart extended to different provinces; and, notwithstanding the opposition it had to encounter, it was embraced by immense numbers of all ranks. Several of our bishops approved of it in their dioceses.

From France it passed into the neighbouring countries; then to the most distant, with a success and rapidity which must have been the effect of divine interposition. The sovereign Pontiffs granted indulgences to the pious associations which were formed in honour of the Sacred Heart of Jesus; and we now reckon above a thousand of these holy sodalities. In fine, Pope Clement 13th, by a decree of the 6th of February, 1765, confirmed this holy devotion, by an authentic approbation of an appropriate Office and Mass, in honour of the adorable Heart.

I shall here mention what is expressed in the Office of the Sacred Heart of Jesus, approved by the Pope:—" The Sovereign Pontiff, Clement 13th, permitted the celebration of the feast of the Sacred Heart of Jesus, to those churches which sought this permission, that the faithful, under the symbol of the Heart, might remember with more devotion and advantage, the love which Jesus Christ testified, by suffering and dying for the redemption of mankind, and instituting, in memory of his death, the adorable sacrament of his Body and Blood."

CHAPTER II.

The Excellence and Solidity of this Devotion, its Object and its End.

CAN there be any thing more holy, more venerable, or more august, than the Sacred Heart of the Son of God; and at the same time, what more attractive, or more amiable? We adore the Body and Blood of

Jesus Christ: how, then, can we refuse our homage to his Sacred Heart, the seat of all virtues, the source of all graces, the object of the complacencies of the Eternal Father; to this Heart, always abounding with goodness, with tenderness, and with love for us?

But we ought not to rest satisfied in contemplating the Heart of Jesus, as the most amiable and most tender of Hearts; we must likewise view this divine Heart as the most afflicted, and the most unworthily treated; for every one knows, that few there are who make any return to Jesus Christ, and love him sincerely; the greater part repay his benefits and love with the most profound forgetfulness and stupid insensibility. How many are there who insult it by their sacrileges, irreverences, and by the most criminal profanations!

The particular and precise object of the devotion to the Sacred Heart of Jesus, is the adorable Heart of the Son of God; a living Heart, by its union to the most holy soul; a divine Heart, by its hypostatical union with the person of the Word. It is this Heart, considered, on the one side, as inflamed with an infinite love for man; and, on the other, as outraged by the ingratitude of those very men for whom he has suffered the most bitter and excruciating torments, and for whom he was pleased to be nailed to the tree of the cross. Now, all these different objects united,—objects so sublime, so admirable, so divine, and so amiable,—ought to excite in us two sentiments, truly just and rational, which constitute the particular end proposed in this devotion; namely, an ardent love for Jesus Christ, which should, as far as possible, correspond to the love with which his divine Heart burns for us; and a bitter sorrow for the outrages which are daily offered him; which sorrow may, in some degree, compensate for the ingratitude of men. All the exercises of our devotion to the Sacred Heart of Jesus ought to be directed to these two objects.

We must in the first place acknowledge, by frequent acts of love and adoration, and by every kind of homage, the love with which the Sacred Heart of Jesus has burned, and continues still to burn for us; particularly in the divine Eucharist, which may be considered as the abridgment of all the wonders which he hath wrought in our favour.

We ought, in the second place, to endeavour to repair, in every possible manner; the insults to which this love has exposed him, during his mortal life, and to which he is every day exposed in the adorable Sacrament of the Altar, where he is so little loved, so little known to men, and often so unworthily treated, even by those to whom he is known.

CHAPTER III.

The immense Treasures contained in the Sacred Heart of Jesus.

THE Heart of Jesus is an inexhaustible source, in which you will find all you can desire. It is a furnace of love, where every other love must be consumed, and, above all, our self-love, and the vicious passions it produces, which are human respect, ambition, and self-gratification.—It is by immersing these fatal inclinations in this ocean of divine love, that you will acquire all the assistance necessary for the various states of your soul.

If you are involved in darkness, ignorance, and error, the Heart of Jesus contains all the riches of the wisdom and of the knowledge of God; this divine Heart will enlighten and direct you; it will especially teach you to know and love this object, which alone is worthy of love; it will teach you to know and to hate yourself.

If your distracted and dissipated mind continually wanders on a variety of vain and dangerous objects, and leaves your soul in dryness and disgust, have recourse to the Heart of Jesus; by its solitude and fervour, it will fix your mind and imagination in uniting them to itself.

If you are influenced by pride or vainglory, destroy this pride in the profound humiliations of the Heart of Jesus: this Sacred Heart is an abyss of humility.

When your soul, deprived of real blessings, laments over its poverty and misery, address yourself to the Heart of Jesus: it is the centre of all virtues, it abounds in the most precious treasures, and it ardently desires to communicate them: it will enrich you.

When your mind is in a state of despondence and desolation, you must run to the Heart of Jesus, and lose yourself in this ocean of consolation, without anxiety to experience its sweetness, until it shall please him to grant it you.

If you are terrified at the sight of your infidelities, inconstancy, and many relapses, go often to the Heart of Jesus; you will find it unchangeable in its love and beneficence towards you; and as it is the throne of mercy, and the strength of the weak, it will raise you up and fortify you.

To make amends for your ingratitude to the Eternal Father, for the innumerable favours you have received, offer him the adorable Heart of his Son in acknowledgment of his benefits, and beseech this amiable Heart, in its infinite abundance, to supply your deficiencies.

If you are in trouble or uneasiness, disturbed by impatience and anger, run to the Heart of Jesus; it is the source af meekness and of peace, which it will impart to you.

In your afflictions, in your most bitter sufferings, the Heart of Jesus, which is the refuge of afflicted hearts, and is in heaven the joy and delight of the angels and saints, will console you, and teach you to suffer with patience and constancy.

When you are alarmed or agitated by fear, retire to the Heart of Jesus, as to an assured asylum; it will inspire you with confidence and love, and make you sensible that fear should yield to love.

If you are, as it were, surrounded with the deadly shades of sin, go to the Heart of Jesus; you will there discover the source of life, and thence you will draw new life, in which you will see no longer but with the eyes of Jesus; you will act only by his inspirations, and will love nothing but according to his Heart.

In a word, in every situation rush into this abyss of love and charity, and, if possible, do not depart, until you shall have been penetrated with the fire by which it is inflamed for God and man.

CHAPTER IV.

Consoling and remarkable Words of the Blessed Marguerite Marie, speaking of the devotion to the Sacred Heart.

IN speaking of this devotion, the Blessed Marguerite thus expresses herself:—" I know of no exercise of piety in the spiritual life, better calculated to raise, in a short time, a soul to the highest state of sanctity, or to make it relish the true delight which is found in the service of God, than the devotion to the Sacred Heart of Jesus: Yes, I assert with confidence, were it known how agreeable this devotion is to Jesus Christ, that there is no christian, how little soever he might be influenced by love for this amiable Saviour, who would not eagerly reduce it to practice."

"Endeavour" continues she, addressing the person to whom she writes, "that persons professing the religious state embrace it: for they will derive so many helps from it, that no other means would be necessary to re-establish the primitive fervour in the most lax communities, and to lead the most fervent to the summit of perfection."

"Our divine Saviour revealed to me, that those who laboured for the salvation of souls, will be enabled to soften the most obdurate hearts, and labour with wonderful success, *if* they themselves are penetrated with a tender devotion to this adorable Heart.

"The laity will find, in this devotion, all the helps necessary for their state; namely, peace in their families, comfort in their troubles, and the blessings of heaven in all their undertakings. It is in this adorable Heart that they will effectually find refuge during their lives, and especially at the hour of death.—Ah! how sweet to die, after having had a constant devotion to the Sacred Heart of that divine Being, who is one day to be our Judge! In fine, it is evident, that there is no person in the world, who would not experience every assistance from heaven, had he for Jesus a grateful love, such as is evinced in the devotion to his Sacred Heart."

In another part of her writings, on the same subject, she mentions, "Our Lord discovered to me treasures of love, and abundance ef graces, which should be imparted to those persons who would consecrate themselves, and sacrifice all, to procure for this adorable Heart all the honour, love, and glory in their power; but treasures so great, that it is impossible for me to express them. This amiable Heart, as being the source of all good, ardently desires to be known to men, over whom it wishes to establish its empire, in order to supply all their wants; for which reason, he wishes that they should address him with confidence: and I think that there is no method more efficacious for obtaining what we ask, than by offering it through the mediation of the adorable sacrifice of the Mass."

Having spoken of a particular favour which she received from our Divine Redeemer, she expresses herself thus :—" He revealed to me, that the desire he had of being perfectly beloved by men, had induced him to manifest to them his Sacred Heart; thereby proposing an object so proper to engage them to love him, and to love him sincerely; that in this Heart he opened all the treasures of his love, grace, mercy, sanctification, and salvation, which this Heart contains; that all those who would wish to render to it, and obtain for it, all the love and honour they could possibly procure, should be enriched with a profusion of those treasures, of which this divine Heart is the fruitful and inexhaustible source.

"But what caused me at the same time a degree of anguish, the most acute I ever experienced, was, that when this Heart was presented to me, I heard these words: 'I have an ardent thirst to be honoured and loved by men, in the Sacrament of my love; and, notwithstanding, I rarely find one who endeavours, according to my desire, to allay my thirst, by any return of love.'"

All the foregoing passages have been extracted from the "History of the Venerable Marguerite Marie."

CHAPTER V.

The Practice of the Devotion to the Sacred Heart of Jesus.

Practice for every Year.

THE first and principal practice of devotion to the Sacred Heart of Jesus is the celebration of its festival, which is fixed for the first Friday after the octave of Corpus Christi. This day ought to be solemnized by approaching the sacraments, prayer, spiritual reading, visiting our Lord in the adorable Sacrament of the altar, and other good works.

The preceding evening prepare yourself for this great day, by some acts of penance or charity, to dispose your heart for the reception of grace. On the day of the feast, approach the sacraments of Penance and the Eucharist. In your confession accuse yourself, and detest your irreverences and infidelities towards the most holy Sacrament of the altar. You ought to communicate with peculiar fervour, as your intention should be to repair the negligence and tepidity of all your former communions. After twelve, in a particular visit, which you will make to the Blessed Sacrament, offer to the adorable Heart of Jesus an act of atonement, in reparation of all the insults he every day suffers in the Eucharist, and compensate for those of which you have been guilty.—The other practices you will find in the exercises appointed for this feast.

Practice for every Month.

In addition to the principal feast, which occurs but once a year, the first Friday of every month has been consecrated to honour the Sacred Heart of Jesus; on which day may be performed all or part of the exercises appointed for the feast,—namely, to go to confession, to communion, to visit the most holy Sacrament, to perform acts of atonement, &c.; so that those who have an ardent zeal for the honour of the Heart of Jesus, may consider this first Friday as a feast peculiar to themselves; which at the same time should not prevent them from pursuing their usual occupations, provided they are careful to offer and direct all their actions to the glory of the Sacred Heart, and in the spirit of reparation.

Practice for every Week.

Fervent souls, who wish to obtain more abundant graces, are not content with honouring the Sacred Heart of Jesus once a month; they also consecrate to it one day every week, which is Friday. On this day they practise some devout exercise, and recite some particular prayer, in honour of this divine Heart, according to every one's devotion.

Practices for every Day, and for every Occasion.

These practices are the more estimable, as they may be frequent, and are within the reach of every one. They consist, first, in performing all the actions of the day, in union with the Sacred Heart of Jesus: thus, if you pray, pray with it; if you work, work with it and in it; if you suffer, suffer with it and for it.—Admirable secret for amassing treasures of merit, graces, and glory!—For as there is nothing so great, in the sight of God, as the Heart of his Son, so nothing can be more agreeable to him than the union of our actions and sufferings with those of this adorable Heart. Its dispositions, infinitely holy, will supply our imperfect dispositions; and by this union our actions will become, as it were, of infinite value.

Secondly, think often of this divine Heart, and have recourse to it in all your wants; consult it in your doubts and perplexities; address it in your troubles and afflictions; unfold to it all your thoughts, your views and projects; represent to it your defects, temptations, and passions; beg of it a remedy for all your sufferings; live in it, and breathe only for it; it will be your all, provided you seek all in this Sacred Heart.

Thirdly, approach often to the Holy Table, to unite yourself by a fervent communion to the dearly-beloved of your heart, and endeavour to correspond with the ardent desire he has of giving himself to you.

Fourthly, often visit our Lord in his churches: when you have occasion to pass one, be happy to enter it and once more assure the God of love, who dwelleth therein, that you love him, and that you never will love any other but him.

Fifthly, if the severity of weather, indisposition, or the avocations of your state, confine you to the house, and deprive you of the consolation of going in person to pay homage to the God of your heart, in the sanctuary where he resides; reflect a moment, and fly thither in spirit, or invoke your Guardian-angel to present himself there for you, and in your name to adore, love, and praise your divine Redeemer.

Sixthly, should you unhappily have offended the Lord, or learn that he has been offended, immediately offer to the Divine Majesty, in sentiments of humble compunction, and in the spirit of atonement, some one of the virtues of the adorable Heart of Jesus.

Seventhly, place in your oratory a picture of the Sacred Heart, and every time you enter your house, or at least when you go out, go and salute this divine Heart, and implore its holy benediction. Several persons carry about them a scapular, or a medal of the Sacred Heart, and kiss it frequently in the day. The celebrated and pious Lanspergeus, a Carthusian monk, speaks thus of the picture of the Sacred Heart of Jesus: "I would recommend you to put in such places as you frequently pass some pious picture of this adorable Heart, the sight of which may remind you frequently to renew your devout exercises in its honour. You may even, as you feel interiorly affected, kiss tenderly this picture, with the same devotion that you would the very Heart of Jesus Christ; entering in spirit into this deified Heart, ardently imprinting on it your own heart, and immersing in it your whole soul, desiring that it may be there absorbed, and endeavouring to inhale into your heart the spirit which animates the Heart of Jesus, its graces, its virtues; in a word, whatever is salutary in this Sacred Heart, which surpasses all measure; for the Heart of Jesus is a superabundant source of all goodness. It is a most useful and pious practice to honour, with particular devotion, this adorable Heart, which ought to be your asylum and your resource in all your necessities, that you may thence derive the comfort and assistance of which you stand in need; for when all mankind abandon and deceive you, be assured that this faithful Heart never will deceive you, never will abandon you."

We may here add, that our Lord revealed to the venerable religious whom he particularly raised up to renew this holy devotion, that he wished that this picture should be honoured, and that he would communicate abundantly his graces where it should be revered, and on those who would honour it. Happy those who know how to make use of it, in order to animate their piety in prayer, their confidence in affliction; and to call to their minds the meekness, humility, and all the virtues of which this Sacred Heart is so perfect a model.

Eighthly, enter into a confraternity established in honour of the most Sacred Heart of Jesus, and endeavour to be actuated by the spirit of that body, and to be exact in the pious exercises which they practise.

Ninthly, endeavour to extend this devotion. The more you love the amiable Jesus, the more will you desire that he should be loved; the love which we bear him is a devouring fire, which seeks to communicate itself. Ask then, often, and with fervent prayers, an increase of devotion to the Sacred Heart of Jesus.

Exert yourself as much as your state of life and circumstances will permit, or as far as an enlightened zeal may inspire you, to establish this pious devotion in the cities or places in which you reside. Would it be difficult for a father or mother to inspire their children and servants with this holy devotion, and to teach them to practise it? Could not a master easily influence his pupils to relish this devotion? a prior or prioress, their subjects? a confessor, his penitents? a preacher, his hearers? a friend, his friends?

The ardent love with which some fervent souls are inflamed prompts them to holy exertions. Sometimes they would get sermons preached on this devotion; sometimes they would erect new confraternities, new oratories, new altars, in honour of the adorable Heart of Jesus, or at least they would contribute to them according to their power.

To distribute books which treat of the worship due to the sacred Heart; to get paintings, medals, and pictures executed which represent it, are not these so many means which may be employed, according as the state of every one may permit? Those who are devoted to the Sacred Heart of Jesus are particularly careful to render, and to cause to be rendered by others, as much as they can, to those pious images the respect which is due to them, in order to repair the injury which the devil has done to the adorable Heart of Jesus, in inspiring sometimes contempt for its picture. We shall here quote, for the consolation of souls devoted to this divine Heart, what the Blessed Marguerite mentions in one of her letters:—" I think that the Lord showed me the names of several persons which were written on the Sacred Heart of Jesus, on account of the desire they had to honour it; and on that account he never would suffer them to be effaced."

Tenthly, those who are devoted to the Sacred Heart of Jesus, and those who have the happiness of being received into any confraternity of the Sacred Heart of our Lord, ought to be considered as disciples the most devoted to Jesus Christ, and even as men called to be the friends of his Sacred Heart. From these glorious qualities three inferences may be especially drawn. The first is, to look on themselves as particularly obliged to repair, as much as they possibly can, by their homage and their love, the outrages and reproaches to which love has exposed the Son of God in the course of his holy life, and to which he exposes his love every day in the most holy Sacrament of the altar; and to redouble their love towards a God so good, who gives them more particularly his Heart, to serve as an asylum and retreat against dangers and temptations. For this purpose, they should particularly devote themselves to those exercises, the object of which is, the adoration of the holy Eucharist; namely, visit the most holy Sacrament, hear Mass daily, approach frequently the Holy Table, to edify all by the respect and modesty of their deportment in the churches.

Another effect which should result from these qualities is, to look on themselves as being more obliged to practise charity towards their neighbour, and to make a particular profession of it. "By this," the divine Heart again repeats, "shall all men know that you are my disciples, if you have love one for another."—*St. John* xiii. 35. Wherefore they should pardon sincerely and willingly; they should carefully avoid disputes, and prevent them; they should suppress all feelings of anger, hatred, revenge, aversion, &c., endeavouring to testify more cordiality to those in whom they shall find least conformity and sympathy with their dispositions; they should practise works of mercy, namely, to assist the poor, attend the sick, comfort the afflicted, &c. They should extend their charity to the relief of the souls in purgatory, who are often much neglected. These suffering souls are dear to the divine Heart of Jesus, and he particularly expects that his disciples and his friends will make every effort to comfort and deliver them.

The third effect regards their personal perfection. They must not rest satisfied with ordinary virtues, but they should aspire to the most perfect. The Heart of Jesus is particularly proposed to them as their model, in order that they may possess its spirit, its affections, and its sentiments: let them esteem what this divine Heart esteems; let them hate and despise what It hates and despises. To purify themselves from the smallest faults, and to avoid them; to make frequent examinations of their interior; to love retirement and prayer; to fill their minds with good thoughts and holy affections, by reading good books; assiduity in hearing the word of God, by the consideration of pious pictures, and holy conversations with pious and enlightened persons; to direct to God their actions, their affections, and their undertakings; to accustom themselves to think of his divine presence, of his holy will, of the dispositions of the Sacred Heart of Jesus: these are so many holy practices, which will render them more and more conformable to the spirit of Jesus.

Eleventhly, in a word, in order to animate you still more to augment your devotion to the adorable Heart of Jesus, and revive your fervour, if unhappily it should have abated, devote from time to time half an hour, in reflecting on the urgent motives which should induce you to practise this pious devotion. Consider how just and reasonable this devotion is, how useful and salutary, how sweet and consoling; but reflect, in a particular manner, on the excellence of the adorable Heart of Jesus, its amiable and infinite perfections, the striking proofs of the immense love which the Sacred Heart has for us, and the extreme ingratitude with which we return his love.

Enter more and more into the dispositions suitable or necessary to promote this tender devotion to the Sacred Heart of Jesus. These dispositons are, a great horror of sin, a lively faith, an ardent desire to love our Lord Jesus Christ, and a recollected and interior life. Guard against the obstacles which may deprive you of it: these are tepidity, self-love, inward pride, or any unmortified passion. In a word, exert yourself to overcome these obstacles, by humility, mortification, prayer, by frequent communion, visiting the most holy Sacrament, meditation, and by fidelity in acquitting yourself of the practices, either exterior or interior, suitable to this pious devotion. Address yourself often to the august Mary, in order that she may introduce you to the Sacred Heart of Jesus. Invoke for this purpose the holy angels, especially your angel-guardian; implore the assistance of the saints, and particularly of Saint Joseph, St. John the Evangelist, St. Francis de Sales, St. Francis of Assisium,

St. Bernardin of Sienna, St. Philip Neri, St. Francis Xavier, St. Louis Gonzague, St. Teresa, St. Gertrude, and of so many others, who have been inflamed with so ardent a love for the amiable Jesus, and who are eager to procure for you an entrance into this Sacred Heart, if you pray to them with fervour. Jesus Christ pointed out St. Francis of Assisium as a special advocate to the Blessed Marguerite, and revealed to her that this great saint was particularly united to his divine Heart, and that he had peculiar influence in obtaining favours from It. We shall here relate the words which St. Louis Gonzague addressed to Nicholas Louis Celistini, a novice of the Society of Jesus, at Rome, who, being at the point of death, was suddenly restored, by the intercession of this great saint, the 10th of February, 1765 :—
"Through my intercession," said he, "the Lord grants you life, to employ it for your own perfection, and to extend, as much as is in your power, the devotion to the Sacred Heart of Jesus; a devotion most pleasing to heaven."

It is thus we read in the account of this miraculous cure, which was published at Rome, with the authority of the judicial and authentic forms. Can we therefore doubt but this amiable saint interests himself in procuring for us, by his intercession, the advantages of a devotion to which he himself invites in so extraordinary and miraculous a manner?

CHAPTER VI.

Some particular Devotions in honour of the Sacred Heart of Jesus.

I.

To offer to God, at every hour, the Acts of Love which the Sacred Heart of Jesus, living on Earth, offered to the eternal Father in Heaven.

A PERSON of eminent piety, and of singular devotion to the Sacred Heart of Jesus, observed this practice, which she had learned from her Angel-guardian. At every hour the clock struck, she offered to God for her sins, and for all those which had been committed during that hour, the acts of love by which the Sacred Heart of Jesus had glorified the Eternal Father, during that same hour while this Divine Heart lived on earth.

II.

To go to Communion the nine first Fridays of nine successive Months, in honour of the Heart of Jesus Christ.

The Blessed Mother Marguerite practised this devotion, with which, she observes, she was inspired by our Lord, who gave her reason to hope for those who would practise the same, not only the grace of final perseverance, but also that of receiving the sacraments of the church before their death. This practice consists in going to communion, with this intention, every first Friday during nine successive months.

III.
To unite ourselves to the holy angels, who adore our Lord in the holy Sacrament of the Altar.

In order to practise this devotion, you may recite the following prayer, or some one similar to it:—

A PRAYER.

BLESSED spirits, who surround the holy altars, permit me to unite myself with you in the homages which you render to the Sacred Heart of Jesus. Vouchsafe to join with me in my humble prayers; and, by your respect and your love, supply, I beseech you, whatever is wanting in me to honour worthily my Saviour and my God.

IV.
To offer to the Eternal Father the merits of Jesus Christ, for the Conversion of Sinners.

This practice consists, first, in offering to the Eternal Father the infinite satisfaction which Jesus Christ, on the tree of the cross, made to the Divine Justice for the conversion of sinners, beseeching him to render efficacious the merits of the precious Blood of this Divine Saviour, in all the souls which sin has destroyed; so that being raised from the death of sin to the life of grace, they may glorify God eternally.

Secondly, in offering to him the infinite love of the Heart of Jesus, that he may warm those hearts which are cold in his service, and inflame them with his love, in order that he may be loved and glorified by them for time and eternity.

Thirdly, in presenting to the Eternal Father, the submission of the will of his Son in all things, to his divine will; in order that we may obtain, by the merit of this precious obedience, the grace of accomplishing his holy will.

V.

To make use of the Beads of the Heart, which may be done in the following manner:—

By viewing or pressing to your heart the medal, image, or scapular of the Heart of Jesus, or a crucifix, or a cross, as many times as there are grains on the beads, which is done without saying either Pater, Ave, or any other vocal prayer, except some short aspiration which may flow from the tender feelings of the heart.

They may likewise, at every grain of the beads they pass over, have the intention by this only action, of protesting to the Sacred Heart of Jesus that they adore it, that they love it, return it thanks, implore its pardon, subject themselves entirely to its will, and give themselves up to be guided by it. The same protestations may be made to the Eternal Father and to the Holy Ghost. At other times their intention may be to pray for some particular grace; for example, the love of God, humility, patience. The beads are peculiarly adapted to infirm persons, who cannot recite many vocal prayers, nor apply themselves to mental prayer.

SECOND PART.

EXERCISES AND PRAYERS

IN HONOUR OF THE MOST

SACRED HEART OF JESUS.

[In the collection of prayers which we give, each person can make choice of those which may be most agreeable to his devotion and interior feelings; not supposing it necessary that he recite all that shall be set down in each exercise. But we ought to remember that our prayers will be so much the more acceptable to the Heart of Jesus, as our hearts shall be penetrated with their meaning. Thus, before prayer, reflect for a moment and consider what you are, and what God is, to whom you are about to address yourself. By so doing, you will comprehend the importance of the action you are going to perform, and the sentiments of humility, of sorrow for your faults, of respect, of attention, of modesty, of fervour, of love and confidence, with which your mind should always be filled, when you endeavour to discharge the duty of Prayer. By praying with these interior dispositions, you will glorify God, and merit to be heard by him.]

A PRAYER,

Which may be added to the Morning Prayer.

MOST holy and most adorable Trinity, Father, Son, and Holy Ghost, one only God in three persons, I adore thee, I thank thee, I love thee with all my heart, through the Sacred Hearts of Jesus and of Mary. In union with these holy Hearts I offer thee my thoughts, my words, my actions, my sufferings, and above all my heart; and I beseech thee, by the merits of these same Hearts, to grant me the grace not to offend thee this day, to increase more and more in thy love, to live and die in thy love, under the protection of the Sacred Hearts of Jesus and of Mary. *Amen.*

A PRAYER,

Which may be added to Prayers for Night.

SACRED Heart of Jesus, I adore thee, I love thee, and I thank thee, for all the favours I have received from thee this day and in the course of my life. Oh! my Divine Saviour, penetrated with grief at the sight of my sins, I detest them with all my heart, for thy love. Pardon me them, and bless the repose which I am going to take, to repair my strength, which I do not wish to employ, with the assistance of thy grace, but to serve thee and to love thee. Sacred Heart of Mary, my good angel, my holy patron, adore and love the Sacred Heart of Jesus, and let your prayers ascend to it in my favour; protect me for this night, during the remainder of my life, and at the hour of my death. *Amen.*

Observe the pious practice of examining your conscience every night.

A PRAYER,

To offer our Actions to the Sacred Heart of Jesus.

ADORABLE Heart, which in all thou hast done and suffered on earth, hast sought the glory of the Celestial Father, and the accomplishment of his most holy will, grant that in union with thy merits and with thy most holy dispositions, I may offer to him the action I am about to commence, with the sole desire of pleasing him and doing his will; and grant me the grace to perform it as I ought. *Amen.*

AN ACT OF ATONEMENT,

To the Sacred Heart of Jesus, which may be made in common, or in private.

ADORABLE Heart of my Saviour and my God, penetrated with a lively sorrow at the sight of the outrages which thou hast received, and which thou daily dost receive in the Sacrament of thy love, behold me prostrate at the foot of thy altar, to make an acceptable atonement. O! that I were able, by my homage and veneration, to make satisfaction to thine injured honour, and efface, with my tears and with my blood, so many irreverences, profanations, and sacrileges, which outrage thine infinite greatness. How well should my life be disposed of, could it be sacrificed for so worthy an object! Pardon, Divine Saviour, my ingratitude, and all the infidelities and indignities which I myself have committed against thy Sovereign Majesty. Remember that thy adorable Heart, bearing the weight of my sins in the days of its mortal life, was sorrowful even unto death: do not suffer thy agony and thy blood to be unprofitable to me. Annihilate within me my criminal heart, and give me one according to thine,—a heart contrite and humble, a heart pure and spotless, a heart which may be henceforth a victim consecrated to thy glory, and inflamed with the sacred fire of thy love. O Lord, I deplore in the bitterness of my heart, my former irreverences and sacrileges, which I wish in future to repair, by my pious deportment in the churches, my assiduity in visiting, and my devotion and fervour in receiving the most holy Sacrament of the Altar. But in order to render my respect and my adoration more grateful to thee, I unite them with those which are rendered to thee in our temples, by those blessed spirits who are at the foot of thy sacred tabernacles. Hear their vows, O my God, and accept the homages of a heart which returns to thee with the sole view of loving only thee, that I may merit loving thee eternally. *Amen.*

AN ACT,

Of Consecration of Ourselves to the Sacred Heart of Jesus.

[It is necessary to remark here, that by the words consecration, donation, promise, or other similar expressions, which are sometimes used in this or in other acts, we do not understand them to imply a vow, but merely a purpose or resolution. None ought, without due consideration, to engage himself by vow; and generally it is proper to consult before-hand, on this point, some enlightened and prudent person.]

ADORABLE Heart of my amiable Jesus, seat of all virtues, inexhaustible source of graces, what could have induced thee to deliver thyself up to death for me, and to give thyself to me in the Sacrament of the Eucharist, though thou foresawest that my wicked heart should be stained with a thousand sins, and should feel for thee only hardness and indifference? These incomprehensible proofs of the tenderness of thy love, even when I did not love thee, make me hope that thou wilt accept the desire by which I wish in future to testify my love for thee. Accept then, my adorable Saviour, the ardent desire which I have at this moment, to consecrate myself entirely to the honour and glory of thy Sacred Heart. Accept the donation which I make to thee without reserve, of all that I am. I devote to thee my being and my life, my thoughts, my labours, and my sufferings. Dispose of me as thou pleasest. Receive in particular the offering which I make to thee of my heart, and of all its affections, which I wish to regulate in all things conformably to thy will. Purify, divine Jesus, and consume my sacrifice by the sacred fire of thy love.

Behold me then, O my God, behold me entirely thine; behold me entirely devoted to thy Sacred Heart, and for ever. God of Majesty, how great are thy mercies towards an ungrateful and guilty soul! Ah! what am I, that thou shouldst deign to accept the offering which I make to thee, of my faithless heart, a heart so unworthy in every respect of being presented to thee? The offering is made, then, since thou dost not reject it; my heart shall be only thine; created objects shall have no part in it. Art not thou my King, my Father, my Saviour, my Friend, my Master, my God, and my All? I ought not, then, and I do not wish to live but for thee.

God of my heart, accept the sacrifice

which the most abject of thy creatures has just made to thy divine and august Heart, in order to repair the ingratitude which I have shown in resisting the charms of thy love. In giving thee my heart, the offering, I acknowledge, is small; but at least I give thee all that I can give, and all that thou desirest of me.

Teach me, therefore, Divine Master, the perfect forgetfulness of myself, to the end that thou alone mayest occupy all my thoughts; and as I desire to perform nothing henceforth but for thee, grant that every thing I do may be worthy of thee. Teach me, above all, by what means I shall arrive at the purity of thy love; or rather give me this pure, tender, generous, and constant love for thee. Grant me that profound humility, and unalterable charity for my neighbour, without which I cannot please thee; and accomplish in me thy divine will, during time and eternity. *Amen.*

ANOTHER ACT,

Of Consecration to the Adorable Heart of Jesus.

I GIVE and consecrate to the adorable Heart of Jesus my being, my life, my thoughts, my words, my actions, my pains, and my sufferings. I wish only for life, that my days may be employed in loving, honouring, and glorifying it. I take thee then, O divine Heart, for the object of my love, the protector of my life, the assurance of my salvation, the remedy of my inconstancy, the repairer of all my defects, and my certain asylum at the hour of my death. O Heart, abounding in mercy, turn from me the arrows of the just wrath of the Celestial Father. I place all my confidence in thee; for I fear every thing from my weakness, as I hope for every thing from thy goodness. Destroy in me every thing which may displease and resist thee; implant so deeply thy love in my heart, that I may never forget thee, nor be separated from thee. I conjure thee, by thy infinite goodness, to transform me into a victim entirely consecrated to thy glory, which may be from this moment inflamed, and one day consumed in the fire of thy love. This is the only object of my desires, having no other ambition than that of living and dying in thee and for thee. *Amen.*

AN ACT,

Of Consecration to the Sacred Heart of Jesus, proper for Religious Persons, and which contains the Renewal of their Vows.

MY adorable Redeemer, I give and consecrate myself to thy Sacred Heart in the most unlimited maner I posibly can.

I am as it were nailed to thy cross by the vows of my profession; I renew them in this divine Heart, in the presence of heaven and of earth, and I return thee thanks for having inspired me with them. I confess that thy yoke is neither unpleasing nor heavy, and that I do not feel encumbered by my bonds; I should wish, on the contrary, to multiply them, and bind the knot still closer.

I therefore embrace the amiable cross of my vocation. Until my last breath it shall be my pleasure and my glory. "God forbid that I should glory, save in the cross of our Lord Jesus Christ, by whom the world is crucified to me, and I to the world." God grant that I may have no other treasure but poverty, no other delights but sufferings, no other love but for Himself. No, my Saviour, never shall I disengage myself from thee, but I shall for ever attach myself to thee. The most narrow ways of the perfect life to which I am called have no terrors for me, because thou art my light and my strength. I hope thou wilt vouchsafe to grant me firmness in all temptations, grace to overcome the efforts of my enemies, and that thou wilt extend to me that benevolent hand which has already imparted to me so many graces, and that it may be more bountiful to me. I conjure thee, my adorable Jesus, by thy blood, by thy wounds, and by thy Sacred

Heart, to grant, that by the consecration which I make to thee of all that I am, I may become this day a new and perfect victim of thy love. *Amen.*

AN EXERCISE OF PRAISE AND ADORATION,

In Honour of the Sacred Heart of Jesus.

ADORABLE Heart of Jesus, hypostatically united to the eternal Word, and thereby the true Heart of God; ineffable Heart of incomprehensible perfection, every sentiment and affection of which correspond to the greatness and infinite majesty of God, and therefore worthy of infinite adoration and praise. In thee, O divine Heart, all celestial gifts are united; thou art the inexhaustible source of every good; thou art the principal of all the virtues, the most pure, the most sublime, the most heroic; thou art the throne of the created and eternal charity; thou alone has been a victim worthy of the divine justice, alone capable of satisfying it; thou art, by all these titles, the most worthy object of the praise, homage, and adoration of angels and of men. Prostrate in thy presence, with the most profound submission of which my heart is capable, I acknowledge with joy and admiration thy greatness and unbounded excellence. I am sorry I cannot, by my homages, my adorations, and praises, procure for thee the glory which is thy due. O that I could captivate with thy love all those who do not know thee, who do not adore thee; and engage them to render to thee the worship and the honour which thou dost deserve! But, alas! as I am very sensible that the affections of my heart are nothing, that they are unworthy of thee, I offer thee, in order to supply my unworthiness and my inability, all the honours and all the praises which thou receivest from the angels and from the saints; I offer thee that which is still more acceptable, namely, the Heart of the august Mary. I unite my misery to this sublime Heart, which, as far as a pure creature can do it, is alone capable of honouring and praising thee. Supported by these merits, I offer myself entirely to thee, and I consecrate to thy glory all that I am. Hear my vows, O adorable Heart, receive me under thy amiable and all-powerful protection. *Amen*.

AN EXERCISE OF LOVE,

Towards the Sacred Heart of Jesus.

MOST amiable Heart of Jesus, which uniting to the divine perfections proper to the Son of God, all the human perfections proper to the son of man! Heart the most noble, the most powerful, the most liberal, the most magnificent of all hearts, and at the same time the most sweet, the most humble, the most pure, the most innocent, the most patient, and the most charitable! Heart of our God, of our Redeemer, of our Benefactor! Heart of our Friend, of our Brother, of our Father, of the Spouse of our souls! worthy, by these amiable titles, of all our tenderness: thou art the true and solid lover of men: not only the just but sinners are included in thy boundless charity. Thou wast pierced with a lance on the cross for our love. Thou art open to be the refuge of pure souls, and the place of their repose. Thou hast been the innocent victim of our sins, and, in order to expiate them, thou wast immolated to the Divine Justice with inexpressible anguish. O Sacred Heart, which by all these qualities art the most worthy object of our love, of our gratitude, and of our tenderness, I wish I were able to consume myself for thy love! Yes, from this moment, assisted by thy grace, I love thee with all my heart, with all my soul, with all my strength, and I would wish to make thee loved by all men. I rejoice for the infinite perfections which thou possessest, and for the homages, praises, and benedictions which thou continually dost receive from the angels and saints. How much do I grieve, that I have hitherto loved thee so little! Enkindle in my heart a flame which may atone for my former tepidity, and which may always increase, until I shall have the happiness of being entirely and perfectly inflamed with thy love in a happy eternity. Amen.

AN EXERCISE OF CONFIDENCE,

Towards the Sacred Heart of Jesus.

DIVINE Heart of Jesus, thy wisdom infinite, thy power boundless, thy love immense; thou knowest all my wants, thou art able and willing to supply them; I will therefore have recourse to thee, with an entire confidence; I will expose to thee all my miseries, that thou mayest vouchsafe to assist me; and my hope shall not be confounded.

I beg, O Heart infinitely merciful, that thou intercede with the Eternal Father, to obtain for me the pardon of my crimes; but hast thou not merited this pardon for me, I do not say by all the blood thou hast shed, but by the weakest of thy sighs? Ah! could the Eternal Father refuse to grant me grace and the absolution of my sins, at the request of the Heart of his beloved Son, the object of his most tender complacency? Are not the wound in thy sacred side, and the adorable blood which flowed from it, which the Eternal Father still beholds, more powerful voices than that of my sins? I hope then to obtain, by thee and from thee, the pardon of my iniquities, how detestable, how innumerable soever they may have been. Yes, thou shalt be my refuge in the day of his wrath, and I will hide myself in thy adorable wound, which is a most secure asylum for all those who detest their sins in the sincerity of their hearts.

I will have recourse to thee, O Heart full of sweetness and goodness, in all my dangers, my pains, my difficulties, my weaknesses; thou wilt be my strength and my defence in temptations; thou wilt place me beyond the assaults of the enemies of my salvation, and enable me to triumph over them.

In the most severe afflictions I will run to thee with so much the more confidence, as I know that thou hast a peculiar tenderness for afflicted hearts; and remembering then the bitter sorrow with which thou didst permit thy divine soul to be overwhelmed, to expiate my sins, I shall be ashamed that my heart should rejoice, whilst thine has been delivered up to agony for the love of me.

In prosperity, in affluence, and even in the most innocent pleasures, I will remember that thy Heart, O life of my soul, never rejoiced but in God, and that mine also should rejoice *only in him.*

I further hope, O Heart, infinitely holy, that thou wilt teach me to be humble amidst honours, poor in spirit and in heart in the midst of riches, moderate and mortified in the most necessary relaxations.

Finally, I hope to obtain from thy Heart so infinitely liberal, meekness, humility, charity; the facility of forgetting injuries, and compassion for the misfortunes of others; a perfect conformity to the will of God, and, generally, all the virtues which are necessary to please him, and to obtain eternal life.

I hope for all these things from thee, because I know that thou art the inexhaustible source of all graces, and that thou desirest more ardently to communicate them to me than I do to receive them. But I do not desire these virtues or this sanctity, but in order to satisfy the desire which thou hast to see them in me, and thereby merit to love the Celestial Father for ever and ever. *Amen.*

ASPIRATIONS,

To the Sacred Heart of Jesus.

I.

SACRED Heart of Jesus, admirable Heart, worthy of the majesty of God and of the mercy of the Redeemer, how little are thy perfections known! Enlighten my soul in the knowledge of thine unbounded excellence, that I may render to thee the glory and the praises which are thy due.

II.

O HEART of my Jesus, infinitely amiable! possess my heart, unite it so closely to thee, that it may never be separated from thee.

III.

O HEART, infinitely holy, model of all hearts! sanctify my heart, and render it like to thine.

IV.

O SACRED Heart, inexhaustible source of graces! enrich my soul with the treasures which are contained in thine.

V.

O SOVEREIGN King of hearts! submit to thy sweet empire my ungrateful and rebellious heart.

VI.

O HEART of Jesus, always inflamed with the divine love, the most pure and the most perfect! enkindle in my heart thy divine charity.

VII.

O HEART of Jesus, the most delightful object of the complacency of the Eternal

Father! make me become worthy of his benign countenance, perfect my affections with thine, and deign to supply, by the sanctity of thy works, the imperfection of mine.

VIII.

O DIVINE Heart, the seat of all virtues! teach my heart to relish and imitate these virtues.

IX.

HEART sorrowful unto death for the sins of the world! penetrate me with sorrow for my sins.

X.

AMIABLE Heart, pierced with a lance for the love of me, and open to serve as a refuge for pure souls! purify me, in order that I may be admitted into this holy and pleasing abode.

Ant. Sacred Heart of Jesus, abounding in goodness and tenderness for us, may all in us be consecrated to thee!

V. Jesus, meek and humble of Heart,
R. Render our hearts like to thine.

A PRAYER.

GREAT God, who hast reposited all the treasures of grace and of science in the Sacred Heart of thy well-beloved Son, open to us this plentiful source of all gifts, and make us worthy to receive the influence of its superabundant merits. *Amen.*

PII AFFECTUS
Ad Cor Jesu.

COR Jesu, verbo Dei substantialiter unitum,
Cor Jesu, Dei majestate dignum,
Cor Jesu, Dei sanctitate sanctum,
Cor Jesu, Dei bonitate bonum,
Cor Jesu, adoratione Deo debita adorandum,
Cor Jesu, amore Deo digno amandum,
Cor Jesu, ineffabile,
Cor Jesu, incomprehensible,
Cor Jesu, Patris Æterni templum dignissimum,
Cor Jesu, verum ac proprium Spiritus Sancti habitaculum,
Cor Jesu, Sanctissimæ Trinitatis sanctuarium,
Cor Jesu, charitatis æternæ dignissima sedes,
Cor Jesu, in quo habitat omnis plenitudo divinitatis,
Cor Jesu, in quo sunt omnes thesauri sapientiæ et scientiæ,
Cor Jesu, thesaurus numquam deficiens,
Cor Jesu, dives in omnes qui invocant te,

Divino amore quo ardes, inflamma cor meum.

Cor Jesu, de cujus plenitudine omnes nos accepimus,
Cor Jesu, pax et reconciliatio nostra,
Cor Jesu, fons aquæ salientis in vitam æternam,
Cor Jesu, puteus aquarum viventium,
Cor Jesu, principium et origo virtutum omnium,
Cor Jesu, in quo sibi Pater bene complacuit,
Cor Jesu, hostia vivens, sancta, et Deo placens,
Cor Jesu, propitiatio pro peccatis nostris,
Cor Jesu, amaritudine repletum propter nos,
Cor Jesu, saturatum opprobriis,
Cor Jesu, attritum propter scelera nostra,
Cor Jesu, usque ad mortem crucis obediens factum,
Cor Jesu, lancea perforatum,
Cor Jesu, fons totius consolationis,
Cor Jesu, solatium peregrinantis animæ,
Cor Jesu, refugium nostrum in die tribulationis,
Cor Jesu, salus in te sperantium,
Cor Jesu, spes in te morientium,
Cor Jesu, cultorum tuorum dulce præsidium,
Cor Jesu, deliciæ sanctorum omnium,
   V. Jesu, mitis et humilis corde,
   R. Fac cor meum secundum cor tuum.

Divino amore quo ardes, inflamma cor meum.

Oratio.

CONCEDE, quæsumus, Omnipotens Deus, ut qui in sanctissimo delecti Filii tui Corde gloriantes, præcipua in nos charitatis ejus beneficia recolimus; eorum pariter et actu delectemur et fructu. Per Dominum nostrum, &c.

Alia Oratio.

DOMINE Jesu Christe, qui ineffabiles Cordis tui divitias Ecclesiæ tuæ novo beneficio aperire dignatus es; concede, ut hujus sacratissimi Cordis amori respondere, et injurias eidem afflictissimo Cordi ab ingratis hominibus illatas, dignis obsequiis compensare valeamus: qui vivis, &c.

Alia Oratio.

ANIMA Christi, sanctifica me.
Cor Christi, accende me.
Corpus Christi, salva me.
Sanguis Christi, inebria me.
Aqua lateris Christi, lava me.
Passio Christi, conforta me.
O bone Jesu, exaudi me.
Intra tua vulnera absconde me.
Ne permittas me separari a te.
Ab hoste maligno defende me.
In hora mortis meæ voca me,
Et jube me venire ad te,
Ut cum sanctis tuis laudem te
In sæcula sæculorum. *Amen.*

SACRED HEART OF JESUS.

The foregoing Devout Affections translated.

HEART of Jesus, substantially united to the word of God,
Heart of Jesus, worthy of the majesty of God,
Heart of Jesus, holy by the sanctity of God,
Heart of Jesus, good by the goodness of God,
Heart of Jesus to be adored with the adoration due to God,
Heart of Jesus, to be loved with the love worthy of God,
Heart of Jesus, ineffable,
Heart of Jesus, incomprehensible,
Heart of Jesus, the most worthy temple of the Eternal Father,
Heart of Jesus, the true and proper abode of the Holy Ghost,
Heart of Jesus, the sanctuary of the most Holy Trinity,
Heart of Jesus, the most worthy seat of eternal charity,
Heart of Jesus, wherein dwelleth the plenitude of the Divinity,
Heart of Jesus, in which are all the treasures of wisdom and knowledge,
Heart of Jesus, a never-failing treasure,
Heart of Jesus, bountiful to those who invoke thee,
Heart of Jesus, of the fulness of which we all partook,

Inflame my heart with thy divine love.

Heart of Jesus, our peace and reconciliation,
Heart of Jesus, the fountain of living waters springing up to eternal life,
Heart of Jesus, the beginning and origin of all virtues,
Heart of Jesus, in which the Father was well pleased,
Heart of Jesus, the living sacrifice, holy and pleasing to God,
Heart of Jesus, the propitiation for our sins,
Heart of Jesus, filled with sorrow on our account,
Heart of Jesus, treated with ignominy,
Heart of Jesus, struck for our crimes,
Heart of Jesus, become obedient even to the death of the cross,
Heart of Jesus, pierced with a spear,
Heart of Jesus, the fountain of all consolation,
Heart of Jesus, the solace of afflicted souls,
Heart of Jesus, our refuge in the day of tribulation,
Heart of Jesus, the safety of those who hope in thee,
Heart of Jesus, the hope of those who die in thee,
Heart of Jesus, the safeguard of those who worship thee,
Heart of Jesus, the delight of all saints,

Inflame my heart with thy divine love.

SACRED HEART OF JESUS.

V. Jesus, meek and humble of Heart,
R. Make my heart according to thine.

A PRAYER.

GRANT, we beseech thee, O Almighty God, that we who glory in the most holy Heart of thy beloved Son, and call to mind the principal acts of his love towards us, may not only rejoice in their participation, but also in their fruits. Through our Lord, &c.

Another Prayer.

LORD Jesus Christ, who hast, by a new benefit, vouchsafed to open to thy Church the unspeakable treasures of thy Heart; grant that we make some return for this love, and by our homage and adoration, atone for the insults offered by ungrateful men to thy most afflicted Heart. *Amen.*

Another Prayer.

SOUL of my Saviour, be my guide;
　　Feed me, O Jesus, with thy flesh;
Wash me with water from thy side,
　　And with thy blood my thirst refresh.

Benignant Jesus, hear my prayer,
  Do not permit my steps to stray;
But save my heart from every snare
  Which the malignant foe can lay.
Make me enjoy thy blessed sight,
  When the last sigh of life is o'er,
That with thy saints I may delight
  To sing thy praise for evermore. *Amen.*

INVOCATIONS,

Of the Sacred Heart of Jesus for every Hour of the Day.

At Seven o'clock.

HEART of Jesus, worthy and true adorer of the Most High, teach me to adore him with thee and by thee, in spirit and in truth.

At Eight o'clock.

HEART of Jesus, perfectly humble, subdue my pride, and annihilate all that is arrogant in me.

At Nine o'clock.

HEART of Jesus, wounded and inflamed with love for me, grant that in my turn I may love only thee in all things, and all things in thee.

At Ten o'clock.

HEART of Jesus, the only victim worthy of God, unite me to thy state of suffering and of sacrifice, by the exercise of a generous and continual denial of myself and of all creatures.

At Eleven o'clock.

HEART of Jesus, penetrated and oppressed with sorrow for the sins of men, grant me the grace to weep and lament, as I ought, for the guilt of mine.

At Twelve o'clock.

HEART of Jesus, perfectly submissive and ever in conformity to the will of thy Celestial Father, grant that in all things my will may be happily obedient to thine.

At One o'clock.

Heart of Jesus, infinitely pure, give me a perfect purity of body, of heart, and of intention.

At Two o'clock.

BENEFICENT Heart of Jesus, model of meekness and of charity, render my heart meek, charitable, and beneficent, that it may resemble thine.

At Three o'clock.

HEART of Jesus, the school whither all faithful souls go to learn the science of the saints, make me one of thy most constant and docile disciples.

At Four o'clock.

HEART of Jesus, consumed by the ardour of thy zeal for the glory of the Most High, inflame my heart with a pure and ardent zeal for the glory of God and the salvation of souls.

At Five o'clock.

HEART of Jesus, obedient unto death, and even to the death of the cross, be thou the vanquisher of my rebellions, and subject me to the sweet yoke of a perfect obedience.

At Six o'clock.

HEART of Jesus, burning with zeal for my salvation, animate me with the same zeal to labour for my sanctification, with fervour and without relaxation, until the last moment of my life.

BEADS

Of the Sacred Heart of Jesus.

THESE are composed of five large Beads, in honour of the five wounds of Jesus Christ, and of thirty-three smaller ones, corresponding to the number of years which the Saviour lived upon earth.

On the cross the Creed is said; on each of the large beads the following prayer:—

I adore thee most Sacred Heart of Jesus Christ. Inflame my heart with the fire of thy divine love.

On every small bead say :—

O most sweet Jesus, give me a heart according to thy Heart.

This form of prayer is finished with a Pater and Ave.

AFFECTIONATE SENTIMENTS,

Of St. Gertrude, towards the Sacred Heart of Jesus.

O LOVE, O my King, O my God, O Jesus, the only object of my love, receive me even at this hour under the amiable protection of thy Sacred Heart, that I may live entirely in thee.

At this moment receive me in the immense ocean of thy infinite charity. Plunge me into this furnace of thy love, that I may be there consumed with its celestial ardours. There, O my sweet Saviour, console me with thine amiable presence; there make me know the price of the blood which redeemed me; there let me hear the sweet voice of thy delightful affection, and call me to thee; there, in the sweetness of thy spirit, draw me within thyself, and immerse me in the abyss of thy perfect charity; there, in fine, grant me the happiness of enjoying eternally thy presence, for my soul desires thee alone.

O Love, thou art this living water for which I thirst; behold my heart is carried towards thee with an ardour which torments it; open to me the salutary entrance to thy Sacred Heart. Behold mine: I no longer wish that it should be at my disposal. O Jesus, my sweet hope, may thy divine Heart, already pierced for love of me, and ever open to all sinners, be the first refuge of my soul at its departure from the body; and there, in the abyss of thy love, may all my sins in a moment be absorbed and consumed.

Extracts from different Passages of the Life of
ST. GERTRUDE.

AN EXERCISE,

To Honour the most Holy Trinity by the Sacred Heart of Jesus.

SUPREME and adorable Trinity, Father, Son, and Holy Ghost, one only God, I adore thee with the most profound respect.

God the Father, Sovereign Creator, Father infinitely powerful, the heavens and the earth are thy works; and thou hast created me to thy likeness. All that I have, I possess from thy bounty; and all that I am, is already thine.

God the Son, divine Word, my Redeemer, my Model, my Salvation, thou hast delivered me from hell, thou hast opened Heaven to me in shedding thy precious blood and in dying for me.

God the Holy Ghost, essential Charity of the Father and of the Son, consoling Spirit, thou hast sanctified me, imparting to me the inestimable gifts of thy grace, and coming to dwell in me.

O sovereign Trinity, infinite Majesty, it is in thy name that I received in my baptism the character of Christian. From that time thou didst adopt me for thy child, and I contracted with thee the most glorious alliance and the most ineffable union. Receive, Holy Trinity, infinite and incomprehensible greatness—receive, I beseech thee, the most lively sentiments of my gratitude. I thank thee, I praise thee, I glorify thee with all my heart, and I bless thee for all the inestimable benefits of my creation, redemption, and regeneration. I bless thee for all the goods with which thou hast loaded me, and which thou dost incessantly impart to me, both in the order of nature and of grace. I bless thee for all the goods which thou hast destined for me in thy eternal mercy, in virtue of my adoption, and of which I have rendered myself unworthy by my innumerable infidelities. I bless thee with all those who bless thee in heaven and on earth. I bless thee for all those who do not know thee, and who, knowing thee, do not bless thee, and I wish that we all together may bless thee eternally in heaven.

But as we can never sufficiently acknowledge thine infinite mercies, O most Holy Trinity, permit me, in order to supply the deficiency, to thank thee through the adorable Heart of Jesus, and to offer to thee the acts of thanksgiving which it has rendered thee, the praises which it has given thee while it lived upon the earth, and which it will continue to give thee for all eternity.

The pleasing recollection of thy innumerable benefits shall never be effaced from my mind; and by the return of a grateful heart entirely devoted to thy service, I will endeavour to prove to thee my gratitude. But, alas! O Father infinitely good, I here acknowledge in thy presence, with the most lively sorrow, that I have been an ungrateful and an unnatural child, and that I have dishonoured thine image by a thousand sins. O Word made Flesh, I have neglected, I have despised thy holy maxims, to follow those of the world; and I have rendered unavailing to myself the price and infinite merits of thy life and death. O sanctifying Spirit, I have rejected thy gifts and thy inspirations; I have grieved thee by my infidelities. I acknowledge, O Holy Trinity, the enormity of my offences; they are innumerable. I have violated the promises which I made to thee; I have forgotten my most sacred and solemn engagements; I have basely forsaken thee, to become a slave to the world and the devil.

Penetrated with sorrow at the sight of my sins, I earnestly desire to atone for them, and do most humbly implore thy pardon.

But, O Holy Trinity, O my God, shall I dare to appear before thee without the precious robe of innocence with which thou didst clothe me in my baptism, and which I have lost by my sins? And canst thou yet acknowledge me for thy child? I confess that I am unworthy of so glorious a name; but if I have ceased to be a child submissive to thy law and docile to thy voice, thou hast not ceased, O Holy Trinity, to be the God of mercies. It is thy mercy which I implore, and I implore it by the adorable Heart of the Divine Jesus. This Sacred Heart was always perfectly subject to thy will, and obedient unto death, even to the death of the cross; it was always filled with an ardent, perfect, and infinite love for thee. I offer thee, in reparation of my offences, the bitter sorrow which the Heart of thy Divine Son experienced at the sight of my sins, and the blood which it shed, in order to expiate them. It entreated thee to grant me grace, and I firmly hope that thou wilt hear its prayers and desires. In this sweet confidence, I ratify and renew with all my heart the engagements and the promises of my holy baptism; I renounce for ever the devil and his works, the world and its pomps, and I detest its pernicious maxims; I embrace, with all my soul, thy holy yoke, and I desire to live henceforth in a manner worthy of the august name of Christian, with which thou hast honoured me.

Animated with a desire of fulfilling more perfectly these holy resolutions with which thy grace inspires me, I entreat thee to accept the entire consecration and dedication which I make of myself to thee. Almighty and eternal God, Father, Son, and Holy Ghost, adorable Trinity of Persons, Unity of Essence, Sovereign Creator of all things, who hast given me being, life, and all that I am, prostrate before thine infinite Majesty, with the most humble sentiments, and the most lively gratitude, in union with the love with which the Sacred Hearts of Jesus and of Mary offered themselves to thy supreme and infinite greatness, I offer and consecrate myself to thee by an entire dedication, to the end that I may apply myself henceforth entirely to know thee, to love thee, and to serve thee; and, by this particular dedication, I desire to obtain from thy boundless goodness abundant graces, which may enkindle throughout the universe the lights of faith, at a time when they are weakened and obscured by so many errors and crimes, which continually outrage thine adorable Majesty. With this view, I unite in a holy alliance with all those who have the same intention of loving thee alone; and in order to put myself in a state of living henceforth with them in the faithful practice of this holy love, I make thee an entire sacrifice of my body and my soul. I submit myself in all things to thy good pleasure, wishing sincerely to lose my will in thine; to give up all my interest, that I may have nothing at heart but thy glory; to deprive myself of all things, that I may entirely depend on thee, and seek only what will be most agreeable to thee. I wish, in fine, to the utmost of my power, to augment thy love in all hearts; to the end, that being all united on earth by the ties of this holy love, we may one day be united by it in heaven, to possess thee, to bless thee, and to love thee, for all eternity. *Amen.*

A PRAYER,

To ask for a Change of Heart.

ONLY Son of the Eternal Father, Divine word, permit me to say to thee, from the profound abyss of my nothingness, that thou hast not taken a heart like mine, but in order that my heart should become like thine.

Grant then, if thou pleasest, my adorable Redeemer, that thy admirable designs may be accomplished in me. Thy heart is pure; may mine be pure. Create a clean heart in me, O God—" Cor mundum crea in me, Deus."—*Ps.* 50.

Thy Heart is humble; may mine be humble.

Thy Heart is patient; may mine be patient.

Thy Heart is docile; may mine be docile.

Thy Heart is sincere; may mine be sincere.

Thy Heart is exempt from all evil; may mine be exempt from all evil.

Thy Heart is all love and sanctified love; may mine be all love and all holy love.

May thy Heart, O my Jesus, entirely possess mine.

May mine, O my Jesus, be entirely absorbed in thine; may it be a faithful heart, a contrite heart, a generous heart, a charitable heart, a perfectly Christian heart. Ah! my divine Saviour, I will henceforth endeavour, with the assistance of thy grace, to have nothing in my heart but that which is in thine; namely, purity, humility, patience, docility, fortitude, meekness, charity; to possess only Jesus and his love. My heart is no longer mine, it belongs to Jesus. Open it, close it, inflame it; it is thine. Alas! it has not always been so; but O Heart of Jesus, O love of Jesus, it is so at present by thy grace, and I trust that it shall be so for ever. Jesus, Jesus, Jesus.

A PRAYER,

To Ask for a Happy Death, and to prepare ourselves for it.

[A happy and holy death is the last of graces, the most precious grace, which perfects all others. We cannot merit it, but we may obtain it. Ask it often with fervour, and endeavour to dispose yourself to die the death of the saints. The best preparation which you can have for that awful moment is a regular life, sanctified by prayer, good works, and the frequent reception of the sacraments. Moreover, employ one day every month to prepare yourself for it. Consider this day as the last of your life. Go to confession and communion, if you can, as if it was for the last time. Meditate on some one of the great truths of religion. Examine what might cause you the most anxiety at the hour of death, and remove it immediately. Accustom yourself to think and to act, as you would wish to have thought and acted at the hour of death, when the veil of the passions shall be taken away, and when you shall judge of all things according to truth and religion. The following prayer contains the acts which the sick and dying ought to endeavour to make. This prayer may be read slowly to them, if they are in a situation to hear it; or at least let some person suggest to them the acts which it contains.]

O AMIABLE Saviour, whose Heart is still open to receive me and hear my prayers, I come, deploring the wanderings of my past life, to beseech thee to grant me the grace to finish it well, and to die in thy holy love. I acknowledge that the bad use which I have made of my life, renders me unworthy of the grace which I ask of thee; but I pray thee to grant me in thy mercy what thou mayest refuse me in thy justice.

From this moment I desire to begin, and with thy holy grace do begin, a new life. Grant that this change may be true, entire, and constant until death, in order that I may henceforth live and finally die in thy holy love.

I believe, O my God, all that which thou hast revealed to thy Holy, Catholic, Apostolic, and Roman Church; because thou, who art truth itself, hast revealed it, and I wish to live and die in this belief.

I hope to obtain thy holy grace in this life, and heaven in the next; because thou art infinitely good and faithful to thy promises, and because the merits of my Saviour are infinite. I love thee, my God, with all my heart for thy sake, because thou art infinitely perfect and infinitely amiable. I love my neighbour as myself, for the love of thee. I pardon him sincerely all the injuries he may have done me, or wished to do me.

Deign then, I beseech thee, to pardon me also my past iniquities. I detest them in the bitterness of my soul, because they displease thee; and I am resolved to amend my life for the future, with the assistance of thy holy grace, on which alone I rely, since of myself I can do nothing.

I adore thee, Sovereign Majesty, and I acknowledge thee for my Lord and my God, my Creator and my last end. I unite my adorations with those which are rendered thee by the angels and saints in heaven. I thank thee most humbly for all the graces, as well general as particular, with which thou hast favoured me. I thank thee particularly for giving me the means of preparing for death. I entreat the angels and the saints to thank thee for me, and I ardently desire one day, in union with them, to render my acknowledgments perpetual.

Eternal Father, O my God, in union with the sufferings and death of my divine Redeemer, and with that of the most holy Virgin, my good Mother, I accept of sufferings and of death; first, to acknowledge thy supreme power and sovereign dominion, by the humiliation and destruction of my body; secondly, to acknowledge thine infinite goodness, and to thank thee for all the spiritual and temporal goods which I have received from thy liberal hand, by depriving myself of all worldly goods; thirdly, to satisfy thy divine justice and expiate my offences, by the sacrifice of my life; fourthly, to obey thy will, infinitely equitable, and to repair all my disobedience to thy holy law; fifthly, to obtain from thy mercy the graces necessary to die well; sixthly, to evince to my divine Saviour my love and gratitude in wishing to die like him, for him, and with him; seventhly, in a word, to be in that happy state in which I can no longer offend thee, and in which I shall love thee eternally. O bounty, O infinite greatness of my God! Father, Son, and Holy Ghost, have pity on me, grant me mercy. Into thy hands I commend my soul.

Jesus be to me a Jesus, now and at the hour of my death. O Mary, protect me in these last moments; thou, who art the Mother of mercy, and who hast obtained for me so many graces. I return thee thanks, and beseech thee to obtain for me a happy death.

Sacred Hearts of Jesus and of Mary, ah! may my heart be united with yours, during my life and at my death. May I live and may I die inflamed with your holy love.

Great St. Michael, who hast conquered the infernal spirit, and who, I trust, shalt one day present my soul to the Sovereign Judge, obtain for me the victory over all my enemies, principally at the hour of my death.

My holy angel-guardian, who hast shown so much zeal for my salvation during my life, accept my just acknowledgments, and protect me particularly in these last moments.

Great St. Joseph, patron of the agonizing, obtain for me to die, as thou didst, in the arms of Jesus and of Mary.

My holy patrons (N. N.), who have assisted and protected me during my life, assist and protect me particularly at the hour of my death.

All ye holy angels and saints of heaven assist me now, every moment of my life, and above all at the hour of my death.

O my Sovereign Lord, I beg of thee a happy death, through the merits of Jesus Christ my Saviour, and through his adorable Heart; through the intercession of the most holy Virgin, and through her most revered heart; through the intercession of all the holy angels and blessed in heaven. *Amen.*

A PRAYER,

Which, consisting of short sentences, may be repeated often, after the manner of Ejaculations, in order to pray for a Happy Death, and to dispose ourselves for it.

OMNIPOTENT and most Holy Trinity, O my God, grant me the grace to live well and die well. Into thy hands I commend my soul.

I believe in thee, O my God; I hope in thee; I love thee with all my heart, because thou alone art worthy of my love; I adore thee, I thank thee, and I submit myself to thy will in all things.

I detest all my sins, because they displease thee. Forgive them, I entreat thee, through the merits of Jesus Christ, thy beloved Son. I pardon with all my heart, for thy sake, all those who have offended me.

Jesus, be thou my strength and my consolation at the hour of my death. Be to me a Jesus now and at my death.

Sacred Hearts of Jesus and of Mary, be my refuge and my abode during my life and at my death. To live in you and for you, to die in you, are the most ardent desires of my heart.

St. Michael, my holy angel-guardian, all ye holy angels, assist me during my life, and especially at the hour of my death.

Great St. Joseph, my holy patron, all ye saints of heaven, obtain for me the grace of loving and praising my God eternally with you. Jesus, Mary, and Joseph.

ASPIRATIONS,

In the form of a Litany, to pray for a Happy Death.

LORD Jesus Christ, God of goodness, Father of mercies, I present myself before thee with a contrite and humble heart; to thee I recommend the last hour of my life, and the decision of my eternal doom.

When my eyes, dim and troubled at the approach of death, shall cast their sorrowful and dying looks upon thee—Merciful Jesus, have mercy on me.

When my lips, cold and trembling, shall pronounce for the last time thy adorable name—Merciful Jesus, have mercy on me.

When my cheeks, pale and livid, shall inspire the beholders with pity and dismay; when my hair, bedewed with the sweat of death and stiffening on my head, shall announce my approaching dissolution—Merciful Jesus, have mercy on me.

When my ears, about to be closed for ever to the discourses of men, shall be opened to the sound of thy voice, which shall pronounce the irrevocable decree, which is to cut me off from the number of the living—Merciful Jesus, have mercy on me.

When my imagination, agitated by dreadful spectres, shall be sunk in an abyss of anguish; when my soul, affrighted with the sight of my iniquities and the terrors of thy judgments, shall have to fight against the angel of darkness. who will endeavour to conceal thy mercies from me and throw me into despair—Merciful Jesus, have mercy on me.

When my weak heart, overcome by the pains of sickness, shall be seized with the horrors of death, and when I shall shed the last tear, receive it as a sacrifice of expiation for my sins, to the end that I may expire the victim of penance; and in that dreadful moment—Merciful Jesus, have mercy on me.

When my friends and relations, assembled around me, shall shed the tear of pity over me, and invoke thy clemency in my behalf —Merciful Jesus, have mercy on me.

When for the last time I shall kiss thy adorable cross, accept this homage as a profession of my faith, of my hope, of my love, and of sorrow for seeing thee so often offended; receive me then into thy Sacred Heart, as an asylum of salvation, and— Merciful Jesus, have mercy on me.

When I shall have lost the use of my senses, when the world shall have vanished from my sight, when my agonizing soul shall feel the pangs of death—Merciful Jesus, have mercy on me.

When my last sighs shall summon my soul to depart from the body, accept them as proceeding from a holy impatience of going to thee, and—Merciful Jesus, have mercy on me.

When my soul, trembling on my lips, shall bid an eternal farewell to this world, and shall leave my body lifeless, pale, and cold, accept the dissolution of this body, as a homage which I willingly pay to thy divine Majesty, and—Merciful Jesus, have mercy on me.

When, at length, my soul appears before thee, and shall, for the first time, behold the splendour of thy Majesty, turn it not away from thy presence, but—Merciful Jesus, have mercy on me. *Amen.*

A PRAYER,

To Offer our Sufferings to the Sacred Heart of Jesus, and to pray for Patience.

ADORABLE Heart, refuge of afflicted hearts, permit me, in the afflictions which I experience, to have recourse to thee. Thou hast been, for my sake, overwhelmed in the bitter sea of affliction and grief; and though thou wast the purest and the most holy of hearts, thou has been nevertheless the most afflicted. Is it not just, then, that a heart, criminal as mine is, should experience sufferings and afflictions? But grant, O divine Jesus, by thy grace, that I may render them advantageous to my soul, and acceptable to thy celestial Father. It is with this intention that I come to unite them to thine, to lay them up in thy Sacred Heart, and there to seek fortitude and consolation. Vouchsafe to look down with pity on the deplorable state to which I am reduced; sorrow wrings my heart; I am a burthen to myself; afflictions weigh me down, poverty and want press me on all sides; my character is injured by detractors and calumniators; my enemies persecute me; my friends forsake me; temptation importunes me; my passions disturb me; the past, the present, and the future affright me, and plunge my afflicted soul into deep consternation. O adorable Heart, it is to thee that I have recourse, it is in thee I place all my hope. Thou wilt alleviate my misfortunes, or at least thou wilt assist me to support and sanctify them. Fortify me, I entreat thee, against myself; support my weakness, and strengthen my dejected courage. Make me a partaker of thy magnanimity, of the submission with which thou didst suffer the most lively pangs, the most bitter sorrows. Give me that love of sufferings with which thou wast incessantly inflamed. Grant that I may conceive so high an esteem for them, that I may fear being deprived of them. Teach me, after thine example, to adore the paternal hand which strikes me, and to know the spiritual advantages of the afflictions with which thou art pleased to visit me. Thou hast chosen humiliation, poverty, and grief, in preference to riches, pleasure, and glory; and thou treatest thy friends as thou hast wished to be treated thyself. Grant, then, O my amiable Saviour, that henceforth walking in thy footsteps, my glory and all my delight may be to suffer for thee and like thee. I adore the dispensations of thy Providence in my regard, without a wish to investigate them. Thou art a God infinitely just, infinitely merciful; I will throw myself into thine arms, and submit myself in all things to thy will. That such may always be the disposition of my soul, I beg of thee, O Jesus, by the submission of thy adorable Heart, and I hope for it through that infinite love which thou hast shown for me. *Amen.*

A PRAYER,

To obtain the Conversion of Hearts.

HEART of Jesus, legitimate Lord of hearts, deign to subject to thy obedience all our hearts. Possess them all, even those which are rebellious to thy law; induce them by the attractions of thy grace to submit themselves to thy dominion. Never suffer them to withdraw an obedience so just, so necessary, and so glorious for them. Render them docile to thy will. Be thou, O most holy and perfect of all hearts, the model of ours. Make them become like to thine,—humble, pure, meek, and patient. Restrain the passions which agitate them; purify them from terrestrial desires, which defile them; settle their inconstancy; soften their hardness; enrich their poverty; elevate their desires to heavenly pursuits; inflame them with the fire of thy divine love; in a word, render them such as will make them agreeable to thee, that they may honour, love, and imitate thee, and thereby possess thee eternally. *Amen.*

A PRAYER,

For the Confraternity of the Sacred Heart of Jesus.

MY Adorable Jesus, who rejectest no person, and who openest thy Sacred Heart to all contrite and humble sinners, grant, through thy infinite bounty, mercy to all those who invoke thy holy name. Propitiously hear the most humble supplications of those who desire sincerely to adore thee in spirit and in truth. May all those who have the happiness of being joined together in the holy society of thy Sacred Heart, partake in a special manner of thy mercies. Behold them with looks of tenderness and compassion; vouchsafe to support and increase their fervour and zeal, and grant them perseverance. Impart thy graces to all those for whom I ought to pray; destroy in them whatever displeases thee, and accomplish all the designs of thy bounty in their favour; that we may all, during eternity, render honour, glory, and benediction to thy Heart, supremely merciful, which has been sacrificed in order to enrich us and to make us eternally happy. *Amen.*

A PRAYER,

For the Souls in Purgatory, and in particular for those of the Confraternity.

JESUS, whose merits and love are infinite, we implore thee for the souls which love thee, and which thou lovest. If thou dost punish them with justice to render them worthy of possessing thee, thou wishest that we should implore thy mercy in their favour, to shorten the time of their sufferings. Hear favourably the prayers which we address to thee in their favour. Remember in particular, we conjure thee, those who on earth were devoted to thy Sacred Heart, and zealous for its glory. O amiable Jesus, suffer them no longer to be deprived of thy presence. They are dear to thy Heart, and it is through this same Heart that we beseech thee to put them in possession of the happiness which alone they desire, and which thou hast merited for them by the effusion of thy precious blood. *Amen.*

EXERCISES
FOR THE
FEAST OF THE SACRED HEART OF JESUS.

[We have explained in the commencement of this book the exercises of piety for the Feast-day of the Sacred Heart of Jesus; read them attentively, and dispose yourself to celebrate it by the following Novena, which begins the eve of Corpus Christi, and may serve to sanctify the octave. The Visits to the Blessed Sacrament ought to be as frequent as possible.]

A NOVENA

In Honour of the Sacred Heart of Jesus.

EVERY day unite your prayers and adorations with those of the most holy Virgin, and of one of the nine choirs of angels and saints, to honour some one of the dispositions of the Sacred Heart of Jesus, and to practise some virtue in its honour.

THE FIRST DAY.

With the Blessed Virgin, the Seraphim, and the Holy Patriarchs.

Adore often the Sacred Heart of our Lord Jesus Christ in the most Holy Sacrament, humble yourself before the infinite majesty of God the Father, and offer continually to him the purest and most profound homages.

Practice.—Renew in your soul the most lively sentiments of respect and adoration for God, and frequently make these acts.

THE SECOND DAY.
With the Blessed Virgin, the Cherubim, and the Holy Prophets.

Adore the Sacred Heart of Jesus, which solicits, night and day, the mercy of God in our favour, and incessantly offers itself in sacrifice for the expiation of our sins.

Practice.—Recall to your mind, in the bitterness of your soul, the enormity of your sins; implore this Sacred Heart to give you a true contrition for them, and unite the sorrow which you endeavour to conceive with that which our Lord experienced in his adorable Heart.

THE THIRD DAY.
With the Blessed Virgin, the Thrones, and the Holy Apostles.

Adore the Sacred Heart of Jesus, presenting to the Eternal Father our good works and our prayers, and supplying our deficiences towards the infinite Majesty of God.

Practice.—Thank God for having given

you so powerful a Mediator, and endeavour to conform daily more and more to the sentiments of this Sacred Heart.

THE FOURTH DAY.
With the Blessed Virgin, the Dominations, and the Holy Martyrs.

Adore the Sacred Heart of Jesus burning with love for you, and asking as a favour that you love it.

Practice.—Pay some visits to this Sacred Heart, to return it thanks for the love it bears towards you, and to testify your love for it.

THE FIFTH DAY.
With the Blessed Virgin, the Virtues, and the Holy Doctors.

Adore the Sacred Heart of Jesus, endowed with all the virtues, and making their practice easy to you, by the efficacy of its merits and the force of its example.

Practice.—Meditate on that virtue which you particularly require; apply yourself to practise it, and let not the day pass without making some acts of this virtue.

THE SIXTH DAY.
With the Blessed Virgin, the Powers, and the Holy Confessors.

Adore the Sacred Heart of Jesus, containing within itself the plenitude of graces, and opening to diffuse them abundantly on those who address themselves to it.

Practice.—Humble yourself in the presence of your Saviour for having so often abused his mercies, and with new ardour and perfect confidence implore him to grant you grace.

THE SEVENTH DAY.

With the Blessed Virgin, the Principalities, and the Holy Virgins and Widows.

Adore the Sacred Heart of Jesus, which delights to be with the children of men, and which with tenderness pities our miseries and our wants.

Practice.—Esteem the happiness you enjoy in being able to converse with Jesus Christ in the most Holy Sacrament; and avail yourself of this advantage as often as you can, without neglecting the duties of your state.

THE EIGHTH DAY.

With the Blessed Virgin, the Archangels, and the Holy Innocents.

Adore the Sacred Heart of Jesus, which is sensibly afflicted with the outrages and impieties of those who are rebels to the Church and good morals, and which desires to find faithful Christians who will endeavour to repair these disorders.

Practice.—Perform some penance, some generous act of virtue, in reparation of the outrages which he receives.

THE NINTH DAY.
With the Blessed Virgin, the Angels, and the unknown Saints of all States.

Adore the Sacred Heart of Jesus, who complains of the coldness and indifference of the lukewarm, and who promises so much to fervent souls, who have generosity to relinquish all, in order to love him without reserve.

Practice. — Endeavour to discover the cause of your want of devotion and of your tepidity; adopt such measures as will enable you to arise from this state, and embrace every means which may contribute to render you more agreeable in the eyes of Jesus Christ.

[This Novena may be practised in the course of the year, as each person's fervour may inspire or wants demand.]

[*An important Observation.*—It is hoped that persons devoted to the Sacred Heart of Jesus will perform this Novena the nine days of the Carnival, to the end that they may repair the injuries which this holy Heart receives particularly at that time, and obtain the conversion of sinners. They should communicate once during the Novena.]

A MEDITATION

For the Feast of the Sacred Heart of Jesus.

FIRST PREPARATION.—After having put yourself, with as much devotion as possible, in the presence of God, and having adored him, represent to yourself our Lord Jesus Christ, who offers you his Heart, and demands yours, in saying to you, "*Præbe, fili mi, cor tuum mihi.*"—Prov. 23.—" Son, give me thine heart."

SECOND PREPARATION. — Beg of Jesus Christ the grace of knowing the infinite perfections of this adorable Heart, and the immense love which he has for you; and that he will enkindle in your heart the fire of his divine love. Make afterwards an act of contrition, in order that your soul may be the better disposed to hear the voice of the Lord, and to remove the obstacles which your infidelities may have opposed to his graces. Implore likewise the assistance of the Blessed Virgin and of your Angel Guardian.

[You may prepare yourself in the same manner for other meditations.]

THE FIRST POINT.

The Sacred Heart of Jesus is the most amiable of Hearts.

CAN we doubt that the Sacred Heart of Jesus is the most amiable of Hearts, since it possesses all perfections in the most sublime degree? First, this Sacred Heart is the most meek, the most humble, the most generous, the most tender, the most compassionate, the most charitable. O divine Heart, what heart can be compared to thine? What heart so amiable, considering only thy natural perfections!

Secondly, but grace gives much more brilliancy, more lustre, more beauty, than all that is beautiful in the order of nature, either in heaven or on earth, in angels or in man. If the least of graces imparts so much beauty, what will several graces conjointly effect? How great, therefore, is the beauty of the hearts of the faithful, and of the saints!

How great shall it be where all the graces are re-united in one single heart! This is what takes place in the amiable Heart of Jesus: the plenitude of the Holy Ghost, the abundance of his gifts repose on it; all the graces, all the virtues capable of rendering a heart amiable, are found in this adorable Heart in all their perfection. Yes, this Sacred Heart contains within itself more virtues and graces than all the angels and men together; and it contains them in all the perfection of which they are capable. How wonderful the beauty and riches of this divine Heart! What excessive love for God the Father and for men! What treasures of humility, patience, meekness, charity, &c., which render the Heart of Jesus infinitely amiable!

If this divine Heart possesses the plenitude of graces, it is itself their source. It is thither that faithful souls must go to obtain the graces of fortitude and magnanimity in labours; of courage and patience in combats and temptations; of light in uncertainties and darkness; of submission and resignation in crosses and sufferings; of consolation and support in the severest trials. It is there that the sweet confidence of pardon springs up to the sinner; it is there that he feels that lively contrition which tends to purify the heart and efface sin; there the just find that sacred and divine fire which animates and supports them. Consoling retreat for interior souls! purest abode of peace! amiable Heart! it is in thee that these generous souls, of whom the world was unworthy, have established their dwelling. In honouring thee in spirit and in truth, and in rendering thee love for love, they consume themselves for thy glory in that pure fire of divine love which thou hast enkindled in their hearts. When shall I be so happy as to be myself consumed? When shall the time arrive, O divine Jesus, when thy Sacred Heart, which thou hast given me as the model of mine, shall be my only rule; since in reality my heart cannot be pleasing to thy heavenly Father, but inasmuch as it will be conformable to thine? What regret, what confusion, when I reflect on the days of my mispent life!

Thirdly, as grace surpasses nature, so glory greatly surpasses grace. What admirable beauty, what excellence, then, in those great saints, in the angels, in the Blessed Virgin! but what prodigy, what excess, what subimity of infinite and boundless glory in the adorable Heart of Jesus, before which heaven, earth, and hell bend the knee!

What glory, what sublimity of glory in the divine function for which it has been formed, which is nothing less than to burn eternally for God, with the purest and most ardent love! a glory truly worthy of this Supreme Being, since it is really infinite. Yes, the adorable Heart of Jesus, by the love with which it is inflamed for God, loves itself in God, honours itself in God, because he loves it with an infinite love: thus it may be said with truth, that for all eternity God shall be loved, as far as the boundless extent of his infinite perfections demand.

Fourthly, in a word, the Sacred Heart of Jesus is united hypostatically to the person of the Word; an union which, consequently, renders it the Heart of God. It is the Heart of God; it is the Heart of the most tender

Father, of the most charitable Redeemer, of the most faithful and most generous Friend, of the most powerful Protector, of the most liberal and most magnificent King. Now do not the endearing qualities which these titles and a thousand others contain, render this divine Heart infinitely amiable ? It is the Heart of God ; it is therefore holy, by the sanctity of God ; it is therefore good, by the goodness of God himself ; wherefore it is supremely good, infinitely holy, infinitely amiable !

Ah ! Sacred Heart, do men know thee, when they do not love thee ? O Heart of Jesus, how amiable art thou ! amiable, since thou containest all the gifts and perfections of nature and of grace, which have made thee the master-piece of the hands of the Creator, and the inexhaustible source from which are drawn the most precious graces ; since thou possessest the most exalted glory, and all the majesty and amiable perfections of the Divinity.

Thy perfections infinitely exceed the love which angels and men bear to thee. Being creatures and finite, they cannot love thee as much as thou oughtest to be loved. If I cannot love thee as much as thou art worthy of being loved, at least I wish to love thee as much as I can, with the assistance of thy grace, and according to the extent of this same grace.

THE SECOND POINT.

The Heart of Jesus is the most loving Heart.

THE love of this adorable Heart for men is, first, a consuming love. The fire of this divine love, enkindled in the Sacred Heart of Jesus, was so lively, so ardent, that at every instant it would have deprived him of life, had not his power preserved it.

Secondly, it is an incomprehensible love. Yes, this Sacred Heart has loved every one of us more than all fathers and mothers together have loved their children; it loves us more than all the angels and saints of heaven, and even more than the cherubim and seraphim love God himself.

Thirdly, it is a tender and compassionate love, which charitably searches for sinners, kindly receives them, mercifully pardons them, and requires in return only their hearts.

Fourthly, it is a strong and generous love, which knows no exception, and which sacrifices itself for our sake. All the affections of this charitable Heart, from the first moment of its existence until its death on the cross, were occasioned by its solicitude for us. To what excess of mortal anguish was it not reduced in the Garden of Olives? If he caused the anguish which he suffered there to appear, it was in order that men might judge of that sorrow with which his sacred soul was continually afflicted. This Heart finally was pierced with a lance; and does it not discover, by this sacred wound, which becomes our asylum, the most unheard-of generosity and tenderness?

But to what excess of kindness and mercy for us has not the ardent love of this adorable Heart carried the divine Jesus? What has it not induced the amiable Saviour to undertake—what has it not made him perform? Could we ever have imagined it—could we ever be able to comprehend it? What! for the love of man, Jesus offers himself a sacrifice; the master for the slave, the King for the subject, the Creator for the creature, the innocent for the guilty! He sacrifices to this love his repose, his honour, his life. He suffers the most outrageous ignominy, the most severe and multiplied afflictions, the most cruel and most shameful death; and that for the gratuitous love with which his adorable Heart is inflamed for man. What goodness, what tenderness, what love!

Holy by nature, Jesus cannot suffer for his own faults. It is for our crimes that he suffers; and these crimes are, our having offended him: and it is not upon us, as we merit, but upon himself, that he avenges our offences; and it is by our own hands that he is immolated. He is offended by us, and he is punished by us and for us. And why? To deliver us from the greatest misfortunes, and to procure for us inestimable good. O love, love! can we attempt to fathom thy depths without losing ourselves?

Jesus could have satisfied for us by a word, by a sigh, by the lightest suffering; but that which would have satisfied the divine Justice, could not satisfy the love of his Heart; and it was this love which delivered him up to all sorts of ignominy, afflictions, and torments; and it was this same love which made him anticipate, promote, and augment his sorrows, that he might soon begin to suffer, in order to suffer more, and to convince us of the excess of his love. Ah, how Jesus loves us! Ah, how much are we loved by Jesus!

But for this admirable love with which his Heart is inflamed, for the innumerable sufferings which it endured, for so many evils from which it delivered us, for the inestimable good which it procures for us, what does he demand, or rather what has he not a right to demand, and what are we not obliged to grant him? What does he demand? He requires, that we love him. Provided we love him he is content, he is satisfied.

In a word, when after all that we unhappily offend him, he is ready to pardon us our crimes and infidelities, to forget the past, and to impart to us every blessing, provided we love him. How wonderful this love! how excessive! O admirable love of this Sacred Heart for ungrateful and guilty wretches!

Fifthly, it is an infinite love. The immense love of this Sacred Heart, in immolating itself, has likewise immolated Jesus for us. This divine Redeemer, gloriously triumphing over death and hell, ascends to his Father. Will he leave us orphans on the earth, henceforth deprived of his presence? O admirable invention of love! He ascends to his Father, and he remains with us; and in order to comply with the infinite love which impels him, his wisdom and infinite power re-unite to perform the greatest miracle of his love. He institutes the adorable Sacrament of his Body and Blood, that he may remain really with us, nourish us truly with this celestial Bread, and make us find there, at the very source, all the graces of which we stand in need; that he may unite us with himself in the most ineffable and miraculous manner, and thereby enable us to live on his very life; in a word, that he may continually offer himself in sacrifice for us, as a most holy victim, to appease the wrath of God, and cause to descend upon us an abundance of the most precious gifts and graces. O prodigy! the greatest gift he could bestow upon us, since he gives himself his very Heart;—infinite gift! as great as the love which influences him. But, in order to effect this, he must overturn the established laws of nature, and perform the most surprising miracles. Nothing is too great for the infinite love with which his Heart is inflamed for us; he has performed these miracles, and his love induces him to renew them every day.

Now, does he confine his presence to one single place on the earth, as he did in his mortal life? No, his love makes him descend from the bosom of his Father, and become really present, in the adorable Sacrament of the Altar, to all the nations of the earth, in every temple of the same city, in order to satisfy the immense and infinite desire he has of dwelling with the children of men. But is it for any length of time that Jesus will reside on the earth? The love which captivates him under the sacramental veils shall retain him upon our altars while there shall be men in the world.

But these ungrateful men will not correspond to so unheard-of a favour: he shall be even outraged, insulted, profaned, in the sacrament of his love. He foresaw it, and his love has not been stopped; this view did not prevent the execution of his designs; he listened only to the voice of his Heart. O love! without doubt so much the more astonishing, as we were unworthy of it. It is this love which continues to perform so many united miracles at the moment of consecration. The substance of the bread and wine is changed; the accidents continue, without any subject to support them; the Body of Jesus Christ, without ceasing to be in Heaven, is on earth in a thousand different places; he is entirely concealed under every sensible particle of the Host; he is there deprived of the use of his senses, and invisible, though composed of flesh and bone like us; and, under these frail accidents, Jesus holds himself captive for the love of men. Always ready to hear them and converse with them —always ready to give himself to them, if they are always in a state fit to receive him.

O! who, with a soul capable of comprehending, and a heart of feeling, all these wonders of Divine Charity, would not burst into ecstacies of admiration, of gratitude, and love; he would find no happiness but at the foot of the altar; there he would wish to live and die, meditating on the unbounded charity of the Sacred Heart of Jesus, and offering himself as a victim, in order to atone for the insults which the Redeemer receives in the sacrament of his love.

O Jesus! adorable Heart, how hast thou

loved us; I shall repeat a thousand times, O Jesus, how hast thou loved us!

The Son of God expiring on the cross for the love and salvation of man, and giving himself entirely for our nourishment in the Sacrament of the Eucharist. Behold how this Sacred Heart loves us:—"*Ecce quomodo amabat.*"—John, 4. Behold the prodigy of a Heart penetrated by the most extraordinary love; behold this prodigy of love, which the angels and the saints, without ever being weary, shall admire and praise during eternity. Man is insensible to this love, and even abuses it; this is a prodigy of ingratitude and malice, perhaps equally inconceivable; a prodigy, which hell and all its tortures shall not be able to efface for all eternity. Ah! Jesus, do not suffer my heart to be such a prodigy of ingratitude: grant that it may be henceforth all love for thee, as thine is all love for me; this is what I wish. So may it be with the assistance of thy holy grace, which I implore and hope from thy Sacred Heart, and from its infinite love for me.

Sixthly, in a word, it is a continual and constant love. Since the first moment of your existence has it ceased to grant you favours, and to load you with its graces, notwithstanding your ingratitude and infidelities? If you have not been a thousand times precipitated into hell, as you merited; if, perhaps, even now hell is not open under your feet, to whom are you indebted for your preservation? Is it not to the love of which this adorable Heart bears you—a love which holds you as it were suspended over this abyss, into which your sins incessantly demand you should be immersed? Is it not to this love which urges you to return from your wanderings, and to put an end to this lukewarm and languid life which dishonours it? Is it not, in fine, to this Heart, which loved you before you existed, and since you received a being? Is it not to this Heart, which, not content with the goods with which it has loaded you, though you have abused them, is nevertheless always disposed to grant you much greater, if you wish to be faithful to it? Yes, the amiable Jesus wishes that the benevolence of his Sacred Heart should continue during all eternity, provided you place no obstacle in the way—provided, in a word, that you love him sincerely. Have we ever seen such incomprehensible love?

O what greatness, what goodness, what perfection, clemency, tenderness, and love, are included in the sacred name of Jesus and Heart of Jesus! Were this Sacred Heart even not infinitely amiable in itself, it should, notwithstanding, challenge our love from this motive alone, *that it loves us infinitely.*

O divine love, O Sacred Heart, O Jesus! Is the heart which refuses to love thee, the heart of a man? No, it is rather the heart of a demon: is it not formed, if we may use the expression, even of the mire of hell? Anathema to him who does not love thee. "*If any man love not our Lord Jesus Christ, let him be anathema.*"—1 Cor. xvi. 22. Ah! may my heart be annihilated, if it should ever be insensible to thy love; but no, Lord, it shall not be said, that I will be always ungrateful. Sacred Heart of my Jesus, adorable Heart, wounded on the cross for my sins, wounded in the Eucharist through love for me and by my ingratitude, I love thee entirely with the assistance of thy grace, and I wish that my love for thee may increase every moment of my life. If the sight of my sins alarm me, the remembrance of thine infinite love, and of thy precious blood shed to expiate my crimes, shall always enliven and strengthen my confidence. May it daily increase, I beseech thee, and likewise the bitter sorrow for my sins, and the ardent love which I wish henceforth to have for thee.

THE THIRD POINT.

When shall the Heart of Jesus be most loved?

SUCH is the desire of the true lovers of this adorable Heart. They know that it is infinitely amiable and infinitely loving, and, consequently, worthy of the love of all hearts; they are, therefore, little satisfied with the love which they bear towards it themselves; they would wish to influence all hearts to love it, and they incessantly sigh with new ardour to see all hearts inflamed with a love so just and so holy. But, alas! what grief for them to be obliged, on the contrary, to cry out Love is not beloved. It is true, and it is their only consolation in this affliction, that this Sacred Heart is beloved by the Eternal Father, and that it is the object of his complacency. This God of sanctity orders his angels to adore it, and he only loves men in the Heart of the amiable Jesus.

It is beloved by the Holy Ghost, who sheds his gifts from all parts to promote this love. O love of the Father and of the Holy Ghost, necessary and infinite love, love truly worthy of this adorable Heart!

It is beloved by the exalted Mary, and in the heart of this Blessed Virgin there is more love for the Sacred Heart of Jesus than in the hearts of all other creatures.

It is beloved by the angels and saints; the happiness of the blessed in heaven consists in a continual and ineffable love for it.

It is beloved on earth by many faithful and zealous servants. But how much greater is the number of those who do not love it, who even insult and outrage it.

Am I not perhaps of this number? Have I loved this infinitely amiable, infinitely loving, infinitely adorable Heart? How many times have I offended, have I despised it? O inexpressible anguish!

Ah! Sacred Heart, how couldst thou love so contemptible and so hateful a wretch?

Ah! my heart, how couldst thou love with so little ardour an object so amiable; how couldst thou resolve to offend the Heart of thy God, of thy Father, of thy Saviour, of the most powerful, the most faithful, and the most tender friend? But how, after so much indifference, after so many offences, does Jesus deign to stretch forth his arms and open his Heart to receive me!

Ah! I throw myself into this charitable Heart, burning with love, and I exclaim, in all the anguish of a heart rent with sorrow: Pardon me, Sacred Heart, pardon me, amiable Jesus, my past transgressions. I acknowledge my injustice, and detest, in the bitterness of my soul, the number and enormity of my crimes.

I love thee now, and always will love thee, adorable Heart; yes, I love thee with all my heart, or at least I ardently desire to love thee.

For the future I wish to love thee more and more; and to endeavour to promote thy love, I offer thee the love of all hearts which love thee sincerely; and I desire that all those who do not love thee, may henceforth love thee ardently and constantly. I rejoice, adorable Heart, that thou wilt be, during all eternity, infinitely amiable, infinitely loving, and infinitely beloved.

CONVERSATION

Of our Lord Jesus Christ with the Disciple on these words:

"MY SON, GIVE ME THY HEART."

Prov. xxiii. 26.

JESUS CHRIST.—My son, I ardently desire that thou wouldst make me an offering. All that which thou hast is mine; I could deprive thee of all thou possessest; but what I desire to receive from thee will be deficient in the beauty which attracts me, if thou dost not thyself present it. I wish to receive it from thy hands. Canst thou refuse me what I demand of thee; thou whom I have loved with an eternal love; thou who art indebted to me for all that thou art?

Disciple.—Ah! my God, could I refuse thee any thing I possess, if thou didst vouchsafe to ask it of me? No, Lord, speak, thy servant heareth. My body, my soul, the blood of my veins, are all thine by the right of creation, of conservation, of redemption, and by a thousand other titles: all is thine by the offering I make of all to thee.

Jesus Christ.—My son, give me thy love, give me thy heart. "*Præbe, fili mi, cor tuum mihi.*" If thou refusest me, I am irritated; if thou dividest it, I am jealous.

Disciple.—O miracle! A God, whose voice I have a thousand times despised, still seeks me, and asks my heart! Ah! what a heart, an ungrateful, perfidious, and rebellious heart; a heart so long an enemy to God: and for what? for trifles, for nothings. Thou alone, O my God, my Master, thou alone art capable of a love so excessive.

O my loving Saviour, who am I, that I can be so dear to thee, that thou deignest to command me to love thee? "*O pie Domine, quid tibi ego sum, ut amari te jubeas a me, et mineris mihi ingentes miserias, si non faciam.*" S. Aug. The desire which thou hast of being beloved by me is so ardent, that thou dost threaten me with the greatest misery if I do not love thee; as if the punishment of being deprived of thy love is not sufficiently great. Oh, how jealous art thou of my heart! Thou art grieved when I refuse it to thee; thou dost promise me great treasures if I give it to thee. Is my love so precious to thee? Have we ever known a great king seek a vile slave, and say to him, —I love thee with all my heart; love me, I pray thee, with a reciprocal love, and I will give thee one of the most beautiful provinces of my kingdom? Divine Heart, how generous art thou! I know not which I ought to admire most—thy solicitations, thy promises, or thy menaces. Thou dost entreat me to love thee; this is an excess of sweetness and goodness. Thou dost promise me eternal rewards; this is an excess of magnificence. Thou commandest me under the strictest penalties; this is a rigour which originates in the most lively source of divine love; which compels me, by an amiable violence, to deliver myself up to thee, and to yield to the sweet attraction of thy love. I can no longer resist; I will this day enter on a new life, and without delay comply with so pleasing a precept. What thou demandest of me is that which I entreat thee to accept: I give thee my heart, but a heart contrite and humble for so much resistance.

Jesus Christ.—But, my son, in giving me thy heart, dost thou well comprehend the extent of thy engagements? In demanding it of thee, I demand all; I consider, that in possessing it, I shall possess all; for all is subservient to the empire of the heart.

Disciple.—Yes, my divine Jesus, I comprehend what thou requirest of me, in demanding my heart; and it is with a perfect knowledge that I confirm the offering which I have made to thee of it.

Jesus Christ.—My son, does thy heart correspond with thy words? Does not an agreeable illusion deceive thee? It is easy to make a general offering in words; but it is difficult to make it in particular and in practice. Hast thou renounced thy conveniences; and art thou disposed to suffer the effects of poverty? Free from all attachment to health, reputation, and life, art thou disposed to receive with resignation, sickness, contempt, and death? Hast thou given me thy time, not wishing to employ it but agreeably to my will. Examine thyself, and endeavour to know, in reality, the secret thoughts of thy heart.

Disciple.—In giving thee my heart, O my amiable Jesus, I resign to thy hands, and give up entirely to thy providence, my interests, my health, my happiness, my fortune, my time, and my life.

Jesus Christ.—Thou hast, then, given me all. O my son, thou hast resigned up all to me; but hast thou done so with all thy heart? It is neither the gift in itself, nor the hand that offers it, which I consider; it is on the heart that I fix my eyes. The value of whatever is done for me or offered to me depends upon the dispositions and affections of the heart.

Disciple.—Consoling reflection for a miserable creature like me! In my situation, I can neither do much, nor perform great things; but the little that thou askest, O divine Jesus, I can do with all my heart, and with great affection. How good a Master art thou, O my divine Saviour! Happy those who have forsaken all, to be entirely thine! but without quitting the state of life in which I am placed, I can with thy grace, in fulfilling my duties, merit heaven and glorify God, as much as those who bear the burthen and heat of the day. It is only necessary to give to God my whole heart. Does he not merit it, and with what creature should I divide it?

Jesus Christ. - But canst thou with truth say, that thou hast given me all thy love, all thy heart, and all thy affections, when thou art still influenced by self-love, seeking thyself and yielding to so many base views and imperfect motives?

How canst thou say that thou hast given me thy whole heart, whilst thou dost continue to grieve the Holy Ghost, by resisting his graces, and committing so many faults, though they may be venial?

When thou prayest with so much negligence, and labourest with so much indolence, canst thou say that thou hast given to thy God what he demands of thee, and what he merits; namely, all thy love and all thy heart?

Disciple.—Behold, my God, how I have lived till now; but I renounce my misspent life with all my heart. Generous and perfect love, enkindle thy fervour in my soul; destroy, as much as it is possible, all self-love and self-seeking; influence all the powers of my soul; animate my negligence; warm my tepidity; support me under the weight of sin which oppresses me, and transform me into a victim inflamed with thy celestial fires.

Jesus Christ.—Observe, my son, that I have not said to thee, Lend me thine heart; but, *Give me thy heart.* He who lends anything to another, considers it still as his property; he merely grants the use of it for a certain time; and when this time is expired, he has a right to claim it. On the contrary, whatever is given belongs not to the original possessor, but is transferred to the dominion of another; and, without injustice, without a manifest robbery, he cannot be deprived of it.

Many faithless and ungrateful Christians content themselves with lending their heart to God. What fervour in prayer; what indolence in action! entirely devoted to God in communion, but to themselves in practice! What fine projects are formed; and how are they executed? New men in confession, but always the same in conduct. They receive and they reject grace; they drive it away, and they retain sin. What shameful inconstancy! Do not, my son, be of the number of these base, fickle, and faithless souls.

Disciple.—I acknowledge, to my confusion, O my God, that I cannot but discover my resemblance in the portrait you have drawn. I blush at the painful thought; for to whom does my heart justly belong? Who is its true master? Is it God? Is it myself? No, I am not my own; I belong to God, I am the possession of God. This great God, in giving me a being, could not deprive himself of the essential and continued dominion he has over my heart. I am therefore his, all his, and at all times I belong to him. When he lent me to myself, he has fixed and determined the use I ought to make of his property. I cannot then, in any moment of my love, rob him of my love or of my heart, without depriving him of a right which he demands, and which essentially belongs to him.

Thou knowest better than I can express, O my divine Jesus, the excess of levity and inconstancy to which sin has reduced my heart. All evil as it is, it belongs to thee; I place it in thy hands. Thou hast not asked it, that it should be refused thee. I present it to thee, and thou acceptest of it; receive it as consecrated to thee. Replenish it with thy graces; grant that it may know neither reserve nor inconstancy towards thee; preserve it so carefully, that nothing may rob thee of it, that nothing may weaken the ardent love which I desire to have for thee. *Amen.*

[You may sometimes use the meditation which precedes the foregoing entertainment, as a spiritual lecture, and the entertainment as a subject of meditation, divided into three points:—1st, God demands my heart; 2ndly, He demands my whole heart; 3rdly, He demands it for ever.]

FIVE VISITS

For the Festival of the Sacred Heart of Jesus.

FIRST VISIT.

THIS should be to thank our Lord Jesus Christ for the infinite love which he has shown us, in instituting the Sacrament of the Eucharist.

SACRED HEART OF JESUS.

SECOND VISIT.

IN thanksgiving for all our communions, and for all the particular favours he has granted us.

THIRD VISIT.

To make an act of reparation for all the outrages which he has received in this august Sacrament, on the part of infidels, and those who are out of the bosom of the Church.

FOURTH VISIT.

TO repair, as much as it is possible, by a profound respect and due homage, the irreverence and sacrileges committed towards our Lord, by the faithful themselves.

FIFTH VISIT.

WE ought to be particular to adore, in spirit, Jesus Christ in all the churches, whether in the country or city, where the most holy Sacrament is kept, and where it is so much neglected, so rarely visited, and so universally forgotten.

[Every person may recite in each visit the prayers which shall be most conformable to the intention he proposes.

If a person cannot acquit himself of these visits, let him at least endeavour to supply them, as we have directed in the practices for each day, page 15. One may likewise engage some pious person to perform these prayers for him.]

P

AN ACT OF ATONEMENT.

To be repeated aloud and in common on the Festival of the divine Heart of Jesus, and the first Fridays of every month, in the churches where this edifying custom is established, or where it may be hereafter established.

O JESUS, our divine Master, adorable Saviour of all men, who hast vouchsafed to veil thyself under the appearance of this Host, by an incomprehensible effect of the love of thine amiable Heart, behold us criminals, prostrate in thy presence, deeply penetrated with anguish for the offences which have been committed against thy Sovereign Majesty. We are here assembled in order to offer up a public and solemn act of atonement, and to repair, as much as is in our power, the innumerable injuries committed against thy sacred person, during the whole course of thy holy life and doleful passion, and all the insults offered thee in the adorable Eucharist, which is the great miracle of thy love for men. O that we could shed tears of blood over our ungrateful and perfidious conduct towards the most amiable of all Kings, and the meekest of all Hearts!—divine Heart, which, by the generosity of its love, hath redoubled its tenderness, even when we were treating it with the utmost contempt. Pardon, O Lord, pardon so many unworthy and sacrilegious communions, so many profanations, sufficient to excite the horror and execration of all ages, so many acts of irreverence in thy sacred temples. Pardon, O Lord, the hardness of our hearts, and our many distractions; pardon the forgetfulness in which we have lived, of thy goodness and of thy love.

Come ye ministers of the Most High, come all ye faithful people, come ye virgins, spouses of the spotless Lamb, let us adore God, who has formed us to his image; let us prostrate ourselves before him; let us weep together, at the foot of the holy altar, over the griefs we have caused, and the wounds we have made, in the adorable Heart of Jesus, who has redeemed us with his blood, sanctified us with his grace, loaded us with kindness, in generously giving us all that he has, and all that he is; let our cries and lamentations ascend to heaven, and let us never cease to mourn. No, Lord, we shall no longer wish for human consolations; we desire no pleasure but in the observance of thy law, of thy maxims, and of thine examples; no affections but those conformable to the sentiments of thy adorable Heart, to which we consecrate ours, in order to love it and to adore it in time and eternity, and by it to render to thy heavenly Father the worship which we owe him. *Amen.*

INVITATION,

To give ourselves up in Spirit to the Sacred Heart of Jesus.

WE invite all faithful adorers of the Sacred Heart of Jesus, to offer themselves up every day in spirit, at nine o'clock in the morning and at four in the afternoon, to this divine Heart, by addressing to it some of the following aspirations, or something similar :—

O divine Heart of Jesus, I love thee, and I invoke thee with all my associates, for every moment of my life, but especially for that of my death.

Cor Jesu, amore nostri vulneratum, divino amoris tui vulnere transfige cor nostrum. Cor Jesu, flagrans amore nostri, inflamma cor nostrum amore tui.

As the practices best calculated to honour the Sacred Heart of Jesus, are the Holy Mass, Confession, Communion, the frequent exercises of the Love of God, and Visits to the most Holy Sacrament, we shall point out several methods for these different exercises, all relative to the Sacred Heart of Jesus, and which each person may make use of according to his devotion. The Second Exercise for Mass, much wished for, which we have added in this edition (page 122), may serve likewise as a pious entertainment on the Passion of our Lord Jesus Christ.

EXERCISES

FOR THE

HOLY SACRIFICE OF THE MASS.

FIRST EXERCISE,

To unite ourselves to the Sacred Heart of Jesus during the Holy Sacrifice of the Mass.

Let your thoughts and affections be conformable to the principal actions and prayers of the Priest.

THE Holy Sacrifice of the Mass is, of all the actions of the Christian religion, the most glorious to God, and one of the most useful to the salvation of man. Jesus Christ there renews the great mystery of the redemption; he there offers himself in a true, though unbloody Sacrifice, as our victim, and comes in person to apply to each one in particular, the merits of that adorable blood which he shed for us all on the cross. What more proper to inspire us with an exalted idea of the Holy Sacrifice of the Mass?

Let us assist at it, if possible, every day, and remember that to assist at it with irreverence, wilful distractions, without modesty, without attention, without respect, is to renew, as much as as in us lies, the sorrows of Calvary, and to dishonour religion. Never fail, then, to assist there with the recollection, modesty, and devotion, which the supreme greatness and tender charity of him who immolates himself for us, exacts.

A PRAYER BEFORE MASS.

I PRESENT myself, O my adorable Saviour, before thy holy altar, to assist at thy divine sacrifice. Deign to apply to me all the fruit thou wishest me to derive from it. I detest, for thy love, all that which impedes the progress of thy grace. Supply, I beseech thee, by thy mercy and by the merits of thy Sacred Heart, the dispositions which are necessary for me.

At the Beginning of the Mass.

JUDGE me, O Lord, according to thy great mercy, and do not treat me as thou treatest the impious; destroy in me the empire of the devil, of pride and self-love; in order that being illuminated with thy light, purified with thy grace, and inflamed with thy love, I may with confidence approach thy sacred altars.

At the Confiteor.

ETERNAL Father, Father most holy, if my crimes provoke thee against me, turn away thine eyes from a wicked servant;

look on thine only Son, this dear object of thy complacency and of thy love; behold this innocent Lamb, about to offer himself as a sacrifice, to efface the sins of the world; and viewing his merits, forget my crimes and perfidies. I detest them from the bottom of my heart, for thy love. Remember that I am most dear to the Sacred Heart of this divine Saviour, who willingly died for me on a cross, and who, for me, is now going to offer to thee the unbloody sacrifice of his adorable body.

At the Introit.

THY Church, O Lord, prepares herself for the Sacrifice of the Mass, in praising thee and imploring thy mercy; unite me to thy divine Heart, that by it I may worthily praise thy eternal Father, and receive the marks of his paternal goodness.

At the Kyrie Eleison.

SWEET Jesus! may thy divine Heart have compassion on my misery; do not reject me, how great soever a sinner I may be; I shall not cease humbly to cry out, Jesus, Son of David, have mercy on me.

At the Gloria in Excelsis.

WE render to thee, O Lord, the glory which is due to thee alone; give us that peace and joy which proceed from a perfect charity. We bless thee, we give thee thanks. We acknowledge that we cannot acquit ourselves of these duties in a manner worthy of thee, but through thine adorable Son, who is with thee, the only Holy, the only Most High, the only Lord, in the unity of the Holy Ghost, to whom be all honour and glory for ever and ever. *Amen.*

At the Collects or Prayers.

ALL the Church prays to thee, O my God, by the mouth of the priest. I unite myself with this holy Church, in order to beg of thee the graces which are necessary for us. It is true I do not merit to be heard by thee; but consider that I ask these graces through the Heart of Jesus, desiring that the designs of his love may be eternally accomplished.

At the Epistle.

ENLIGHTEN my mind, O Lord, and give me the knowledge of thy divine scriptures, and the love of thy holy law. Assist me to keep it to the smallest point, and conduct me to Jesus Christ thy Son. It is he whom I desire to know, to hear, and to follow.

At the Gospel.

MAY I never be ashamed, O my Saviour, of thy Gospel or thy cross; may I never fear openly to profess what I firmly believe in my heart; may thy divine word produce in us fruits of grace and of salvation; and grant me, dear Jesus, as much courage to accomplish it, as thou inspirest us with firmness to believe it.

At the Credo.

YES, my God, I believe all the truths which thou hast revealed to thy holy Church. There is not one of them for which I would not willingly shed my blood; and it is in this entire submission, that uniting myself entirely to the profession of faith which the priest makes to thee, I now confess in heart and in spirit, as he pronounces aloud, that I firmly believe in thee, and all that thy Church believes. I affirm, in the presence of thy altars, that I wish to live and die in the sentiments of this pure faith, and in the bosom of thy Holy, Catholic, Apostolic, and Roman Church.

At the Offertory.

RECEIVE, O most holy Father, the Sacred Heart of Jesus thy Son, our divine Redeemer. We present it as a holocaust, the most agreeable and worthy of thy greatness, in order to render to thee, through it, our homage, our thanksgiving, and the satisfaction which we owe to thy justice for our sins, and to obtain from thy bounty all the graces necessary to secure eternal salvation. Remember the labours, the sufferings, the death of this dearly-beloved Son, and the ardent love with which his Sacred Heart was inflamed for us, when he died for our salvation on the tree of the cross; and regard favourably our sacrifice, that it may be to the glory of thy divine Majesty, and useful to all the faithful. Vouchsafe likewise, O my God, to permit me to consecrate to thee all my thoughts, all my desires, all my words, and all the actions of my life. I submit myself entirely to thy divine will. I unite the sacrifice which I make to thee of myself, with the perfect sacrifice which thy Son, my Saviour, offered to thee on the cross, and which he continues to offer on our altars. I take from this moment the sentiments of his Sacred Heart as my rule and model; deign to apply to me his merits, in order that my sacrifice may be agreeable to thee.

At the Lavabo.

PURIFY me more and more, O my God, from the sins I have had the misfortune to commit. I detest them all with my whole heart, because they displease thee. I beseech thee by the sorrow which the adorable Heart of thy Son experienced, to pardon me my sins, and to give the innocence and sanctity which this spotless Lamb demands, who is going to be immolated on the altar.

At the Orate Fratres.

MY God, may the sacrifice at which I have the happiness to assist serve to extend the glory of thy holy name; may it tend to my sanctification, and draw down thy benedictions on thy holy Church.

At the Preface.

DISENGAGE us, O Lord, from all things here below; elevate our hearts to heaven, fix them on thee alone. In the union which is at present made of the Church triumphant and militant, we enter in spirit, O divine Saviour, into the sanctuary of thy Sacred Heart, to be there consumed by the fire of thy holy love; through it we adore thy infinite sanctity; we unite ourselves in heart and in mind with the celestial Hosts, confessing with them that thou art Holy, Holy, Holy; the immortal God, to whom belong benediction, glory, wisdom, thanksgiving, honour, and power, for ever and ever. Amen.

At the Canon.

WE adore thee, O Father, infinitely merciful, and we entreat thee, through the Heart of Jesus, a most holy victim, to receive our oblation. We offer it to thee by the hands of the priest, for thy holy Catholic

Church, for our holy Father the Pope (N.), for our Prelate (N.), and for our pastors, for our Queen and all the royal family, for our governors, magistrates, and other superiors. We supplicate thee also for all our relations, our associates, our friends, our enemies, our benefactors, and all those for whom we are obliged to pray. We implore thee to grant perseverance to the just, consolation to the afflicted, relief to the suffering souls in Purgatory, and conversion to bad Catholics.

O Jesus, who didst die for all, bring back to the bosom of thy Church those who are separated from it by schism or heresy; enlighten infidels and idolaters; bless the efforts of those who labour to instruct and convert them. Give to them all, O Lord, thy grace, thy love, and eternal life.

When the Priest spreads his Hands over the Chalice.

LORD, since the imposition which the priest makes with his hands, denotes the possession thou takest of thy victim, which is going to be offered for us, we should no longer consider ourselves but as victims destined to death; grant us, then, the grace continually to die to ourselves, in consecrating to thee all our thoughts, words, and affections, in order to live in a continual spirit of sacrifice to the glory of thy holy name.

At the Consecration.

LORD, grant us the grace, that as the bread and wine are going to be changed into thine adorable Body and precious Blood, so we may be transformed into thee, to become the same spirit with thee. Change our hearts, that they may resemble thine, and that they may have no other desire, no other will but thine.

At the Elevation of the Sacred Host.

SALUTARY Host, which openest to us the gate of Heaven, I adore thee with the most profound respect: strengthen me against the enemies of my salvation.

O Jesus, holy Victim, I adore thee, I love thee, and I implore thee, through thy Sacred Heart, to purify me, to sanctify me, and to inflame me with thy sacred love.

At the Elevation of the Chalice.

O PRECIOUS Blood, fountain of grace and mercy, I adore thee. Flow into my heart, O most pure source, to extinguish there the fire of my passions, and wash me from all the stains of sin.

After the Elevation.

O MY God, what may I not hope to obtain through this spotless victim, sacrificed for us on this altar? It is through

Christ our victim, and through the merits of his precious blood, that we dare to pray and hope for the pardon of our sins, the spirit of penance, a profound humility, an ardent charity, and final perseverance.

At the Memento for the Dead.

LORD, we beseech thee, through the merits of thy holy death and passion, and through the love of thy Sacred Heart, to deliver from Purgatory the souls which are there detained, and in particular those of our parents, friends, associates, benefactors, and all those for whom we are obliged to pray. Grant them, dear Lord, the eternal repose after which they so ardently sigh.

At the Nobis quoque Peccatoribus.

HEAVEN, O my God, where thy saints reign, is likewise our inheritance; Jesus, the amiable Jesus, has merited it for us by the effusion of his precious blood; and he at present offers it to thee on this altar, to merit for us the pardon of those sins which shut the door of Heaven against us. Hear the voice of this precious blood, which supplicates mercy for us; hear the prayers of his adorable Heart; pardon us, and grant that we may reign eternally with thy saints.

At the Pater Noster.

THOUGH I am but a miserable sinner, great God, yet I take the liberty of calling thee my Father, as thou desirest. Grant me the grace, O my God, not to degenerate from the quality of thy child, and do not suffer me to do anything unworthy of the title. May thy holy name be sanctified throughout the universe. Reign from this moment in my heart, by thy grace, that I may perform thy will on earth, as the saints do in Heaven, and that I may reign eternally with thee in glory. Thou art my Father; give me then, I beseech thee, this heavenly bread with which thou dost nourish thy children. Pardon me, as I pardon from my heart, for thy sake, all those who have offended me, and never permit me to fall into any temptation; but grant, with the assistance of thy grace, that I may triumph over all the enemies of my salvation.

At the Agnus Dei.

LAMB without spot, holy victim, who takest away the sins of the world, purify my heart from all those sins of which I know I have been guilty, and those I do not remember. I detest them all with my whole heart, for thy sake, and I am sorry for having committed them, because they displease thee, who art infinitely amiable. Give me a new heart, O divine Jesus, a heart conformable to thine. Remove from the world all iniquity, destroy vice, make thy holy religion triumph, convert and save sinners, and give us eternal peace.

At the Domine non sum dignus.

IT is true, O Lord, I am not worthy that thou shouldst enter into a soul so miserable as mine; but my miseries and pressing wants make me desire to eat of this heavenly bread, and oblige me, in the hunger which presses me, to have recourse to the tenderness of thy paternal Heart, to draw from that divine abundance wherewith to supply all my wants, and to fill the void of my soul. Come, then, O Jesus, take possession of my heart, and render it worthy of being united to thine.

[If you do not actually communicate, you must do so spiritually, and make the following acts:]

An Act of Desire.

COME, O divine Jesus, the well-beloved of my soul, come and take possession of my heart. The thirsty deer does not sigh with more ardour after a refreshing fountain, than I do for the happy moment when I shall receive thee.

An Act of Supplication.

GIVE me at least, O Lord, the crumbs which fall from thy table. Give me that profound humility which the sight of my nothingness ought to produce. Clothe me with the nuptial robe of charity, that I may enter with the just into the banqueting-hall, to eat there the bread of the elect: give me an ardent desire for this food, and remove every obstacle which may retard my happiness, and prevent me from participating at thy sacred table.

At the last Prayers.

GRANT us the grace, O my God, to dwell and to live in Jesus Christ, who gives himself in these divine mysteries. Grant that we may receive and preserve the fruit of this awful sacrifice which we have offered to thy Sovereign Majesty, we beseech thee, through the intercession of the Blessed Virgin, of the angels, and of the saints whom the Church particularly honours on this day.

At the Benediction.

DIFFUSE on us, O eternal Father, thy most abundant benedictions, and grant us to hear from the voice of thy divine Son, at the day of avenging justice, these consoling words: "*Come, ye blessed of my Father,* *possess the kingdom which has been prepared for you from the creation of the world."*

At the last Gospel.

ADORABLE Word, without beginning and without end, grant us the grace to know thee, to hear thee, to love thee, and to imitate thee all our life, in order that we may adore thee and contemplate thee eternally with thy Father, in the unity of the Holy Ghost. *Amen.*

An Act of Thanksgiving and Reparation after Mass.

I RETURN thee thanks, with all my heart, O my amiable Jesus, for thy goodness in permitting me to remain in thy divine presence, whilst thou didst offer thyself in sacrifice on this altar for my sake. I most humbly ask pardon of thee for the little attention and devotion I have had at these divine mysteries. Penetrated with sorrow, I desire to make some reparation to thy Sacred Heart, for all the acts of irreverence which are ever committed during this august sacrifice; and I conjure thee to grant us the grace always to feel the effects of it, to preserve the fruit of it, and to assist at it every day with increasing fervour.

SECOND EXERCISE,

To unite ourselves to the Sacred Heart of Jesus during the Holy Sacrifice of the Mass.

A PRAYER BEFORE MASS.

To dispose our hearts to assist at it with advantage, the mind should be fixed on the Mysteries of the Passion.

DIVINE Jesus, true Son of God, holy Victim, Peace-offering, Lamb without spot, who, by thy precious blood, hast satisfied the divine justice for the sins of the world; Redeemer, infinitely merciful, to what excess hath the infinite love of thine adorable Heart carried thee, to save me, to sanctify me, and to render me eternally a partaker of thy glory! Not content with having immolated thyself on the tree of the cross, thou hast likewise instituted the august Sacrifice of the Altar, where, by the true though mystical and unbloody renewal of the sacrifice of Calvary, thou every day appliest to us thine infinite merits: grant me the grace to assist there with the sentiments of respect, love, and gratitude, which thou requirest of me; and teach me to render, through thee and with thee, to thy heavenly Father, the homage which I owe to him, to satisfy his divine justice for my sins, to acknowledge the inestimable benefits with which he incessantly loads me, and to draw down on me more and more the effects of his mercy. *Amen.*

FROM THE BEGINNING OF MASS TO THE EPISTLE.

Jesus in the Garden of Olives.

I ADORE thee, O my divine Jesus, prostrate in the presence of thy Father in the Garden of Olives, and delivering up thy Heart, for my sake, to fear, sorrow, and the most bitter anguish. Thou waitest not the fury of the Jews to shed thy blood, thou dost commence to shed it thyself, and, by a prodigious effect of thy unspeakable grief, thy blood flows in abundance from all parts of thy body.

O precious Blood, which bedewest the earth, I adore thee with the most profound respect. Thou art shed through an effort of love, and thou oughtest to wash away the stains of our sins: wash, purify my heart from all my iniquities.

O profound grief, which dost penetrate with the most overwhelming anguish, the most sanctified, the most amiable of hearts, penetrate mine likewise. It is I who am guilty: Jesus is innocent. What regret, what affliction for me, O adorable Heart, when I reflect that it is I—that it is my crimes that have cast thee into this mortal anguish! I disavow, I detest, I abhor, with all my heart, these unhappy sins. O that I could expiate them here below, with a sorrow like to thine! Have mercy on me, O my divine Saviour, and grant that, as I have sinned against thee, I may expiate my iniquities by weeping over them with thee.

Eternal Father, it is the sight of thy divine majesty offended, of thy glory insulted, of thy sovereign greatness and infinite perfection outraged, by the sins of men and by mine, which has forced from thy well-beloved Son these deep sighs, bitter griefs, and sorrowful complaints: it is to expiate our perfidies, our abominations, and our innumerable sacrileges, that he bedews the earth with his precious blood. O merciful Father, let thine anger be appeased, and let the mortal anguish of his adorable Heart satisfy thy justice for all our deficiences; grant to the Blood, grant to the Heart of thy dearly-beloved Son, a pardon which we do not merit, but which he has merited for us.

King of heaven and of earth, amiable Redeemer, source of the felicity of the saints in heaven, joy and consolation of the just on earth, in thy most overwhelming grief thou dost, for my sake, willingly deprive thyself of all consolation. Prayer is thine only succour, and thou dost persevere in it with constancy, without attending to the repugnance of nature; and thou deliverest thyself up to the most cruel torments and to the most ignominious death. Shall I never profit, O my divine Model, by the examples which thou givest me, and the love which thou showest for me?

Since it is from thee, O my sweet Jesus, that I ought to expect consolation and fortitude in the crosses which thy love ordains for me, why, blind as I am, have I not recourse to thee? Divine love, faithful love, who art never nearer thy servants than when they are in tribulation, it is in thee alone that I place my confidence. Deign to fortify me in my conflicts, and to console me in my afflictions. By the merit of the submission with which thine adorable Heart submitted to the will of thy heavenly Father, grant that mine may be perfectly submissive, and that it may be ever ready to suffer all that this Father, infinitely holy, pleases, as he pleases, because he pleases, and as long as he pleases. *Amen.*

Jesus betrayed and taken in the Garden.

JESUS, my glory and my sovereign good, thou dost commence to prove the ardent desire which thou hast to die for us, when thou dost permit the blackest, the foulest treason. Judas, whom thou hadst chosen for one of thine apostles and confidants, whom thou hadst admitted to thine intimate friendship and to thy sacred table —Judas, the traitor Judas, sells thee for vile interest, betrays thee with a kiss, and delivers thee into the hands of thine enemies. But, alas! how often have I not imitated his ingratitude and his perfidy! O my Lord and my Master, I feel my heart penetrated with the most lively sorrow. Pardon me my past infidelities, and do not suffer me to relapse any more. Root out of my heart whatever may prevent me from being entirely thine; grant me the grace to be in future of the number of those who love thee sincerely, ardently, and constantly; and since thou hast suffered, for my sake, the treason of a perfidious friend, give me courage to support patiently the pains, mortifications, and injuries which I shall have to encounter. Grant that I may never allow myself to be puffed up by the esteem of men, nor dejected by their infidelity.

In the meantime, O my amiable Master, thou deliverest thyself up to thine enemies; they rush upon thee like furious lions, they load thee with chains, they trample thee under their feet. But these chains do not keep thee; it is the desire of doing the will of thy Father, and the love which thou hast for me. O divine hands, ever abounding in mercy, how unworthy soever I may be, do not depart from me, I beseech you. The chains which bind you, do not confine your power; make it appear in favour of this ungrateful soul. O my divine Saviour, since thou art thus bound only to procure my liberty, break, I beseech thee, the chains which still attach me to the world and to myself, and bind me for ever to thy holy law and to thy service, with the chains of thy love. May my mind and my heart be ever engaged with thee, and may I find no repose but in thee alone, O my love, O my life, O the only hope of my soul!

FROM THE EPISTLE TO THE OFFERTORY.

Jesus conducted to the different Tribunals.

PERMIT me, O my adorable Master, to follow thee in spirit to the different tribunals whither thou didst wish to be conducted, in order that I may profit by the examples thou there givest me. Thou appearest there as a criminal, thou the Sovereign Judge of the living and of the dead; they accuse thee of being the disturber of the public tranquillity, thou who art the Prince of Peace, and who descended from Heaven to reconcile all, and to re-establish peace upon the earth; they contemptuously insult and treat thee as a fool, thou who dost possess the treasures of eternal wisdom; they sentence thee to death, thou by whom all things were made, and by whom they have life, animation, and existence. I adore thee with the most profound respect, even in the midst of the outrages which thou receivest.; and I acknowledge thee as the Word of the Father and his infallible Word; as the eternal Wisdom, who dost preside over the designs of the Most High, and dost govern the universe; as the true Son of God; as the Eternal God, almighty, infinitely wise, and infinitely good. O Jesus, I acknowledge thee and I adore thee as the way, the truth, and the life. It is thou I desire to follow, it is thou I wish to hear, it is by thee I desire to live. Be thou blessed a thousand times for having called me to the knowledge of thy holy Gospel. Grant me the grace to relish the sacred maxims which thou there teachest me, that my conduct may be ever conformable to them. Preserve in my heart that pure faith, that perfect submission of heart and mind which I owe to thy Church, and in which I wish to live and die.

But, my divine Master, what instruction ought I not to derive from thy invincible patience, thy unalterable meekness, thy perfect tranquillity, thy heroic silence in the midst of false witnesses, of outrages the most bloody, of affronts the most ignominious, to which thine infinite love for me has exposed thee? O boundless charity! whilst these barbarians think only of destroying thee, thou art entirely occupied with a desire of suffering for them; and thine adorable Heart is full of tenderness and love, even for those who treat thee with so much indignity. Whilst their fury seeks new means of outrage against thee, thou dost labour for their reconciliation and for mine, and thou art solicitous only for the consummation of thy sacrifice. O when shall I be instructed by thine example, when shall it affect me and suppress in my presumptuous heart the sentiments of aversion, of spleen, of anger and revenge, which spring up in me when I experience the slightest mark of contempt? Ought I not to think myself very happy, O my divine Model, to have any share in thine ignominies, and to be able to sacrifice my honour and my reputation, to the solid glory and true consolation which are found in resembling thee? Give me, I beseech thee, O my adorable Master, the love of contempt and humiliation; make me a partaker of thine invincible patience, and of these sentiments of tenderness which thine adorable Heart preserved even for those who treated thee with the utmost contempt. *Amen.*

FROM THE OFFERTORY TO THE SANCTUS.

A Prayer.

THOUGH I acknowledge that I am unworthy of presenting myself before thee, O my God, permit me to offer thee, by the hands of the priest, this sacred and spotless victim for the expiation of all my sins, and for the entire and perfect change of my heart. I offer it to thee for the living and the dead, that it may procure for all the happiness of eternally enjoying thy presence in the mansions of the blessed. *Amen.*

Barabbas preferred to Jesus.

A THIEF, a seditious wretch, a murderer, is judged more worthy of living than thou, O divine Jesus, who art the essence of goodness, wisdom, and holiness; and among so many witnesses of thine irreproachable conduct, there is not an individual who will give testimony in thy favour, or speak a word in thy defence: all have lost the remembrance of thy miracles, of thine examples, and of thy virtues; they have forgotten the meekness with which thou didst receive them, the wisdom with which thou didst instruct them, the power with which thou didst heal them, and all the love which thou didst testify for them. O perverse world, how false and deceitful is thy friendship! how unjust and unreasonable are thy judgments! But, alas! O my adorable Redeemer, what confusion for me, when, reflecting on my past conduct, I call to my recollection how often I have preferred the friendship of this world to thine. I have forsaken thee,

O the God of my soul, for vain honours and vile interests; I have banished from my heart thy divine Spirit, to make the spirit of sin and darkness reign there; I have exchanged thee for death, O the Life of my soul; to thee I have preferred a blind and extravagant world, O eternal Wisdom; I have quitted thee to walk in darkness, O divine Light. How shall I dare to appear before thee, how can I raise my eyes to thee, after having thus insulted thee? Pardon me, O merciful Father, such enormous indignities, and so monstrous a preference. O that I could, at the expense of my life, repair the injury I have done thee! I detest my attachment to the world and my pride, which have been the cause of my crimes. Confound above all, O my Jesus, this insupportable pride, which is the source of my disorders, and grant me the grace henceforth to love nothing so much as humiliations. *Amen.*

Jesus Scourged.

MY adorable Jesus, no form of justice is observed with regard to thee: Pilate acknowledges thine innocence, and delivers thee up to be cruelly punished as if thou wert guilty; thou consentest to it, O my amiable Saviour! The sacred fire which burns in thy Heart is insatiable; its activity knows no bounds, because it desires to consume all, and thou consumest thyself for my salvation.

O divine love, is it possible that thou hast so much power over Jesus, and so little over me? O my divine Jesus, burn not alone with this divine fire; grant that I may be inflamed with it, and be consumed with thee: thou wishest it, and canst do it. Lord, do what thou canst, and permit me not to resist what thou wishest.

Thy love has not permitted that thine enemies should treat thee with any sort of humanity. They fasten thee to a pillar, they scourge thee cruelly; they have no pity on him who had compassion for all the miserable. Instead of forty stripes, as ordained by the law, the executioners weary themselves in scourging thee, and relieve one another successively. Thy sacred body, thus buffeted and torn with whips, is but one single wound.

Behold, O my divine Jesus, the melancholy state to which my crimes have reduced thee; behold what my disorderly self-love has cost thee. I wish to have no other pleasure in future, O thou love of my soul, than to burn with love for thee, to return thee incessant thanks for thy ineffable charity, to embrace this sacred pillar as the support of all my hopes, to suffer continually with thee, to unite my penance with thy sufferings, and to expiate, by the mortification of my criminal body, my own sins, for which thine innocent body has suffered such cruel torments.

Jesus crowned with Thorns.

I ADORE thee, O Lord, now humbled and suffering for me. I adore thy divine head crowned with thorns; this head, which the most brilliant stars in the firmament would not be worthy to crown. I adore thine eyes, full of that divine light which imparts joy to the blessed in Heaven, and which are at present concealed under a veil, and bathed with tears. I adore thy majestic countenance, which the angels can never cease to contemplate, and which I at present behold covered with spittle, livid and disfigured, for the love of me. I adore thee as the sovereign King of Heaven and earth; I submit with joy to thine amiable dominion, and I am heartily sorry for having withdrawn from it so often. Reign alone in me henceforth, O Prince of Peace; pacific Monarch, possess alone all the affections of my heart. Banish from it these cruel tyrants, these fatal passions, which dispute its possession with thee, and dispose of me according to thy holy will. I consecrate to thee all that I am and all that I can do. Receive me by thy mercy; govern me by thy wisdom; defend me by thy power; enrich me by thy liberality; chastise me by thy justice. Dispose of me as thou pleasest; but do not permit I should ever cease to be in the number of thy faithful subjects.

O King of Glory, become for me the man of sorrows, and loaded with reproaches! is it possible, when fixing mine eyes upon thee, that I do not acknowledge how great is my injustice, in refusing, burdened as I am with innumerable sins, to taste one single drop of that bitter chalice which thou, my Redeemer, hast drunk even to the dregs? I have frequently sinned, and my crimes are enormous: why, then, should I not wish to discharge even a small part of the great debts I have contracted in sinning? O Lord, I conjure thee, through the love which induced thee to suffer so much for me, to enlighten, to inflame, and enable me to imitate thee. Divest me of this criminal self-love, and replace it with thy holy love; and may I seek in future as ardently for sufferings, as I have for the past time avoided them; that resembling thee here by my patience, I may attain to thy resemblance in glory. *Amen.*

FROM THE SANCTUS TO THE ELEVATION.

Jesus is shown to the People, and condemned to Death.

THOU appearest before the Jews, O my Saviour, all covered with wounds, exhausted of blood and of strength, overwhelmed with sufferings; and these furious Jews, far from being affected by the lamentable state to which thy love for us has reduced thee, insist, with loud cries, to have thee crucified. Alas! my Jesus, thy divine Heart was deeply affected by the ingratitude of this cruel people, whom thou hadst preferred to all others on earth, enlightened with thy divine instructions, and loaded with thy greatest benefits. But, alas! my amiable Redeemer, was I not then present to thy thoughts, among the number of those ungrateful wretches? Were not the cries of my sins intermixed with the cries of this infuriate populace who demanded thy death, and which pierced thine amiable Heart with the keenest sorrow? Pierce mine, O my God, with the shafts of lively contrition; grant that it may burst forth in sighs and grief for having caused thee so much affliction. In the meantime, Pilate pronounces against thee the sentence of death, and condemns thee to the punishment of the cross. Thou acceptest it, O my divine Jesus, with a prompt and generous will, in obedience to the will of thy Heavenly Father: thou submittest to it with joy, in order to save me from eternal damnation, which I have deserved; and in delivering thyself up to the will of thy executioners, thou committest to them the power of making thee suffer as many different torments as their cruelty can invent.

After such profusion of love, hast thou not every right to require, O my amiable Saviour, that I should abandon myself to thee without any reserve and without any division? I surrender myself entirely and for ever to thee, O my love and my only hope. I give up to thee my soul, my body, my strength, my honour, my life, and all I possess; but, above all, I commit and consecrate to thee my will, with a firm resolution to fulfil thine in all things. To whatever sufferings thou wouldst permit or desire I should be condemned, to them I submit willingly, ever attentive to thine example. Strengthen me only with thy grace, that I may joyfully accept both losses and disgraces, insults and afflictions, through the sole desire of pleasing and imitating thee.

What shall I render to thee, O eternal Father, for this infinite charity, which has induced thee to deliver up for me thy beloved Son, and to sacrifice him for my salvation? In him thou givest me every blessing, —a remedy in misfortunes, relief in sufferings, comfort in afflictions, and an all-powerful mediator to support my petitions. O infinite Mercy, be thou ever praised and blessed by all thy creatures! I receive from thy paternal hand, with heartfelt gratitude, this dear Son, the object of thy complacency, and I offer him to thee, and myself in union with him. Through him thou wilt pardon my sins, fortify my weakness, dispel my darkness, instruct my ignorance, heal the wounds of my soul, inflame my lukewarmness, and preserve me in thy love and in thy grace. Do not permit, O my God, that I ever separate myself from thy beloved Son, or lose the fruit of his sufferings; for without him I am lost, and in him only I find my life and salvation.

Jesus carrying his Cross.

AT length the hour is come, O divine Redeemer of the world, when, by an incomprehensible effect of thine infinite goodness and mercy, thou condescendest to open to us and point out the way which leadeth from earth to Heaven. The cross to which thou art to be fastened is placed on thy lacerated shoulders; its weight and its infamy do not terrify thee; thou embracest it with tenderness; and though exhausted by the blood thou hast shed, by the torments thou hast undergone, by the wounds with which thou art covered, thou joyfully loadest thyself with this instrument of our salvation. O God of goodness, nothing appears hard or painful to thy love. In the meantime, the cries of the populace, the cruelty of the executioners, the outrages, the insults of thine enemies, renew all thy torments; thy wounds are again opened, sweat and blood trickle down from all parts of thy body. Thy strength fails, thou sinkest under the weight, and renewest thy love, thy obedience, and thy desire to suffer and die for me. More oppressed with the weight of my crimes than that of the cross, thou teachest me that the only way to render it light to thee, is to weep over mine own iniquities. I beg of thee, my adorable Master, to grant me these salutary tears, that deep regret, that bitter sorrow for the offences I have committed against thee. By the cross thou hast merited pardon of them for me, and by the cross I desire to expiate them myself. If thou go before me with a cross so heavy, shall I think I do much in following thee with a cross, which becomes very light by thy grace? O sacred and venerable cross, inheritance of the elect and friends of God, assured asylum of the afflicted, receive me into thine arms, and may I be united by thee to him, who has redeemed me by thee. *Amen.*

AT THE ELEVATION OF THE HOST.

ADORE thee, O Son of the living God, O God of my heart, O love of my soul; I firmly believe that thou art really present in this sacred host. I adore thee, O divine Redeemer, O thou glory of the just, the crown of the blessed, the source of eternal good. I adore thee, O holy Victim; spotless Lamb, that takest away the sins of the world, I conjure thee to take away mine, to inflame and consume me for ever with thy love.

AT THE ELEVATION OF THE CHALICE.

I ADORE in this chalice, O my divine Saviour, this precious blood which thou hast shed for the redemption of all mankind: wash, with this adorable blood, every stain in my soul that can offend thine infinite sanctity, that there may be nothing in me to withdraw me from thee.

AFTER THE ELEVATION.

Jesus elevated on the Cross.

I ADORE thee, O amiable Jesus, elevated on the cross; I acknowledge thee for my Deliverer, and the divine Redeemer of the world. Cast on this miserable sinner thine eyes of mercy, and one of those affecting looks which entirely changes the heart. I prostrate myself before thee with the most profound respect; I acknowledge that thou art my salvation and my life, that in thee I discover all riches, and a Heart ever ready to grant me assistance. I love thee, O Saviour of my soul, and my greatest affliction consists in not having loved thee more ardently. Why cannot my eyes become two fountains of continual tears, and my heart a furnace of love everlasting? Remember, O my Jesus, that thou hast promised to draw all to thyself, when thou shouldst be raised from the earth. Though I am nothing in thy sight, and though my sins render me more insignificant than that nothing, I am, notwithstanding, the work of thy hands. Draw me then to thee, O my God, and change me into thee. Triumph over me, as the love which thou hast for me has triumphed over thee. Display thy glorious power and the riches of thy goodness, by making me die to myself, so as to live only in thee. Destroy in me my wicked spirit, and give me thy divine spirit; the spirit of humility, the spirit of mortification, the spirit of oblation, the spirit of love, the spirit of resignation to the divine will, the spirit of understanding, to comprehend thy heavenly doctrine, the spirit of fidelity, in order to follow thine example. May thy holy spirit live in me, and may it for the future influence all my actions. O divine Saviour, live and reign alone in my soul, and grant that I may live crucified in thee. May all my glory consist in dying for thee, and all my happiness in living in thee. Grant, from this moment, that all created objects be, with regard to me, as if they were not, and that nothing may remain dear to me but thou alone, O crucified Jesus; for thou art the love and the life of my soul, my only treasure and all my happiness.

Thou art all mine, O my Saviour; thou art all things to me, entirely sacrificed for my wants and my salvation. Thou givest me thy divine nature, which communicates infinite virtue to all thou doest, and to all thou hast endured for my salvation. Thou givest me thy human nature, immersed in an abyss of sufferings. Thou givest me thy divine head crowned with thorns, thy cheeks livid and bruised, thine eyes obscured and bathed in tears, thy mouth drenched with gall and vinegar, thy hands and feet bored with nails, thy flesh mangled, thy nerves overstrained, thy bones dislocated; thou givest me thy thoughts, thy desires, thy life; and in consuming thyself thus entirely for me, thou reconcilest me to thy eternal Father, thou communicatest to me thy merits, thou offerest me mercy, that satisfiest for me to the divine Justice, thou diest to make me live, thou hast shed the last drop of thy blood to purify me, and thou workest all these miracles through the extreme love thou hast for me. I cannot have for love so excessive either the esteem or gratitude which it deserves; but I adore, I bless it, as much as I possibly can. O that I had as much ardour and purity as all the angels and saints of Paradise, as all the just upon earth, that I might love thee as they do, and correspond, at least in some degree, to the excess of thy charity! But thou doest all these things, O my God, in a manner proportionable to what thou art, that is, with infinite perfection; but, as I am a miserable creature, all I do is miserably done. Yet, knowing our wretchedness, thou art content with our good desires, and the little we are able to do. I resign to thy hands, O my God, all that I am and possess: I offer up all to thee, since from thee I have received all,—my body, my soul, my senses, my strength, and my life. I consecrate for ever to thy service all the gifts of nature and grace which I have received from thee, and place them at the foot of thy cross. O holy cross, faithful companion of my Saviour, may I continue henceforth attached to thee and to him; may I never be deprived of him or of thee: and that thus the old man may be renewed, and I may begin to live in the newness of the spirit of Jesus. *Amen.*

FROM THE PATER NOSTER TO THE DOMINE NON SUM DIGNUS.

Jesus promises Paradise to the penitent Thief.

MY divine Saviour, I acknowledge with the penitent thief, that thou art the Sovereign King of heaven and earth. On the cross I behold thee covered with blood and wounds; on it I adore thee as my God, and the only Son of the eternal Father. Remember me, O my Saviour, when thou art in thy kingdom, and grant that I may there occupy the place which thy love has destined for me. By the cross thou hast merited it for me, and by the cross also I desire to render myself worthy of it; since it is in reality the channel of thy mercies, and the pledge of eternal glory. Grant that I may be a partaker of the cross, on it to become like thee, to live and die on it in thy love and for thy love. *Amen.*

Jesus afflicted at the Sorrows of his Blessed Mother.

AMIABLE Jesus, O innocent Lamb, Thou feelest not only thine own, but also the torments of thy holy Mother. O Heart of the Son, O Heart of the Mother, pure Hearts, Hearts full of grace, Hearts inflamed with love, Hearts so united and so deeply afflicted, associate me to partake in your sufferings. Thou sensibly feelest, O holy Virgin, the innumerable sorrows of thine holy Son, because thou art the most tender of mothers. Thou feelest most sensibly, O divine Jesus, the interior torments of thy holy Mother, because thou art the most grateful and generous of all sons.

O amiable Hearts, you suffer for each other, and you feel, without a ray of comfort, your mutual sufferings. O Hearts abounding with justice and goodness, I can bear no longer the reproach of having reduced you to this condition: either pardon me, O Sacred Heart, or avenge thyself. Since all creatures obey thee, command them to punish me. Make me a partaker of thy sorrows: it is only just I should share them, as I have brought them upon thee. O Jesus, the love of my soul, O Mary, my hope and my refuge, deprive me of the sweets of life, and do not permit mine to terminate, without having relished the salutary bitterness of the cross.

What shall I render thee, O God of my heart, for all the blessings with which thou hast loaded me? I could wish never to cease blessing and praising thee, when I consider the admirable works of thy infinite love. Thou turnest everything to my advantage: even thy sorrow in beholding thy afflicted Mother, becomes a source of benedictions to me. Thou givest me this holy

U

virgin for a mother, and wishest I should be her son, that she might compassionate my miseries and wants, as she compassionated thee when reproached. How greatly are thy views superior to ours, but how replenished with goodness to us! It is because Mary is the Mother of the Saviour, that she is to be also the mother of sinners! Were we not miserable children, how could she be the mother of mercy?

Most holy Virgin, Queen of martyrs, it was at the foot of the cross that thou hast been given to me for a mother. Protect me, I beseech thee, since I have cost thee so much; have always for me the tender feelings of a mother, and do not suffer thy unworthy son to perish. *Amen.*

Jesus abandoned on the Cross.

TRUE comforter of afflicted hearts, only hope of dejected minds, faithful friend of desolate souls; O Jesus, the strength of the weak, and the refuge of those who are forsaken! what then is this abyss of woes in which I see plunged? Thou art more solicitous for me than thou art for thyself, and thou art forsaken, that I may not be so. Ah! because I have abandoned thee, thou art thus abandoned by thy Father: thou expiatest the forgetfulness of

God in which I have lived, by the state of dereliction in which thou diest. Pardon me, Lord, all my sins, which have reduced thee to that state in which I behold thee. I return to thee, O Father of mercy; receive me, O God of all consolation; support me by thy grace, and grant that so many sufferings may not be useless to me. I do not ask thee not to afflict me, but not to abandon me in afflictions; to teach me to have recourse to thee in these as my only comforter; to support my faith, to fortify my hope, and to perfect my love in afflictions. Grant me the grace to acknowledge thy hand in them, and not to desire any other consolation than what cometh from thee. Humble me, then, as much as thou pleasest, and comfort me not, but that I may suffer and persevere until death in sufferings. Since the graces I request are the fruits of thy dereliction, show forth its power in my infirmity, and glorify thyself in my misery, O my Jesus, thou only refuge of my soul. If thou hear me, what praises will not the angels give thee? what fruit wilt thou not draw from thy blood poured out so profusely? How glorious for thine almighty hand, to strengthen so the dust of which I am composed, that I might be proof against the most violent attacks! I expect this grace from thy bounty, and I begin from this moment to return thanks, in the hope of doing so for endless ages. *Amen.*

Jesus says, "I thirst!" and they present him with Vinegar.

MY divine Saviour, there is nothing that thou dost not wish to suffer for the cure of my disorders! Thou endurest a burning thirst, that the seat of thy tender mercies, to which the scourges and nails could have no access, may not be exempt from torment. But, O God of love, thou sufferest another thirst incomparably more violent: it is an ardent desire that I should love thee with a sovereign, predominant love, which should be superior to all other love; that is, the desire to possess my heart; and notwithstanding my insensibility and ingratitude in refusing it to thee, thou ceasest not to desire and to ask it of me. Ah! Lord, my divine Master and my Father, I resist no longer; this heart shall be thine, which belongs to thee by numberless titles, and which merits destruction when it is not devoted to thee; it shall be thine by thy grace, without either reserve or division. Deign, this day, to take possession of it, and reign in it with absolute power. Yes; should any one ask admittance, I shall answer,— My heart is no longer mine, it belongs to my Jesus, to whom I have given it for ever.

O Saviour of my soul, since this heart is thine, never give it me back again; for I cannot confide in myself when it is in my hands. Deign, then, to give it a secure place in thy Sacred Heart, that it may learn to love thee in that furnace of love; may this sacred fire purify all its affections, consume all its coldness, fix its inconstancy, banish all its reserve, regulate, sanctify all its movements, all its inclinations, and may I live solely influenced by this holy love. No, Lord, let no other passion reign in me henceforth but that of loving thee. O that I was all soul, all heart, all sentiment, to live only by thy love! Why have I not, were it possible, as many hearts to love thee as thou hast amiable perfections? But if I have but one heart to offer thee, at least, O my God, it shall be henceforth entirely thine, without reserve, without division.

O my charitable Saviour, thy desire for our salvation, and the thirst which consumes thee, to see us happy in Heaven, regard all mankind, and even the cruel executioners who put thee to death. O infinite charity, permit me, after thine example here, to entreat thee for all men, and especially for those for whom thou desirest I should offer up my prayers; I recommend all to thee. Pour down thy blessings on thy holy Church, and on all her members; on all our superiors, ecclesiastical and secular; on my relations, friends, enemies, benefactors, associates. Grant, likewise, that the souls in Purgatory may experience thy mercy, especially those for whom I particularly intend to offer up my prayers to thee; grant them to feel the fruits of the blood which redeemed them, and render them eternally happy by thy divine presence. *Amen.*

AT THE DOMINE NON SUM DIGNUS.

The Prayer.

THAT I was sufficiently pure, O my adorable Saviour, to be able to feed on thy sacred flesh! What an advantage for me, could I at this moment possess thee in my heart, pay thee in it my homage, expose to thee my wants, and participate in the favours thou grantest to those who really receive thee: but I acknowledge myself most unworthy, on account of my sins. Pardon me, Lord, I conjure thee: I detest them with all my heart, because they displease thee. Accept my sincere desire to partake of thy sacred banquet, and create in me that pure heart, so necessary to receive thee worthily in this sacrament of thy love. In expectation of this happiness, grant at least that I may receive thee spiritually by a lively faith, a firm hope, and an ardent charity. Yes, my adorable Jesus, I firmly believe thou art really present in this august sacrament. I hope thou wilt make me partake of its admirable effects. I love thee, and desire to love thee for ever with all my heart. Purify it from all sin, and take from it whatever is displeasing to thee; that by the frequent and holy use of this bread of life, which the love of thy Sacred Heart has given us, I may be transformed into thee, live only by thee, in thee, and for thee. *Amen*.

FROM THE LAST ABLUTION TO THE END OF THE MASS.

Jesus dying.

JESUS, the Author of life, the Redeemer of men, the Son of the living God, our Master, our Model, our only Hope, I adore thee consummating thy sacrifice on the cross; I adore thee overwhelmed with sufferings, exhausted of strength, commending thy spirit into the hands of thy Father; I adore thee dying and dead. How happy should I be, could I die for thee as thou hast died for me; and to shed my blood for thee as thou hast shed thine for my salvation! But thou dost not require I should die like thee, by a verdict of human justice, and in the hands of executioners. Thou consentest that I should live, and thou only desirest I should not live enslaved by my passions, and abandoned to my own will. Thou desirest I should live, and be entirely thine; that, according to the liberty of a child of God, I may follow the law of thy spirit, and the influence of thy love. Ah! Lord, if that be all the return thou askest of me, I shall not die ungrateful.

From this moment I look on myself as one dead to sin; from this moment I wish to die to all impulsions of sin, to my evil habits, to my inclinations, and to my own will. Assist me, my God; give me thyself this stroke of death, which I shall receive as a particular benefit. From this moment I shall begin to live by faith: faith shall regulate my thoughts, my affections, my words, my actions, my entire conduct. I will live no longer to myself; I will live to God alone in Jesus Christ; I will live now, not I—but Jesus Christ crucified will live in me. *Amen.*

Holy Virgin, Queen of martyrs, Mother penetrated with the most lively sorrow at the sight of thy dear Son expiring on the cross, obtain for me a spark of this divine fire with which thy Sacred Heart was inflamed, that my heart being inflamed for Jesus my Saviour, I may always retain the tender remembrance of his sufferings and death; bear in me, with courage and constancy, the sacred characters of his cross and mortification, and one day participate in his eternal glory.

O blessed spirits, O all ye saints of Paradise, who now contemplate this divine Lamb, glorious, impassible, immortal, and who possess him with a certainty of never losing him, obtain for me the grace not only to seek him on earth, but to become like this adorable Saviour, to the end I may merit to be crowned in the mansion of his glory. *Amen.*

AN ACT OF THANKSGIVING AND REPARATION AFTER MASS.

I THANK thee, O my divine Saviour, for the favour thou hast granted me this day, in permitting me to assist at thy adorable Sacrifice; in recalling to my mind the precious remembrance of thy sufferings and death, and exciting in my heart new desires of serving and loving thee. O my amiable Jesus, preserve in me these holy desires; deign to render them firm and efficacious. I am sincerely sorry for the coldness and indifference I have had this day in thy presence, and so frequently heretofore at the foot of thine altars, and for all the irreverences I have ever been guilty of. I desire to make all possible atonement to thee, with sentiments of the most lively compunction: forgive me these irreverences, and grant me the grace to repair them, by the respect, the recollection, and the fervour with which I shall assist henceforth at these divine Mysteries. *Amen.*

EXERCISES FOR CONFESSION.

FREQUENT Confession is one of the most necessary and effectual means of advancing in virtue; because this sacrament not only confers sanctifying grace to efface the sins which have been committed, but likewise actual grace to preserve from future relapses—a grace which God communicates so much more freely, as we shall prepare ourselves for confession with more care, and endeavour to make it with more perfection; to which the following practices may be conducive.

A PRAYER,

To beg of God the Grace to know our Sins, and to grant us Contrition to detest them.

MY God, who knowest my guilt, and that I am, of myself, unable to know the number and enormity of my sins, and to conceive a salutary sorrow for them, enlighten my mind, soften the hardness of my heart, render it docile to thy grace, and sensible to thy infinite goodness, that I may weep and detest them, because they displease thee and offend thy Sovereign Majesty. And thou, O Sacred Heart of Jesus, that hast experienced so lively a sorrow for my sins, and implored the pardon of them with sad and bitter lamentations, inspire me with that sorrow to which thou didst condescend to subject thyself for love of me, especially in the Garden of Olives, where, pierced with mortal anguish, thou satisfiedst the justice of God for all the sins of the world.

A PRAYER,

To the most Holy Virgin, to our Guardian-Angel, and our holy Patron Saints.

HOLY Virgin, Mother of grace, and assured refuge of sinners, intercede for me, that by the confession I am going to make, I may obtain both pardon of all my sins, and the grace to commit them no more.

Holy angels, and thou in particular, faithful and zealous Guardian of my soul; ye happy saints of Paradise, and thou, above all, my holy Patron (N.), assist me to rise from this state of sin, and obtain for me the grace never again to relapse.

After having called to mind your different sins, with the number and the circumstances necessary to be explained in confession, you may go over the following Reflections, to excite yourself to a true and sincere Contrition; at least you can read them the evening or the day you intend to confess:—

REFLECTIONS,

Which may excite us to Contrition.

SINNER, hast thou ever seriously reflected, that by mortal sin thou devotest thyself voluntarily, as an unhappy victim, to hell and its devouring flames; that thou didst choose, in preference to Heaven, the infernal dwelling for thine eternal habitation; that thou didst take the devil for thy father; that thou didst look on thyself as his child, and didst become the brother of all the unhappy reprobates, that is, of all the profligates and impious wretches that have ever been on earth, to dwell eternally with them in that abode of horror and despair?

2. Hast thou ever reflected that thou didst renounce, with full consent and for ever, the beautiful mansions of Heaven, this abode of peace and felicity, that eternal inheritance which the love of thy God had prepared for thee; that thou didst deprive thyself for ever of the possession of the sovereign good, which alone can render thee happy, and didst renounce the prospect of joining the society of the august Mary, of the angels and saints,

that is, of all the truly wise, virtuous, and holy that have ever existed?

3. But adopt motives more noble still, and more disinterested. Consider, that by mortal sin thou hast dared to revolt against God himself, to rise up, like Lucifer, against thy Sovereign Lord and the absolute Master of all things, and to refuse him the obedience which is essentially due to him from all creatures. What rashness, what insupportable pride! What! thou, dust and ashes, a mere nothing, thou insultest God himself, and darest insolently to contemn his orders and his law; darest to outrage him; to incur, without fear, his displeasure and indignation; to brave, as I may say, his anger, and to defy his just wrath! This terrible Judge has only to speak to exterminate thee, and to cast thee headlong into hell; and thou hast been thus rash to insult him in his presence and under his eyes! O blindness and folly! O horror and execration!

4. This Father of all, this most tender, this benevolent and merciful God, has not ceased to load thee with his benefits. From all eternity his love has spoken to him in thy favour; and thou, encompassed on all sides with his most precious gifts, hast forgotten his blessings and despised his graces. What do I say? thou hast even made use of

the gifts he conferred on thee, to rise up in opposition to him and to insult him. What abuse of health, of riches, of talents! what abuse of the sacraments, of his grace and inspirations! What ingratitude could be blacker or more deserving the just vengeance of God? A thousand times hast thou been snatched from eternal flames; since he delivered thee as often from them, as he could, with strict justice, have cast thee into them, after thy sin. Vile prey of devils, where wouldst thou be now, were it not for his infinite mercy?

5. Thou hast dared to compare the God of all greatness and sanctity to thy silly passions and sordid interests, and thou hast given them the preference: how impious! how very outrageous! The God of our mind and heart is what our minds esteem, and what our hearts love above all things. Thus, the God of the miser is gold and silver; the God of the intemperate is his appetite; consequently, every sinner, as much as he can, dethrones, destroys, and annihilates God, and sets up a new and abominable deity, whom he adores like a slave, whose will he follows, often at the expense of his honour and property; to this deity he sacrifices his immortal soul, formed to the image of God, and destined to possess him for ever. What a crime! what an abominable act!

6. Sin, this horrible monster, as hateful as God is amiable, is the only enemy of God; it is the only object that God hateth; but his hatred to it is eternal, necessary, and infinite. He hates sin as much as he loves himself. Yes, sin is something so abominable and hideous, that his horror of it would occasion his death, were he mortal and passible : so that if God could die, thou wouldst have caused a thousand times his death by thy sins. Conceive, if thou canst, any malice equal to that. And yet this God has not crushed and destroyed, (when a thousand times provoked,) this ungrateful wretch, this traitor, perjurer, deicide! Imagine, if possible, a greater act of mercy. Wouldst thou still continue to insult a God so infinitely good; not to love him so infinitely amiable, henceforth, with all thy heart? Wouldst thou refuse him thy heart, which he asks, and on which he has every claim? Ah! rather die a thousand deaths.

7. Look, O sinner, on the Lord of glory, the divine Jesus, covered with contempt and reproach, overwhelmed with sorrows, expiring on the tree of the cross.

It is sin that has reduced him to that state; it was, in particular, to expiate thy crimes that he suffered such cruel torments and an infamous death.

It is sin that renders ineffectual in thee

the fruits of the sufferings of this redeeming God; and whilst thou art given up to sin, the merits of the divine Saviour, though of infinite value, will yet be of no avail for thy salvation. O enormity! O malice of sin! who shall be ever able to know thee, ever sufficiently able to detest thee?

Return then speedily to thy God, O sinner, whoever thou art. The mercies of thy God are greater than thy crimes. He expects, he calls, he eagerly seeks thee. Jesus, the amiable Jesus, extends his arms to thee; he opens his Heart to receive thee; he desires the conversion, and not the death of the sinner. Return to him with sorrow and confidence.

As for thee, who hast been already so happy as to return to thy God, never forget his mercies to thee. Weep for thy past sins, without intermission; expiate them more and more. Reproach thyself for thy slothfulness in the service of a God so good, who has pardoned thee with so much mercy. Be filled with confusion and grief at the sight, the multitude and malice of those other sins, which, though venial, as thou didst suppose them to be, are nevertheless injurious to God, and so prejudicial to thy salvation. Yes truly, venial sin offends God, is displeasing to God, is repugnant to the interests and glory of God, is a crime against God, an evil, consequently, of a superior order to all other evils; so great an evil, that it would be better to let the whole world perish, than wish to save it at the expense of one single venial sin.

Venial sin grieves the spirit of God, cools the friendship of God with regard to us, tarnishes the brilliancy and beauty which grace imparts to our souls, makes us lose the fruit of our good works, in rendering them vicious, and insensibly disposes us to mortal sin. Venial sin deprives the soul of a new grace which it would have received, of a degree of glory which it might have acquired, of a degree of love which God would have conceived for it. Venial sin will destroy for ever the happy fruits which an act of charity, whose place it usurps, would have always produced; and God will be the less glorified, less loved, and will love us the less. O how affecting are these reflections, if deeply impressed on a heart that loves God and desires his glory! What should you then think of the multitude of your venial sins? and what a subject of tears and sorrow should they not be to you!

AN ACT OF CONTRITION.

GOD of goodness and mercy, suffer a poor, contrite, and humble sinner to cast himself at thy feet, and solicit thy grace and forgiveness. Penetrated with the most lively sorrow, I conjure thee to forget and pardon my crimes: they are great and many in number, O my God! but thy mercies are infinite, and thou wilt be more glorified in granting me the pardon I ask. Forget them, I beseech thee, O my Sovereign Lord! I shall never forget them, but always bewail them. O that I could shed tears of blood to efface them! O that my heart is not broken with sorrow and regret at the sight of so many iniquities! O ungrateful wretch that I am, have I received so many benefits from thy mercy, but to offend thee with additional malice and ingratitude! Created to thine image, purchased with the precious blood of the divine Redeemer, nourished with his adorable flesh, loaded with a thousand blessings, is this the return I make for thy mercies? Was there ever ingratitude more atrocious? I cry out for pardon; O God, I cry out for mercy! Pardon me all the insults I have given thee, O God infinitely amiable! How is it possible that I have not loved thee, O supreme goodness? How have I dared to offend thee? Yet, thou hast condescended, O God of love, to preserve my life, and often to snatch me from hell; thou invitest, thou urgest me to return to thee! Ah! I return sincerely to thee, O my God. I detest, in the bitterness of my soul, all my unhappy crimes, because they are displeasing to thee, and thou art supremely amiable; and I am firmly resolved to amend, and to fly the occasions of sin; ready to die a thousand times, rather than offend thee hereafter.

For the love of thyself, O my God, for thy glory, for the joy thou impartest to all the blessed in Heaven, for the consolation of the just upon earth, and to excite the confidence of sinners, pardon me, Lord, how unworthy soever I may be of thy mercy. I confess, O my God, my grief is not lively enough, my hatred to sin is not sufficiently great. Accept, I beseech thee, O God of infinite sanctity, the hatred thou bearest to them thyself; accept the sorrow which the adorable Heart of Jesus has felt for them; accept the infinite satisfaction he has offered thee to atone for them. It is by his death he has merited for me the life of grace which I humbly beg of thee; and it is in virtue of his precious blood that I hope to obtain it from thine infinite goodness. O my amiable Jesus, after the crimes I have committed against thee, shall I dare once more to appear in thy presence? But it is thou who callest me: wilt thou reject me? Thou wishest not the death of the sinner, but rather his conversion. I return then to thee, penetrated with sorrow for all the sins I have committed against thee. It is I—I acknowledge it to my shame, and I blush at thy feet in confessing it—it is I who have plunged, by my crimes, thine adorable Heart into that that sea of affliction in the Garden of Olives. But remember, that even by that same sorrow which thou hast felt for them, thou hast merited for me a sincere repentance, and an entire abolition of them; and it is through this afflicted Heart I beg both these graces of thee.

It is I, unfortunate traitor, who, more cruel than thy very executioners, have made thee endure the vilest treatment and the most insulting outrages. It was I who caused the blood to run from thy veins, and made thee expire on the cross. But thou hast asked pardon for thy executioners; deign, then, to ask it for me. Mercy, O divine Jesus, by this blood, the infinite merit of which belongs to us, as being transferred to us by thy love. Tender Father, be merciful to thy child, penetrated with a lively regret for his sins. Charitable Pastor, receive this poor strayed sheep. Amiable Redeemer, do not lose the fruit of thy sweat, of thy blood, and of thy death. Permit, since thou stretchest forth thy arms and openest thy Heart to me, that I may cast myself into them with confidence. O most amiable Heart, abounding with tenderness for me, how could I not love thee! O divine love, soften this heart of stone, break it with sorrow, inflame it with thy sacred fire. Ah! may the amiable manner in which thou treatest me, after the commission of so many crimes, touch my heart most sensibly! I am firmly resolved, O Jesus, henceforth to burn with the fire of thy divine charity. Alas! were it not for the multitude of thy mercies, I should long since have burned in the fire of hell. From this moment I begin to love thee. Yes, thou art the God of my heart; reign in it as its Sovereign. I love thee with all my soul; because thou art infinitely amiable. I break off for ever from sin. I detest with all my heart those which I have committed, aud I detest them for the love of thee, because they displease thee; and I am firmly resolved not to relapse again into them, with the help of thy holy grace.

But, O divine Saviour, who knowest my weakness, vouchsafe to strengthen me. It is on thy assistance only that I can rely. O my God, my God, who hast given me these good dispositions, bless and strengthen them so, that whatever unforeseen occasions may offer, whatever temptations may attack me, I may never separate myself from thee, or from thy love. *Amen.*

ANOTHER ACT OF CONTRITION.

MAKE me a partaker, O my God, of that horror of sin, of that grief which was felt by the Sacred Heart of my amiable Saviour, when sinking under the enormous weight of my crimes, prostrate before thee on the earth, quite bathed in tears, covered all over with blood, he made condign reparation for me to thy offended Majesty, imploring thy mercy in my favour, with profound sighs and tender lamentations. I desire, at least, this perfect sorrow, and I beg it of thee with all my heart. I renounce all my iniquities; I abhor them because they are displeasing to thee, O my God, who art infinitely amiable and infinitely good. I am heartily sorry for having disobeyed and offended thee. I blush with confusion, O God, supremely perfect, for having preferred some vile earthly interests to thy infinite perfections and love. There is nothing I would not willingly perform or suffer, to expiate so many sins; and I should esteem myself happy to shed the last drop of my blood to make satisfaction to thee. I renounce for ever, not only all sin, but everything likewise that may be to me an occasion of sin; and I make a firm resolution to fly with horror all that has been to this moment a subject of scandal, or a cause of temptation to me, ever ready to sacrifice my dearest interests, rather than expose myself to be guilty of anything contrary to to thy service, or the fidelity which I have promised thee at the sacred font of baptism.

[Approach the sacred tribunal with modesty and recollection, and confess all your sins with humility and sorrow, with sincerity, prudence, and discretion.]

ACTS OF THANKSGIVING
AFTER CONFESSION.

WHAT shall I render to thee, O my God, for the great benefit which thou hast granted me? What shall I do to express my gratitude? Thou hast broken the shameful chains of my sins; and the least I can do to testify that gratitude to thee, is to offer thee this day, and all the days of my life, a sacrifice of praise; to bless, to extol incessantly, the immense extent of thy mercy. I do so with all my heart, O my God, and I shall do so until death, and never be weary of glorifying the most sweet and most amiable of all Fathers.

Sacred Heart of Jesus, it is to thee I am indebted for the favour which the Heavenly Father has granted me. Thou hast appeased his anger, satisfied his justice, and merited my pardon. Confirm the work of my reconciliation, which has cost thee so much; make it steady and constant. For that purpose give me the necessary fortitude and courage to put in execution the holy resolutions with which thy grace has inspired me: I renew these resolutions with all my heart.

Holy Virgin, thou hast interceded for my pardon, intercede for my perseverance, and obtain for me the grace to live and die in the friendship of my God.

O ye holy angels, and thou, in particular, my Angel-guardian; O all ye saints of Paradise, and thou, above all, my Patron Saint, (N.) accept, I beseech you the sentiments of my just gratitude, and obtain for me a constant fidelity in the service of the greatest and best of Masters.

A PRAYER,

How you should offer your Penance to God.

MY Lord and my God, I offer thee the penance I am going to perform, and I unite it to the infinite satisfactions of Jesus Christ my Saviour. Grant that the abundant merits of thy dear Son, and the immense extent of the love of his Sacred Heart, may supply the imperfection and feebleness of the works which I shall perform, and the punishments which I wish to endure, to satisfy thy divine justice.

[Do not delay performing the penance which has been enjoined you. But, in order to testify to God your sincere return, examine into the causes of your sins, and see how you can prevent them. Foresee the occasions you may have to relapse into your ordinary faults; renew your resolutions to avoid them, and impose some penance on yourself, which you must take care to put in execution, if unhappily you should relapse.]

AN INVITATION

To make frequent Acts of Contrition.

THE practice of making frequent acts of contrition is very much recommended by the saints, as being most useful, either for those who only enter the way of perfection, or for such as are more advanced.

In fact this practice contributes, in the first place, to keep us humble, by reminding us of our sins and of hell, from which the mercy of God has preserved us.

2nd. It gives us great confidence to obtain the entire abolition of our sins; for, as St. Jerome observes, "*If you have always your sin before you, God will not have it before himself.*"

3rd. It will be a great subject of consolation to us at the hour of death, to think that by our contrition we have endeavoured to expiate the sins of our past life.

4th. This practice is not only the remedy for our past sins, but it is also a great pre-

"Wash me yet more from my iniquity, and cleanse me from my sin."—*Ibid.*

"Turn away thy face from my sins, and blot out all my iniquities."—*Ibid.*

"A contrite and humble heart, O God, thou wilt not despise."—*Ibid.*

"Remember, O Lord, thy bowels of compassion, and thy mercies, that are from the beginning of the world."—*Ps.* xxiv. 6.

"Jesus, Son of David, have mercy on me."—*Luke* xviii. 38.

"For thy name's sake, O Lord, thou wilt pardon my sin; for it is great."—*Ps.* xxiv. 11.

"If thou, O Lord, wilt mark iniquities; Lord, who shall stand it? For with thee there is merciful forgiveness; and by reason of thy law, I have waited for thee, O Lord."—*Ps.* cxxix. 3, 4.

"Help us, O God, our Saviour; and for the glory of thy name, O Lord, deliver us, and forgive us our sins for thy name's sake."—*Ps.* lxxviii. 9.

"Convert us, O God, our Saviour; and turn off thy anger from us. Thou wilt turn, O God, and bring us life; and thy people shall rejoice in thee. Show us, O Lord, thy mercy; and grant us thy salvation."—*Ps.* lxxxiv. 5, 7, 8.

servative against those which might be hereafter committed.

5th. Finally, it is an exercise of the love of God: since perfect contrition, the motive of which is the love of God, and being nothing else than sorrow for having offended a God so good, so amiable, and worthy of being served, the more we love God, the more we shall grieve for having offended him.

In order to facilitate this holy practice, you may make use of the following Aspirations, extracted from the Scriptures:—

DEVOUT ASPIRATIONS

Of a contrite and humble Heart.

"MINE eyes have sent forth springs of water, because they have not kept thy law."—*Ps.* cxviii. 136.

"My sores are putrified and corrupted, because of my foolishness."—*Ps.* xxxvii. 6.

"Father, I have sinned against Heaven and before thee."—*Luke* xv. 18.

"O God, be merciful to me a sinner."—*Luke* xviii. 13.

"Have mercy on me, O God, according to thy great mercy; and according to the multitude of thy tender mercies, blot out my iniquity."—*Ps.* l. 3, 4.

"Wash me yet more from my iniquity, and cleanse me from my sin."—*Ibid.*

"Turn away thy face from my sins, and blot out all my iniquities."—*Ibid.*

"A contrite and humble heart, O God, thou wilt not despise."—*Ibid.*

"Remember, O Lord, thy bowels of compassion, and thy mercies, that are from the beginning of the world."—*Ps.* xxiv. 6.

"Jesus, Son of David, have mercy on me."—*Luke* xviii. 38.

"For thy name's sake, O Lord, thou wilt pardon my sin; for it is great."—*Ps.* xxiv. 11.

"If thou, O Lord, wilt mark iniquities; Lord, who shall stand it? For with thee there is merciful forgiveness; and by reason of thy law, I have waited for thee, O Lord."—*Ps.* cxxix. 3, 4.

"Help us, O God, our Saviour; and for the glory of thy name, O Lord, deliver us, and forgive us our sins for thy name's sake."—*Ps.* lxxviii. 9.

"Convert us, O God, our Saviour; and turn off thy anger from us. Thou wilt turn, O God, and bring us life; and thy people shall rejoice in thee. Show us, O Lord, thy mercy; and grant us thy salvation."—*Ps.* lxxxiv. 5, 7, 8.

THE PRAYER

Of a penitent Soul to the Sacred Heart of Jesus.

SACRED Heart of my amiable Jesus, thou wast filled with the bitterest sorrow for the sins of mankind, and it is from thee I have imbibed that lively sorrow, these precious tears, which the remembrance of my past sins draws from me. Ah! divine Heart, if I see thee plunged into the most grievous and mortal anguish, should I not reproach myself, convinced that it is my depraved heart which has thus afflicted thee? I detest and abhor these sins and crimes which I have had the misfortune of committing, the sight of which pierced thee with such pain and affliction, and, at the same time, with such tender zeal and compassion for an unworthy sinner.

O Jesus, my Lord and my God, is it thus I have repaid thy love? Can I ever weep sufficiently to wash away my crimes! Ah! that I could unite in my heart the sorrow of the most penitent hearts! Blind as I have been, I sought the friendship of men, and despised thine. I have given them my heart, and refused it to thee, O most amiable Heart; and I have not loved thee, O Jesus, all burning with love for me! Ah! I wish, through the ardour of my love and my heartfelt sorrow, with the assistance of thy holy grace, to make thee forget, if possible, these fatal moments when my ungrateful heart has not been devoted to thee. O Jesus, receive it, I beseech thee, and with it accept all that I am and possess. I give thee all—goods, honour, reputation, health, life; dispose of all according to thy will. Provided I love thee, I am content.

O Sacred Heart, vouchsafe thyself to supply for the want of that sorrow which I ought to conceive for my crimes. It is by thee I detest them; through thee, and for the love of thee, I sincerely grieve for having committed them. Could I, O divine Jesus, present to thy Father a heart more capable of satisfying his justice? Are not thy Sacred Heart, and the bitter sorrow with which thou wast pierced, and all thy merits, assuredly mine? Has not thy love surrendered them to me? O Heart ever open, through love, to receive the sinner, permit me to enter with confidence into thy sacred wound, there to be secured from the anger of the Eternal Father, so justly irritated against me; be thou my assured asylum against the enemies of my salvation, and particularly at the hour of my death.

O sacred, O divine love, how can I express my gratitude to thee? Thou wishest and requirest that I should love thee, and yet I have been cold and indifferent to thee. O love, O generous Heart, pardon mine, which is base and perfidious, but now, by thy grace, contrite and humbled for its baseness and perfidy. O ardent and active love, O Heart of Jesus, still burning with love for me, and desiring my love, pierce thou thyself my heart with one of these inflamed darts with which thou art filled; inflict a deep wound; may it daily increase more and more, and may it remain incurable. O adorable Heart, may my love for thee know neither change nor limits; may my love for thee make me always detest my past life, render me like thee, and both an agreeable and faithful victim of thy love.

Be thou mine, O Sacred Heart, and may I be thine. May my heart, O Jesus, be entirely conformable to thine. May I no longer live, desire, nor love, but according to thy Heart and for thy glory, during time and eternity. *Amen.*

SENTIMENTS

Of a penitent Heart at the foot of the Cross.

I ADORE thee, O Victim of propitiation, who hast been sacrificed for my salvation. Humbled at thy feet, I implore thy mercy. Thou hast shed thy blood to blot out my iniquities; purify my soul still more from its stains. O infinite goodness which has supported me, do not abandon me. Adorable mouth which hast called me, do not condemn me. Sacred hands which have formed me, do not destroy me. Sacred feet which have been fatigued running after the dispersed children of Israel, be thou my asylum and refuge. Heart ever filled with compassion for sinners, Heart ever open to their sincere return, receive me. O Jesus, my life, my beloved, for me thou hast died, for thee I desire to live. Yes, my God, the debts which I have contracted with thy Divine Majesty are immense. I justly deserve to be punished; but look on thy Son, this peace-offering, who offers himself for the sins of the world; hear the voice of the blood of Jesus Christ, my brother, which ascends to Heaven; behold all he has suffered to appease thine anger and satisfy thy justice: put his sufferings in the scale with my iniquities, and thou wilt find that his sufferings will outweigh and ought to blot out these iniquities.

What thanks shall I offer thee, O Jesus my Saviour, when I reflect on all thou hast done for so great a sinner as I am? Thou hast plunged thyself into an abyss of sorrow and ignominy, to draw me from that of my miseries; thou hast died for my salvation. I am doubly indebted to thee, because thou art both my Creator and my Redeemer. How can I express my thanks for such great benefits, except in giving myself entirely to thee, and delivering into thy hands this soul, which thou hast purchased at so high a price? I will love thee then with all my soul, with all my mind, with all my heart, with all my strength. But, alas, this resolution can be effected only by thee; my soul, then, must cling solely to thee, because all its happiness depends upon thee, and cannot be sanctified without thee.

Receive, O divine Saviour, the protestation I now make, in offering to thee my homage and adoration. I prostrate myself before the glorious instruments of thy passion. I adore that cross on which thou hast consummated thy sacrifice. I adore that crown of thorns, the diadem of infamy and sufferings, which thou hast borne to expiate my sins; those nails stained with thy blood; that lance which has pierced thy Heart; those five wounds which have cured the wounds of my soul.

Thy head is inclined to give me the kiss of peace; thy veins extended to embrace me; thy Heart open to receive me; thy body delivered up to death as the price of my redemption; thy merits are mine.

Be merciful to me, O God: that criminal who crucified thee lies now at thy feet, and, through thy sacred wounds and thy precious blood, begs pardon of thee. I have been the cause of the death of my Saviour, which renders me inconsolable. O that I could die with grief, and cancel my crimes with my tears, and wash them away with my blood! I detest them, O Lord, in all the bitterness of my heart, and I make a sincere resolution rather to die than renew thy sufferings, thy passion and death, by new crimes. *Amen.*

AFFECTING REFLECTIONS,

On the Cross of our Lord Jesus Christ.

HOLY cross, ennobled and consecrated by the blood and death of the Saviour, more brilliant than the stars of Heaven, and more precious than all the riches of the earth, I adore thee with the most profound respect. Thou art the termination of his labours, the end of his exile, the commencement of his glory, the trophy of his victory, and his triumphant chariot; but thou art also my patrimony and the precious inheritance which the Lord has bequeathed me. He died in thine arms poor, despoiled of everything, and content in possessing only thee. Thou art the lively image of divine love, and the most faithful mirror of unlimited goodness. I adore thee, O precious cross; thou shalt be in future my treasure, my refuge, light, my knowledge, and all my wisdom. O happy, and a thousand times happy, the soul who never forsakes thee, but penetrates the profound truths which are hidden in thee! Thou art the support of my weakness, the terror of mine enemies, the foundation of my hopes. The Heavens already acknowledge thee; the world reveres thee; hell fears thee; and the devil knows that he who expired on thee is truly the Son of God.

Thou art no longer what thou hast been heretofore; thou hast lost thine ancient hardness; thou art become a light burden, an agreeable yoke, a source of glory, the asylum, the strength, and the repose of those who cast themselves into thine arms; and when they appear dejected, they are supported, relieved, and exalted, by the same burden which overwhelms them.

In thee we find life and salvation, strength of heart, spiritual joy, the perfection of virtue, and the most assured pledge of eternal happiness. By thee the wisdom of the world is confounded, pride is humbled, and humility crowned. Thou that hast confirmed the apostles, consecrated the martyrs, strengthened the virgins, sanctified all the just; thou rejoicest the angels; thou defendest the Church; thou fillest the heavens; and on the dreadful day of general judgment, thou shalt appear with Jesus Christ for the glory of the elect and for the eternal confusion of his enemies.

Nevertheless, O adorable cross, all those who glory in thee should expect to be unknown to the world, despised, hated, and persecuted by the world. They must spend their lives in tears, in want, in sufferings, in contempt, and be trampled under foot by all mankind. But, in depriving them of earthly goods, thou givest them those of Heaven; in taking from them the friendship of men, thou fillest them with divine love; in stripping them of worldly honours, thou makest them children of God; in covering them with infamy, thou crownest them with glory; and, disengaging them from all creatures, thou unitest them to God in an ineffable manner.

I adore thee, O holy cross, O hidden wisdom, O light unknown to the world, the honour of those who follow thee, the security of those who carry thee, the crown of those who embrace thee, the recompense of those who love thee, and the salvation of those who cast themselves into thine arms. To die on thee, is to live; and to live on thee, is to reign. He who loves thee is content; he who desires thee is tranquil; he who possesses thee is rich.

I adore thee, O tree of life, whose fruits are the solid nourishment of the children of

God. I adore thee, O furnace of love; I embrace thee with all my heart; I will never separate myself from thee; receive me in thine arms, support me, purify me, sanctify me: may he who died on thee for the love of me, receive me through thee. *Amen.*

EXERCISES
FOR COMMUNION.

THE divine Saviour gives himself to us in communion, with a great desire to make us partake of his treasures and graces: let us place no obstacles calculated to restrain his liberality, by neglecting to bring the dispositions suitable or necessary to receive the admirable effects of this sacrament of his love. Let us, therefore, bring these proper dispositions:

Remote Dispositions,—which are, great purity of conscience, or, at least, an extreme application to require it; constant fidelity in fulfilling the duties of our station; an ardent desire to correspond to the designs of the Son of God, in giving himself to us; a lively and sincere sorrow for our sins, when we approach the tribunal of penance.

Immediate Dispositions.—From the preceding evening observe a more than ordinary recollection; practise some good works; read slowly and with reflection the following considerations; go and pay a visit to him whom you intend to receive; make interior acts of those virtues which are the most suited to this adorable Sacrament, as acts of faith, of humility, of sorrow for your sins, of desire, of joy, of hope. Finish the day, and endeavour to compose yourself to rest, with this consoling reflection:—*To-morrow I am to receive my God!* Recall this thought the next day when you awake, and meditate in the morning on the happiness you hope to enjoy.

[*Observation.*—Any of the following exercises may serve as a remote preparation for communion, and they may be read on the evening preceding the day you intend to communicate: the others may be used as an immediate preparation during the Mass at which you are to communicate. You need not recite all that is here set down, as if all were necessary; but apply with fervour to those you may have chosen. The same may be said of the other exercises which are contained in this collection.]

REMOTE PREPARATION

BEFORE RECEIVING THE HOLY COMMUNION.

CONSIDERATIONS,

On the inestimable Grace which our Lord Jesus Christ confers on us, in giving himself to us in the Holy Communion.

WHO is he I am about to receive? It is Jesus Christ, true God and true Man, the same that sitteth at the right hand of the Eternal Father, the Lord of Heaven and earth; my Creator, my Redeemer, my Preserver, and he who shall judge me on the last day. O infinite Grandeur! infinite Majesty! infinite Wisdom! infinite Power! infinite Goodness! My God condescends to give me himself as a pledge of his desire to procure my eternal glory. O what should be my respect and my love for him, if I saw him visibly present? Yet I am fully convinced of his presence when I contemplate him with the eyes of faith. Reanimate this faith within me, O Lord; may its light, by enlightening my mind to receive thee with the most profound respect, inflame also my heart to express for thee the most ardent love.

II. To whom does Jesus Christ give himself? To me, who am dust and ashes—to me, a vile, blind, weak, wretched, malicious sinner, who have, by repeated crimes, so often and so basely betrayed him!—to me, an ungrateful wretch, notwithstanding his numberless benefits!—to me, who have so often deserved hell-fire! All the kings of this world, before this God of glory, are less than the worms of the earth: the angels of Heaven do not think themselves pure in his presence. Yet he desires to enter and dwell in my heart: what care, what precautions should I not observe, to prepare him a mansion as worthy as possible!

III. Why does Jesus Christ desire to give himself to me? He desires it for my good and advantage; he desires it to strengthen me against mine enemies, the devil, the flesh, and the world; to heal the deep wounds I have received from them; to strengthen the health of my soul, and to preserve the life which his grace has restored me; to support me in friendship with him against the various objects which might dissolve and snatch it from me; to unite me intimately to him; to transform me into him; to make me partake of his divinity, by rendering me like him. It is, then, most certainly true, that the amiable Heart of Jesus bears me an immense and unlimited love. I wish I had, O Jesus, a heart transported with love, inflamed like a seraph, to express my gratitude for such an unspeakable benefit. I shall make every effort to bring a heart disengaged from whatever displeases thee, and from every created object; a heart given up quite to thy service.

AFFECTING SENTIMENTS,

Extracted from the Holy Scriptures, to dispose ourselves for Communion.

"BEHOLD the bridegroom cometh, go ye forth to meet him."—*Matt.* xxv. 6.

"Behold the King cometh to thee meek."—*Matt.* xxi. 5.

"Yea, Lord, I have believed that thou art Christ, the Son of the living God, who art come into this world."—*John* xi. 27.

"What is man, that thou art mindful of him? or the son of man, that thou visitest him?"—*Ps.* viii. 4.

"Lord, I am not worthy that thou shouldst enter under my roof."—*Matt.* viii. 7.

"Lord, to whom shall be go? Thou hast the words of eternal life."—*John* vi. 69.

"God is my Saviour: I will deal confidently, and will not fear; because the Lord is my strength and my praise, and he is become my salvation."—*Isa.* xii. 2.

"As the hart panteth after the fountains of waters, so my soul panteth after thee, O God! My soul hath thirsted after the strong living God: when shall I come and appear before the face of God?"—*Ps*. xli. 1, 2.

"My heart hath said to thee, my faith hath sought thee: thy face, O Lord, will I still seek."—*Ps*. xxvi. 8.

"I stretched forth my hands to thee: my soul is as earth without water unto thee. Hear me speedily, O Lord: my spirit hath fainted away."—*Ps*. cxlii. 6, 7.

"What have I in Heaven? and, besides thee, what do I desire upon earth? For thee my flesh and my heart hath fainted away: thou art the God of my heart, and the God that is my portion for ever."—*Ps*. lxxii. 25, 26.

"Come, Lord Jesus."—*Apoc*. xxii. 20.

[These affecting sentiments from the holy Scripture contain acts calculated to prepare for communion: the other passages which we quote at the end of this exercise contain some acts proper for thanksgiving after communion. Persons accustomed to meditate, may easily find sufficient to occupy their minds before and after communion.]

DEVOUT COMMUNICATIONS

WITH OUR LORD,

On giving himself to us in the Holy Communion.

MY divine Saviour, thy love for me is truly incomprehensible: thou givest thyself to me, and thou desirest, in thine amiable Sacrament, to furnish me with every blessing. Thou desirest to feed me as my shepherd, to conduct me as my guide, to heal me as my physician, to defend me as my protector, to instruct me as my master, to hear me as my confidant. Thou desirest to dwell in me, and that I should dwell in thee. The most striking mark of tender love which thou gavest to thy beloved disciple was to allow him to recline on thy breast; and thou wishest now to recline on my heart. Ah! since thy condescension is so great, O my God, as to enter this heart, reign in it alone, close it to all other loves but thine.

If thy goodness to me is immense, I sincerely desire that my love for thee may have no limits. If thy goodness to me is eternal, I also desire that my love for thee may have no end. If thy goodness to me is ever the same, I desire that my love may never change, except, O my God, to increase and daily become more ardent. Thou desirest, then, O thou most liberal of all Sovereigns, and it is in compliance with thine order that I approach the banquet-room, that I there appear with the guests, that I take my place amongst the most faithful servants in thy Church, and partake, with these angelical men, of the bread of angels. But, Lord, what art thou doing? Hast thou forgotten that thou art my King? Dost thou forget that I am the vilest and most contemptible of thy subjects? Fearest thou not, that I may either forget myself, or that which I am, when I see myself so highly honoured; or what thou art, in seeing thee so much abased? No, my God, never, by thy grace, shall I forget either my misery or thy grandeur; never shall I forget that I am but dust and ashes, and that in thy most profound humiliations thou art ever equally venerable and adorable.

So far from insulting thee in future, I wish henceforth to attach myself only to thee. Thou wilt reign in me, and reign in me alone and exclusively. I shall make thee reign in my memory by recollecting thy benefits; I shall make thee reign in my mind by a respectful attention to thy holy presence; I shall make thee reign in my will by a perfect conformity to thine, and by the lively and tender affections of my heart. O Jesus, O my King! reign absolute Lord of my soul, which is thine, since it has been created only for thee, and begin to exercise in it all thy prerogatives.

Thou wilt speak, Lord, and thou shalt be heard. What thou wilt condemn, I shall condemn; what thou wilt approve, I shall approve; what thou wilt forbid, I shall avoid; what thou wilt order, I shall execute. My obedience shall be complete: and thou, O my God, thou wilt re-establish me in the treasures of grace which I had lost; thou wilt look on me with a favourable eye, and accept my services; thou wilt support me against the common enemies of thy glory and my salvation; thou wilt give and preserve to me that peace which the world cannot give, and which is only found in thy kingdom.

Thou sayest to me, then, O my Sovereign Lord, as thou didst heretofore to Zacheus: "I must abide to-day in thy house." What a happiness, my God! what an honour! but, at the same time, what a subject of uneasiness for a man so poor as I am! Where shall I lodge thee, O Lord? Is my misery suitable to so great a Sovereign?

When the princes of the earth go to visit their subjects, they send their officers thither to prepare all things for their reception; and, when they arrive, they are received as if in their palaces. Thou canst do the like, O Lord. Yes, O my God, thou canst and wilt do it for the love of thyself. Send thine angels, that they may dispose me by their holy inspirations; order them to encompass me, that they may receive thee when thou comest. Finally, during all the time thou remainest with me, may they form a court such as thou hast in Heaven. Give me all the innocence and sanctity, all the modesty and reserve, all the faith and respect, all the gratitude and love, which thou oughtest to expect from a soul that is for ever and entirely devoted to thee.

ASPIRATIONS

Of a Soul that ardently desires to communicate.

MY divine Redeemer, whom I adore veiled under these feeble species, is it possible that thou hast reduced thyself to this state, for the purpose of visiting me and residing in my heart; and that to induce me to receive thee, thou didst promise me numberless blessings? O God of grandeur and of majesty! O God of love! why am I not all spiritual to conceive such mercy, all heart to feel it sensibly, all tongue to proclaim it aloud?

O infinite goodness, the angels are never tired contemplating thee: shall I not then desire to receive thee into my heart, since thy goodness permits it? Ah! I offer thee this heart. Come, come, O divine Sun of Justice; I am plunged into the fatal gloom of ignorance and sin; come and disperse this obscurity, and illuminate my soul with the divine light of thy grace.

Come, O charitable Physician of my soul;

after having made for me a bath of thy blood, and sanctified me in the fountain of baptism, I find myself, through my own negligence, oppressed with a thousand dangerous maladies, which involve my soul in disgust, weakness, and death: come, then, and heal me; my state is much more deplorable than that of the paralytic, whom thou asked, did he wish to be cured. Yes, my God, I wish it sincerely. Grant, through thy infinite mercy, that the desire I have for it may be more lively and ardent.

Come, O thou most faithful and most tender of all friends, come to my assistance. Powerful enemies rise up against me; my passions are continually at war with me; my own weakness affrights me, and I see myself exposed to the danger of perishing. Delay not, I conjure thee, to help me. Come, thou only art my strength, my life, my hope, my salvation, my light, my consolation.

Come, O thou source of all blessings, come and enrich me with thy treasures; adorn me with thy virtues; dissipate my tepidity; inflame me with thy love. Come, and permit not that I should ever give thee cause to withdraw thyself from me.

AN ACT

To offer up the Communion.

This act contains the principal intentions for which we should offer our Communion and the Sacrifice of the Mass: each person may add those which he shall judge most suitable to the dispositions of his soul. If you make this act the evening before you purpose to approach the communion, it would be well to renew it the next morning.

SOVEREIGN Lord of all things, Almighty God, infinitely holy, infinitely adorable, I offer thee this communion, in union with all the merits of Jesus Christ, thy beloved Son, and of the infinite love of his adorable Heart; in union with the merits of the holy Virgin, and the ardent love of her holy Heart; in union with the merits and the love of the beatified souls who enjoy thy glory in Heaven, and of the just who live upon earth. I should wish, O my God, in order to render myself more pleasing to thee in this communion, to approach with that lively faith, that profound humility, that tender confidence, that pure conscience and ardent love, with which so many holy souls are inflamed in approaching this sacred banquet. I beseech thee to accept my desire, and to supply, by thy mercy, all my deficiencies. I offer my communion to thee, and, at the same time, the divine sacrifice at which thou grantest me the grace to assist, to render thee the honour and glory which are due to thee, O God of majesty; to satisfy thy justice, which I have provoked by so many sins; to thank thee for the innumerable benefits that I have received from thy liberal hand, and which I should have received more abundantly, had I not impeded them by my infidelities; in a word, to obtain from thy infinite mercy the graces which are necessary for me, and, in particular, the grace of subduing this passion, of acquiring this virtue (N. N.), but especially the grace of a happy death.

I offer it to thee, O merciful Father, in memory of the passion and death of thy dear Son, my divine Redeemer, to enter into his views and designs, to accomplish his orders and his will, to love him with more ardour and perfection, to participate in the merits of his labours and sufferings, to acquire his spirit, to imitate his virtues, to model my life by his, to assimilate my heart to his, and to make to his Heart a public reparation, for all the sacrilegious communions, irreverences, and profanations which are committed against him in this august sacrament of his love, and in a particular manner for those of which I have been guilty.

I offer it to thee, O God of supreme liberality, to thank thee for all the graces thou hast granted to men, and which thou wast disposed to grant them, had they not rendered themselves unworthy; to thank thee, in particular, for all those thou hast conferred on the venerable Mary, the angels and the saints, especially on my angel-guardian and patron saint. I offer it to thee, O God, infinitely good, for the triumph of thy holy religion, the glory and propagation of thy holy Church; for the conversion of infidels, heretics, schismatics, and of all sinners. I offer it to thee for the necessities of all my relations, friends, associates, benefactors, and enemies; for the perseverance of the just, the comfort of the afflicted, and the deliverance of the souls in Purgatory; in a word, for all those whom I am obliged to pray for; and I desire to enter into all the intentions requisite for gaining the indulgences which I may obtain by this holy communion.

IMMEDIATE PREPARATION

ACTS AND PRAYERS FOR MASS BEFORE COMMUNION.

AN ACT OF FAITH.

I BELIEVE, O my Lord and my God, that thou art really and substantially present in the most holy Sacrament of the

Altar, and that thou art in it true God and true Man. I believe it, because it is thyself, O eternal Truth, who hast declared it; and I feel more convinced of it than if I beheld it with my eyes. Yes, I believe that thou art the Son of the living God, the Word made Flesh for the salvation of the world; and that in receiving thee, I receive thy adorable Body, which suffered and died for me, which arose triumphant and glorious. I believe that I receive thy precious Blood, which was shed for the salvation of mankind; this holy Soul, the master-piece of the magnificent hand of the Lord; this adorable Heart, the object of his complacencies, the fruitful source of all graces, the seat of all virtues, always burning with love for me; in fine, thy holy and adorable Divinity; thyself, O my amiable Saviour, and thyself entire. Yes, I believe it by thy grace: too happy could I seal with my blood the truth of my belief.

AN ACT OF ADMIRATION.

MY soul, what a miracle, what a prodigy! Jesus, the absolute Lord of all things, the King of glory and all majesty, the God of all grandeur and all sanctity, veils his sovereign splendour under the feeble appearance of bread and wine; reduces himself, and, as it were, annihilates himself for me;

overturns all the laws of nature, and performs at once the most astonishing miracles through his love for me! My mind can never cease admiring these surprising wonders: I can never, O my God, express the admiration with which I am filled. The angels and saints are in profound astonishment. O how true it is, my Lord and my God, that having loved thine own, thou hast loved them particularly at the end of thy mortal life, by instituting this divine and adorable Sacrament. O infinite wisdom, O power unlimited, O love, O excess of love and tenderness, who can ever sufficiently praise and admire thee!

AN ACT OF ADORATION.

IT is with the most profound respect and humiliation that I adore, O divine Jesus, thy supreme grandeur hidden under these frail accidents, and render to thy divine Majesty the most sincere homage. I adore and return a thousand thanks to thine infinite wisdom for having devised means, so admirable and surprising, to feed me with thy adorable flesh, and to give thyself entirely to me. I adore, I praise, and I love, with all the affection of my soul, this adorable Heart, that infinite love which has willingly condescended to exercise thy wisdom and power for the execution of a work worthy of thyself. I adore this adorable Body, this precious Blood, that holy Soul, which I am going to receive from thy liberality, thy magnificence, and thy life. O Jesus, divine Jesus! yes, thou art truly the great and admirable God, the wise and powerful God, the God of sanctity, the God of all perfection; thou art truly the God of mercies, the God of love, the God of tenderness and bounty. I adore thee in this mystery with all thine infinite perfections. May every knee bend before thee; may all creatures bless and praise thee; may all hearts love thee ardently and for ever.

AN ACT OF HUMILITY.

WHO am I, O my God, that thou shouldst so abase thyself as to come and visit me? Ashes and dust, a vile nothing! Shall I even dare present myself before thee? So often rebellious to thy commands, insensible to thy benefits and to thy love, abounding in vices and defects, shall I have the assurance to present thee my heart to be thy dwelling. What alliance can exist between my baseness and thy grandeur, between thy sanctity and the depravity of my feeble, languishing, and criminal soul? Ah! Lord, I am unworthy of the least of thy graces; I am still more so of that which thou desirest to confer on me in giving me thyself. I humbly prostrate myself in thy presence, and I acknowledge, with all the humility of which I am capable, both thy sovereign grandeur and my extreme baseness: I acknowledge the infinite distance there is between thee and me. Thow knowest it infinitely better than I do, O my God, and yet thou invitest me to receive thee. If my unworthiness makes me tremble, thy amiable invitation gives me confidence: deign, I beseech thee, to supply thyself for my deficiencies.

O divine Jesus, seeing myself very remote from the dispositions I desire for receiving thee, I cast myself into thy Sacred Heart, to draw thence that lively faith, that charity, that fervour and purity, which I ought to have. I confess before thee the excess of my misery: enrich me with thy gifts, for thy Sacred Heart is an inexhaustible treasure of graces.

AN ACT OF CONTRITION.

MY God, supremely good and merciful, how is it possible, that after having been so often unfaithful to thee, and often driven thee from my heart to make room for sin, thou condescendest to abase thyself in coming to me? How much do I grieve for having offended thee, O sovereign goodness! I detest, with all my heart, all the sins that I have committed to the present moment, and I detest them for the love of thee, because they displease thee, who art infinitely amiable and worthy of being loved above all things. Efface them more and more; purify my heart from the smallest stains; destroy in me all affection to that which offends thee; give me, O divine Jesus, a new heart, a heart conformable to thine, a pure heart burning with ardent love for thee, and seeking only thy glory.

AN ACT OF LOVE.

JESUS, O amiable Jesus, how shall I repay thy love, except by reciprocal love! To be born and to die for me, to deliver and give thyself up entirely to me. O love! O excess of love! with what transports should I not be seized! Ah! burn, inflame, consume my heart with the sacred fire with which thy adorable Heart continually burns. O adorable Heart, do not suffer my love to languish. If I am unworthy of a great love for thee, grant it to me, because thou art entitled to the most unlimited love of all hearts. O Jesus, O my only love, light up, I beseech thee, in my soul this divine fire, which thou cames to kindle on earth, and with which thou so ardently desirest to inflame our hearts. O thou God of my heart, why have I not the ardour of the cherubim and seraphim to love thee! O thou the most amiable of objects, it is for thyself that I love thee, that I desire to love thee more and more, and ever to be inflamed with thy love. O Father, the most tender of Fathers, the most faithful and generous Friend, the vigilant Pastor, and most charitable Physician, thou art my treasure and my joy, my strength and my comfort, my God and my all! How do I now grieve for having loved thee so little! Grant that henceforth I may be all inflamed with love for thee, and for thee alone! Reign entirely in my heart and remembrance; take possession of them for ever. May I think, speak, and act only for thy love; may I live and die in thy love and by thy love.

AN ACT OF HOPE.

O DIVINE Saviour of souls, that comest to me, and thou comest to fill me with thy gifts and thy graces. What a subject of confidence for me! And what canst thou refuse me, O Jesus, since thou givest thyself! Thou art a faithful God, and thou dost promise to assist me. Thou art the God of wisdom, and thou knowest my wants. Thou art the God of power, thou canst relieve me. Thou art the God of mercy and goodness, thou lovest me tenderly, and thy wish is, in honouring me with thy visit, to enrich me with thy treasures. What may I not expect, possessing in my heart even the Author of all graces? The greater my miseries are, the more I have to hope from thy liberality and goodness. Relying on the fidelity of thy promises, on thy power and thy love, I hope, O my God, for all the assistance necessary to triumph over my enemies, to vanquish myself, and to love thee tenderly to the last moment of my life.

O happy day, O precious moment, I shall possess in my heart the source of graces, thy adorable Heart, O divine Jesus! I shall draw light from it to dissipate my darkness, treasures to enrich my poverty, strength to fortify me against my weakness, consolation to alleviate and support my cross, courage to combat my passions and triumph over them. In it I shall find a remedy for all the disorders of my soul; from it, especially, I shall draw that water of life which blotteth out sin; that ardent and generous love which devours and consumes for its beloved.

AN ACT OF DESIRE.

THE beloved of my soul, O my joy, my life, my treasure, hasten the moment which my heart desires! I sigh, I languish with tenderness and love, in expectation of thy happy visit. Come, O amiable Jesus, come and no longer delay. Come to purify, sanctify, and inflame me. O celestial Bread, when shall I have the happiness to be entirely thine, and be consumed by the fire of thy love? When, O infinite Charity, shall I live only from thee, by thee, and for thee? Come and work this miracle of mercy, in giving thyself to me. O my sovereign Good, disengage, from this moment, my heart from the slavery of its passions and vices, adorn it with thy virtues, extinguish in it every other desire but that of loving and pleasing thee.

I offer thee my heart, O Jesus my love, to receive thee; open thine to me, that I may lose myself in thee, and live only for thee. May thy adorable Heart be my place of prayer, of love, and adoration; may I never go out of it, may I live and die there, consumed with the fire of thy love, O thou God of my heart and my All!

A PRAYER

To the Blessed Virgin, to our Angel-Guardian, and to our Patron Saints.

O HOLY Virgin, august Mary, my holy Angel-guardian, celestial spirits, my holy Patron (N.), all ye saints of Paradise, obtain for me a spark of that heavenly fire with which you burn for my Beloved. He comes, he appears. O Jesus, I humbly adore thee, and I love thee with my whole heart.

ACTS AND PRAYERS

AFTER COMMUNION.

[No time is more precious than that which immediately follows communion: be careful to improve every moment of it. From the moment you have received the sacred Host, enter into profound recollection, and converse with Jesus Christ present. It is then the heart only should speak to Jesus; the language of the heart pleases him. We shall here suggest some sentiments which may be dwelt on, according as the heart may feel more or less affected. The following acts, which we set down more at large, may be afterwards made.]

AFFECTING SENTIMENTS

After Communion.

O LOVE, excess of love! ocean of goodness and mercy; inexhaustible source of all good; God of majesty and glory! I have the happiness to possess thee! I adore thee, and humble myself before thee.

O Jesus, O amiable Jesus, it is thyself, with all thy perfections, that I possess in my heart. What tenderness, on thy part, to come to visit a poor sinner! No, I shall never forget so great a favour.

One heart is too confined to love thee, divine Jesus; one voice is too limited to publish thy munificence. May all Heaven and earth take part in my joy, and sing to thee canticles of praise.

Thou art mine, and I devote myself entirely to thee my Saviour. O love, may this love ever continue! No, I do not desire to live, but I wish Jesus to live in me.

How could I live without loving thee! How have I dared to offend thee! O bitterness, O regret! And yet thou hast condescended to give thyself to me! O Jesus, O my God! Thou alone art capable of such love, and it is only thou who art sufficiently powerful to effect such miracles of love. And shall I not love thee? Shall I place bounds to my love? Ah! may I rather die.

I have found my treasure, my joy, my delight—thy adorable Heart, O Jesus! It is mine; thou hast given it to me thyself. Heart of my God, of my Father, of my Redeemer, I render to thee my most profound adorations.

O Heart the most amiable, O Heart the most loving! ah! when wilt thou be also the most beloved? Take from me, I entreat thee, this ungrateful heart, this heart so tepid, so slothful, so cold in loving thee. Give me a heart to return thee love for love. Thou hast performed many miracles to give thyself to me; complete this one, in giving me a new heart inflamed with love for thee.

Holy Virgin, blessed spirits, holy inhabitants of Paradise, come, partake in my joy; adore, praise, love; pray with me and for me, to your Master and mine. I possess him in my poor heart. Yes, it is himself; he is the source of your happiness in Heaven, and at present, in my exile, he is my strength and consolation.

But when shall I see thee without veil and obscurity, O thou God of my heart? When shall I be united to thee for ever? Hasten, hasten that happy moment, that I may love thee without end and measure.

Ah! what graces am I not to obtain from my amiable Jesus. O my King, thou art all-powerful, filled with love, liberality, magnificence, and generosity; and my innumerable miseries are extreme. Transform my heart, full of vices and imperfections, into a heart ornamented with all virtues, a heart according to thine. Give me thy love, but, at the same time, a love such as thou requirest and expectest from me: on my part, give all, without further reserve or inconstancy. *Amen.*

AN ACT OF FAITH AND ADORATION.

I BELIEVE firmly, O my divine Jesus, that I have received, and possess within me, thy body, thy blood, thy soul, and thy divinity; because it is thyself, the sovereign truth, who hast revealed it: and therefore, humbly prostrate in thy holy presence, I confess and adore thee as my Lord and my God, and I unite my adorations and homage to those which are at present paid thee in Heaven. To thee belong glory, honour, salvation, and benediction. Thou art the legitimate King and the absolute Lord of all beings. As such I adore thee; I render thee my most profound adorations, and I wish that thy reign may be unalterably fixed in all hearts. Establish it particularly in mine, which thou hast made choice of this day for thy dwelling, through thine infinite mercy.

AN ACT OF ADMIRATION AND JOY.

SOVEREIGN and infinite Majesty, how is it that thou hast deigned to visit the least of all thy creatures, and to abase thy incomprehensible grandeur to my misery? Thou, O great God, before whom the angels tremble with respect, and who even at present, when I have the honour to possess thee, art confessed and honoured with the most humble and profound adorations by the highest seraphim, and by all the inhabitants of Heaven; thou, the immortal God, the holy and powerful God, comest and dwellest in the heart of a miserable sinner like me! Ye Heavens, be seized with astonishment; and thou, O my soul, give thyself up to the most lively transports of joy. May thy tender gratitude ascend to Heaven like an agreeable perfume, and join thy praises and benedictions with those of the angels and the saints.

AN ACT OF THANKSGIVING.

HOW great are thy mercies to me, O my God! they are truly incomprehensible. O holy Father, thou hast given me thy beloved Son, the object of thy complacencies. O Word made Flesh, thou desirest that thy adorable Body and precious Blood may become the nourishment of my soul; thou givest me thy adorable Heart, and the inestimable riches which it contains. Holy Spirit, thou deignest to abide in my heart, and to shed in it thy gifts and graces. O infinite goodness; O immense charity; O ineffable love! I wish I could consume myself in praises, in acts of thanksgiving and love. O my soul, bless the Lord, who doeth for thee such great and wonderful things. May all the power of my soul, O my God, unite in glorifying thy holy name; may I never lose the remembrance of so many benefits; may my heart love thee, my tongue celebrate thy magnificence all the days of my life; and since my gratitude cannot be infinite in its vivacity and ardour, grant, O my God, that it may be infinite in its duration, and that I may sing thy mercies for ever.

AN ACT OF LOVE.

O JESUS, who, by an incomprehensible love, hast deigned to suffer and die for me, who condescendest daily to sacrifice thyself on our altars, to appease the wrath of thy Father justly irritated against me, and who hast fed me with thy adorable Flesh, I do not desire to live henceforth but for thee. Grant, O Jesus, that I may be entirely thine; love nothing so much as thee; love nothing but with relation to thee; that nothing may be capable of separating me from thee. Yes, I love thee above all things. O that I could command the hearts of all those who do not love thee, I would consecrate them all to a love so just and delightful. I offer thee, in recompense, the love of all those who love thee in Heaven and on earth. May the fire of thy divine love destroy in it all that can oppose the inviolable attachment I wish to have for thee, who art my supreme good. Thy love and thy grace are the only favours I ask for time and eternity.

ACTS OF
CONFIDENCE AND SUPPLICATION.

MOST holy and eternal Father, almighty and merciful God, who, by an effect of thine infinite goodness, has been pleased to feed my soul with the adorable body and precious blood of thy dear Son, wilt thou refuse me what I ask, after having given me what is most dear to thee? Is not all that I can ask infinitely inferior to the present which thou hast made me? It is true I do not merit to be heard; but the divine Jesus merits it for me, and prays himself in my favour. His prayers, his adorations, his homages, are what I present to thee: it is his adorable Heart which induces thee to hear, particularly at this moment, from the centre of my heart, his wishes, his sighs, his mournings, that thou mayest cast thine eyes of mercy on a strayed sheep, which he has brought back to the fold. By this Sacred Heart, deign to pardon me all the sins of my past life; fortify me so with thy holy grace for the future, that I may never have the misfortune to lose thy friendship; and grant me the grace to accomplish faithfully thy holy will, and in the end to die in thy love.

And thou, O amiable Jesus, who reposest in my heart, and who wouldst not invite me to ask great things, if thou hadst not an extreme desire to grant them to me, behold the favourable moment to display thy liberality. After the favour which I have received from thee, there is none that I do not expect from thine ineffable goodness, how unworthy soever I acknowledge myself of it. I render homage to thy power, and confess there is no weakness which thou art not able to strengthen—no evil so incurable which thou canst not heal—no heart so defiled which thou canst not purify—no heart so poor which thou canst not enrich, so cold which thou canst not inflame, so afflicted which thou canst not console, so abandoned which thou canst not relieve.

Alas! I am devoid of all virtue: I have neither humility, patience, nor love. The slightest occasion seduces me, and makes me soon forget all my good resolutions; I am indifferent, remiss, and inconstant in thy service; my mind and heart are successively the theatre and sport of a thousand different passions. O my amiable Master, thou who art so compassionate, canst thou see so many miseries without being affected with them?

O tender Father, O my divine Saviour, have mercy on thy servant, redeemed with thy precious blood. Thou hast in thy hands the remedy for all my infirmities, and I know that thou lovest me. It is from thy goodness I expect my cure: give me what is most necessary for me, and what is most for thy glory. I do not ask, O my amiable Jesus, the riches and prosperity of this world; give me, on the contrary, a contempt for, and perfect disengagement from them. But give me a profound humility, great purity of heart, of body, and mind; grant me unalterable sweetness, invincible patience, perfect submission to thy holy will, a holy and constant hatred of myself and my passions, fortitude and courage to subdue them—the following in particular. (N.N.) Give me, above all, thy holy love in a supreme degree: this only will comprise all the rest. I beg it of thee for my whole life, but, in a special manner, at the hour of my death.

[Renew your petitions with greater earnestness and fervour. Be persuaded that you will render yourself the more pleasing to our Lord, the more your requests are numerous, great, and offered up with ardour and confidence; for this is the moment of his liberality and greatest mercies.]

AMIABLE Jesus, thy patience is such, that thou art never weary of attending to the cries which my wretchedness, poverty, and the love I desire to have for thee, compel me to express. I shall again raise up my voice to the Lord my God, and I hope he will hear the prayer of his servant.

Thou art entitled to the love of all hearts, O divine Jesus; yet how many are there who do not love thee! Give me, I beseech thee, all the love with which they ought to burn for thee: this favour I beg for thy glory. O Master infinitely great, O Father sovereignly perfect! if, by thy grace, I become a faithful and zealous servant, a submissive child, abounding with tenderness and love for thee, wilt thou not have all the glory? Deign, I conjure thee, to forget mine iniquities, and inflame my heart with thy love. Thy mercy solicits in favour of a sinner the work of thy hands; thy blood shed for me demands that it may not become useless, and that its merits may be applied to my soul; thine adorable Heart incessantly re-echoes its lamentations and sighs to obtain pardon for me. Hear no longer, O my divine Saviour, the voice of my sins; look on them no longer but with eyes of compassion. Behold the great things which thou hast done for me: see the immense love which has this day degraded thee, to honour me with thy visit.

Thou comest to reside in me, O my Sovereign Lord; to load me, no doubt, with thy favours; and to make me experience the effects of thy wonderful mercy: accomplish in me thy designs, I conjure thee. Thou comest to apply to me, amply and efficaciously, the merits of thy life and death, to sanctify my body and soul, to make me live a heavenly life, in some manner like thine. Thou comest to me, that angels and men may discover, by this inestimable communication, the great gifts thou desirest to confer on me—how good, how sweet, how liberal and magnificent thou art. Thou comest to procure for thyself the most just glory, and to render thy labours both abundant and useful. Oh! accomplish in me the work for which thou art come. Amiable Jesus, produce in me all these effects, in an eminent and sublime degree. Wouldst thou have descended from Heaven, wrought so many miracles, overturned the laws of nature, and made so many preparations in vain, for thy glory and my sanctification? O my God, essentially good, all-wise and all-powerful, do not lose the fruits of thy coming. On my part, I detest and disavow, with all my heart, all that can place any obstacle to them. Ah! operate in me that for which thou camest on earth. Dissipate my darkness, support my weakness, enable me by thy grace to get out of this state of tepidity in which I languish, and which might induce thee to reject me. Sanctify my body and soul, all my thoughts, words, actions; and inflame my heart with a pure, constant, and ardent love, until death. May my only regret be henceforth, that I have not loved thee, O my amiable Saviour, or loved thee so little; my only fear be, to forfeit thy love! May it be my sole comfort to love thee ardently; my only desire to increase more and more in thy love; my only interest be to contribute to thy love; and my only hope to love thee for ever in Heaven!

Permit me, likewise, O amiable Jesus, to solicit that the devotion to thy Sacred Heart may extend to all parts, that all mankind may be inflamed with thy love. I recommend to thee also thy holy Church, our spiritual and temporal rulers, my parents, friends, associates, enemies, those who labour in the conversion of souls, all persons whom I might have injured, either spiritually or temporally, and all those for whom I am obliged to pray. In a word, I humbly beg the perseverance of the just, the conversion of infidels, schismatics, heretics, sinners, and the relief of the souls in Purgatory.

AN ACT OF OBLATION.

THOU God of my heart, my whole desire and my only portion consist in loving thee. To thee I also devote myself without any reserve, and for ever. I consecrate to thee my body: purify it more and more, and render it worthy of being the temple of the Holy Ghost. O Jesus, I surrender it to thee: dispose of it according to thy blessed will. I submit to all mortifications and infirmities, to sickness, sorrows, and death itself. I desire nothing but what thou desirest; and however painful the cross may be which thou hast prepared for me, I await it, through thy grace, with entire submission; I shall receive it with lively gratitude, carry it with joy and constancy; happy in being able to say with thy great apostle: "With Christ I am nailed to the cross."

I consecrate to thee my heart: receive it as an acceptable sacrifice. I conjure thee to preserve and unite it to thine; for in it I desire to abide all the days of my life, to live in it unknown to the world, and known only to thee.

To thee I consecrate my will, that it may be conformable to thine in all things. Ah! what should I and can I desire and will, but the will of my Lord and my God! O Jesus, thy will be done, and not mine. May all things happen as thou willest, and not as I will. Let self-will reign no longer in me, O amiable Jesus. Thou art my King, my Lord, my Father; and I am thy subject, thy slave, thy child. Command and thou shalt be obeyed; behold me entirely at thy disposal.

I consecrate to thee my understanding: I shall no longer judge of anything but according to thy divine lights; I shall despise all thou hast despised, and esteem what thou hast esteemed; I shall feel only contempt for the false treasures, the vain honours, the fatal pleasures of this world; I shall desire only the good things of heaven, and the means which conduct to them; disengagement from creatures, humiliations, and crosses; such are the objects of my ambition. O my God, may thy grace work in me the accomplishment of the holy desires with which it inspires me!

I consecrate my memory to thee; it shall always remind me of thy grandeur, thine infinite perfections, thy goodness, thy beauty, thy supreme attractions. I shall place my delight in the remembrance of thy favours, of thy love, and of thy mercy to me. Can I use any means more effectual to penetrate me with love and gratitude towards thee?

I consecrate to thee, O my sweet Jesus, all that I possess: all is thine; dispose of it as thou pleasest. I consecrate to thee all that I can; I am ready to sacrifice all,—cares, pains, labours, fatigues, toils, goods, health, reputation, even life, and the last drop of my blood, to testify to thee my love, and to induce all hearts to love thee.

In a word, O amiable Jesus, I consecrate to thee all that I am: receive me according to thy great mercy and love. I belong to thee, I am thy portion: I am resolved to be thine without reserve or division; to serve thee with joy, with love; to love thee till my last breath, and for endless ages. *Amen.*

ANOTHER ACT OF OBLATION.

RECEIVE, Lord, my entire liberty; receive my memory, my understanding and will. It is thou who hast given me all I have and possess: I restore it to thee without reserve, and commit all to the disposal of thy holy will. Give me only thy love, together with thy grace, and I shall be rich enough; I ask no more.

Do not content yourself with this general offering; enter into a particular detail; and at every communion make to your God a sacrifice of some one of your defects: this will be an excellent method of arriving, in a short time, at great perfection. Pray to your heavenly Master to speak to your heart, and to make his will known to you. Listen with great recollection to the words of life that he shall address to you, and perform generously the sacrifices that he shall require. "Speak, Lord," you may say, "for thy servant heareth."—1 *Kings* iii. "Lord, what wilt thou have me to do?"—*Acts* ix. You may afterwards say the following,—

PRAYER.

IT is very just, O my God, that since thou hast given thyself entirely to me, I should give myself entirely to thee; and that after having presented to thee so many petitions, I should not refuse what thou graciously demandest of thy unworthy servant. Yes, my God, I sacrifice most cheerfully to thee my proud and hasty temper, my vanity, my luxury, my inclination to ridicule, and to speak unfavourably of others; I sacrifice to thee my ease and convenience, ever averse to constraint and contradiction; I sacrifice my delicacy in not bearing to suffer anything; my fear of contempt and humiliation; my immoderate uneasiness for the loss of health or property; my unhappy human respect, which has so often blasted my best resolutions; my worldly prudence; my unfeeling conduct to the sick and indigent; my negligence in tending to the perfection of my state, and in observing its duties and regulations; my slothfulness in acquitting myself of pious exercises; my almost continual dissipation of mind and heart; my tepidity and reserve in thy service; but, I sacrifice to thee, in particular, my predominant passion (N.), the fatal source of so many imperfections.

[Every one may go into a detail with regard to what concerns himself.]

Yes, O divine Jesus, such are my sincere resolutions. Should a heart that desires to be thine dread to sacrifice all things to please thee, and does it not find in thee alone every blessing? Is a divided heart worthy of thee, and will it ever be perfectly happy?

Deign, then, O my amiable Saviour, deign to confirm me in the holy resolutions with which thou hast now inspired me. I ask this favour through thine adorable Heart—I hope it from its infinite love for me.

A PRAYER,

To the Blessed Virgin, to our Angel-Guardian, and to our Patron Saints.

HOLY Virgin, my good Mother, in whom, after God, I place my confidence,—since thou takest so great an interest in the favours which thy dear Son confers on me, deign to thank him thyself for me, I beseech thee, for that which he has now granted me; obtain for me the grace to be faithful to him until death.

Holy angels, and you in particular my guardian-angel, I beg the same favour from you. And you my holy patrons and protectors, deign to join your prayers and thanksgivings to those of this poor sinner.

[Before you retire say the prayers to gain the indulgence, and recite the act of reparation which follows.]

AN ACT OF REPARATION,

To the Sacred Heart of Jesus, after Communion.

ADORABLE Heart of my divine Redeemer, which infinite love has concealed under the eucharistical species, to be the food, the strength, the refuge, the consolation and director of our souls; pierced, as I am, with sorrow, in reflecting on the impious and sacrilegious conduct of many bad Christians, who receive thee in the state of mortal sin, and dishonour thee in such a variety of ways; considering the negligence of many lukewarm Christians, who receive thee without preparation, devotion, and scarce without any reflection; when I think, in fine, of the faults I have so often committed against this august sacrament; I detest all these crimes from the bottom of my heart, and I desire to make thee reparation for them.

Pardon us, O source of infinite love; and to render us more worthy of pardon, change our hearts entirely. Grant us the grace never to approach thy holy table unprepared, through human views or through custom, and that we never absent ourselves through negligence; but that we may always approach with a pure conscience, a lively faith, a right intention, an ardent charity and profound humility. Grant, also,

O God of goodness, that we may have the happiness to receive thee worthily at our death, and live by thee and with thee for a blessed eternity. *Amen.*

[Penetrated with gratitude for the benefit which you have received, endeavour to recall often its precious remembrance. Visit in the afternoon the holy Sacrament, to renew your thanks to your divine Saviour, and to confirm yourself in your good resolutions. Keep yourself more recollected, and observe more vigilance over your senses during the entire day.

The fruits which you should particularly endeavour to draw from your communions are, great purity of heart, determined courage to overcome yourself, true change of conduct, union with our Lord, and great resignation and submission to his will. Foresee the obstacles, and generally endeavour to surmount them.

It is a very holy practice to receive, from time to time, the adorable sacrament of the Body and Blood of Jesus Christ, with the same preparations and the same sentiments as if you were on your death-bed; which is called, receiving the Sacrament by manner of viaticum. There is also a most useful practice, authorised by the holy Fathers, and which may be used daily and every hour of the day, which is, a spiritual communion. It consists in making acts of faith, that Jesus Christ is present in the holy Sacrament of the Altar; acts of hope, to partake in the effects of this adorable Sacrament; acts of love and desire, to receive it really; and acts of humility, acknowledging yourself unworthy of his favour]

AFFECTING SENTIMENTS,

From the Holy Scriptures, which may be made use of after Communion.

"VERILY thou art a hidden God, the God of Israel, the Saviour."—*Isa.* xlv. 15.

"The desired of all nations."—*Agg.* ii. 8.

"The Lamb of God, who taketh away the sins of the world."—*John*, i. 29.

"The brightness of eternal light, and the unspotted mirror of God's majesty, and image of his goodness."—*Wisd.* vii. 26.

"The splendour of his Father's glory, and the figure of his substance."—*Heb.* i. 3.

"My Lord and my God."—*John*, xx. 28.

"Behold he whom thou lovest is sick."—*John*, xi. 3.

"Heal my soul, for I have sinned against thee."—*Ps.* xl. 5.

"Say to may soul, I am thy salvation."—*Ps.* xxxiv. 3.

"This is my rest for ever and ever: here will I dwell, for I have chosen it."—*Ps.* cxxxi. 14.

"I found him whom my soul loveth; I held him, and I will not let him go."—*Cant.* iii. 4.

"My beloved to me, and I to him."—*Ibid.* ii. 16.

"Speak, Lord, for thy servant heareth."—1 *Kings*, iii. 9.

"My son, give me thy heart."—*Prov.* xxiii. 26.

"I love them that love me: and they that in the morning early watch for me shall find me. With me are riches, and glory, glorious riches and justice; and I walk in the way of justice, in the midst of the paths of justice, that I may enrich them that love me, and fill their treasures."—*Prov.* viii. 17, 18, 20, 21.

"But it is good for me to stick close to my God, to put my hope in the Lord God."—*Ps.* lxxii. 28.

"My soul hath stuck close to thee: thy right hand hath recived me."—*Ps.* lxii. 9.

"I live now; not I, but Christ liveth in me I live in the faith of the son of God, who loved me, and delivered himself for me."—*Gal.* ii. 20.

"Benediction, and glory, and wisdom, thanksgiving, honour, and power, and strength to our God, for ever and ever." **Amen.** —*Apoc.* vii. 12.

A CONSECRATION,

Of perfect Love to our Lord Jesus Christ.

[Convinced by the most powerful motives, of the obligation you are under of loving ardently our Lord Jesus Christ, whom you desire to have henceforth for your divine Saviour, choose some of the most solemn feasts to make this consecration, and renew it afterwards from time to time, especially after communion.]

INCARNATE Word! only-begotten Son of God! Sovereign Lord of Heaven and earth, and my most amiable Redeemer; acknowledging that I am created for the glory of God, and consequently for thee, who art by excellence the glory of thy Eternal Father; and desiring to attain that noble end through homage to thy grandeur, gratitude for thy benefits, and in proof of my love; prostrate at thy feet, with the most profound sentiments of respect, in the presence of the glorious Virgin thy Mother, of my angel-guardian, of St. Joseph, and all the court of Heaven, I offer and consecrate to thee this day, my person and life, resolved to live no longer for myself, but to be totally thine the remainder of my days; to make an open profession of living according to thy maxims and spirit; to abandon myself absolutely to thy divine will; to tend with all my strength to perfect myself in thy love, and to practise every day as many acts of divine love as I possibly can.

I conjure thee, O Jesus, my only love, to accept this offering; to consume with thy divine fire this sacrifice which I make to thee of myself; and to grant that all the powers of my soul, my senses, my thoughts, words, actions, affections, desires, may be so many holocausts, to burn continually in the flames of thy charity. Maintain, I beseech thee, O my saviour, thine interests against me; and as I have already the happiness of belonging to thee by numberless titles, offer me with thee and those that love thee, to thy heavenly Father; and grant that my self-love may be no impediment to the perfection thou expectest from me; but that I may render myself capable of it, by the frequent practice of thy love and imitation of thy virtues, particularly of thy profound humility, poverty, mortification, and contempt of the world. From thee alone do I expect them, as well as all other things that are necessary for me, as I stand in great and continual want of thee, O most illustrious Glory of God, my Jesus. Such are the ardent desires of a person who is thine for time and eternity, and who desires to unite and associate with all those who glory in loving thee, and being devoted to thee in a particular manner, O my amiable and divine Jesus! who livest and reignest with the Father and the Holy Ghost for endless ages of ages. *Amen.*

[Pray for those who tend to this perfect love of our Lord Jesus Christ.]

EXERCISES FOR VISITING

THE MOST

HOLY SACRAMENT.

THE palaces of kings are often filled with courtiers; friends often visit and freely converse together; shall the palace of the King of Kings only remain deserted? Is it only the most tender, generous, and faithful friend whom we do not deign to visit, or wish to converse with? It is the particular duty of faithful souls, devoted to the Sacred Heart of Jesus, to idemnify in some manner, this amiable Saviour, for the indifference and tepidity of so many Christians towards him. They find in our churches the Sacred Heart to which they have devoted themselves, and which is the tender object of their love; let them visit it as often as their state of life will permit.—We shall here point out different practices, which may assist them in conversing with this divine Heart, and imbibing from it the abundant graces of which it contains the plenitude.

FIRST EXERCISE

FOR VISITING THE MOST HOLY SACRAMENT.

FIRST PRACTICE.

To Visit our Lord in a Spirit of Love.

IT is love which keeps the Lord in our temples; his Sacred Heart burns with the most ardent and tender love for us; let us, therefore, return him love for love. To enkindle the divine fire in your heart, consider first, the immense love which Jesus expresses, by giving himself to you in the sacrament of the Eucharist; secondly, the innumerable graces which he grants you; thirdly, the extreme desire he has to be with you, since it it his delight; (*Prov.* viii.) the perfections, grandeur, and ineffable amiableness of his divine Heart, which is a furnace of love; the school and the teacher of perfect love, which is all love, and should consequently be the centre of all desires and of all hearts.

Inflamed by these different motives, unite all the powers of your soul and all the ardours of your heart, to express your love to this amiable Saviour. Acknowledge, that whatever you do or suffer for him, will be very little indeed in comparison to what you owe him. As it is impossible for you to love him as he deserves, exult and rejoice in considering that he possesses all the advantages of nature, the riches of grace and glory, all the perfections of Divinity; and that he is exalted for ever to the summit of all greatness, glory, and felicity. Rejoice in contemplating him as the object of the homage, adorations, praises, and eternal love of all the celestial court. Then reflect on yourself; embrace the chains of your blessed captivity, which attach you to this adorable Master; desire to render your dependence on him still greater and more intimate. Exclaim with the Psalmist, "It is good for me to adhere to my God. Whom have I in Heaven? and besides thee what do I desire upon earth?"—*Ps.* lxxii. 28, 25. "Thou art the God of my heart, and the God that is my portion for ever."—*Ibid.* In a word, beg the Sacred Heart of Jesus to inflame you himself with his love, and to render your heart such has he desires. Pray with confidence, pray with perseverance: you will be heard; for such a request is conformable to his desires, and he is still more eager to grant you his love than you can be to obtain it;—but endeavour to oppose no obstacle to it.

SECOND PRACTICE.

To visit our Lord in a Spirit of Praise.

TO praise God is the occupation and employment of the angels in Heaven, and it is also the most excellent and perfect employment of men upon earth. Thus visit our Lord, with the intention of paying him the tribute of praise and benediction you owe him.

For that purpose, consider the glorious titles, the infinitely sublime perogatives and admirable perfections of this divine Saviour; and endeavour to adopt the sentiments of admiration, respect, adoration and praise, which these titles ought to inspire.

Jesus Christ, true God and true Man, is the only begotten Son of the living God, the object of his complacency, and the splendour of his glory. He is the Admirable, the Angel of the great Council, the Father of the world to come, the Prince of Peace. He is the King of Kings, the Lord of Lords, the Beginning and the End of all things; at his name alone every knee must bend, in Heaven, on earth, and in hell. He is our Meditator, our Restorer, our Saviour, our Brother, our Head, our King, our Judge, our High-priest, our Pastor, our Master, our Model, our Physician. He is the Way that we should follow; the Truth which enlightens us; the Door through which we should enter. He is our Life, because he alone gives life to our souls; and he will be our crown, our glory, and happiness, for all eternity.

Considering the greatness and loveliness of your divine Redeemer, pour forth your heart in sentiments of adoration, respect, praise, and benediction. Unite your praises and most profound adorations to those which are rendered to him by the angels and saints in Heaven, and by all the just upon earth. Exclaim with the ancients of the Apocalypse: "Worthy is the Lamb that was slain, to receive power, and divinity, and wisdom, and strength, and honour, and glory, and benediction for ever and ever."—*Apoc.* v. 12. Invite, after the example of the prophet, all creatures to bless him, to praise him, to exalt him with you. Finnally, praise and honour your divine Saviour through his own Heart; for this is one of the pious practices which pleases him most, as he declared to Saint Gertrude.

THIRD PRACTICE.

To visit our Lord in the Spirit of Confidence.

JESUS is your amiable Redeemer, whose love for you was so great, that it induced him to suffer the most cruel torments and the most ignominious death; he resides in our churches for the love of you, and to load you with his graces; he is, at the same time, infinitely rich, liberal, and powerful, and has graciously promised to hear all your prayers. Can any thing more be necessary, to excite you to the most tender, firm, and unlimited confidence in him? Thus, then, open your heart to him without reserve, as to your Father, the best and most tender of Fathers. Converse with him as with the most generous, disinterested, and constant friend that ever existed. Sometimes lay before him your sins, and the principal faults into which you have fallen since your last visit; at other times, your passions, your evil dispositions; sometimes, your pains, your anguish, your vexations, your doubts, your weakness, your fears; for all of which beg pardon, grace, light, counsel, fortitude, support, consolation; and that with the most profound humility, tender confidence, and perfect resignation. Expose to him, sometimes, your actual state, your future apprehension, your desires, your hopes, your designs and intentions; and passing from confidence to resignation, you will abandon yourself entirely to his amiable providence, and deposit in his Sacred Heart all your cares, labours, enterprises, goods, health, life, death, and all your interests; neither desiring nor relishing any thing but his holy will, on which you are firmly resolved to depend in all things.

You may likewise consider yovrself in his presence, first, as a wretch reduced to the greatest misery, at the fect of a Monarch, "who is rich and liberal to all that call upon him."—*Rom.* x. 12.; and you will say to him: "I am needy and poor, O God, help me."—*Ps.* lxix. 6.

2d. As a sick person, apply to this charitable Physician, who during his mortal life healed, with such goodness, all those who addressed him. Say with the blind man of Jericho: "Jesus, Son of David, have mercy on me."—*Luke,* xviii. 38.

3rd. As a weak man, assailed from all quarters by powerful enemies, you will implore the assistance of Jesus, as the vanquisher of sin and the devil; and you will say, "O God, come to my assistance; O Lord, make haste to help me."—*Ps.* lxix. 1.

In a word, filled with the sentiments of a disciple eager to learn the science of the saints, say with St. Peter, "Lord, to whom shall we go," but to thee? "thou hast the words of eternal life.—*John,* vi. 69. Teach me to know and to hate myself; teach me to know and to love thee.

FOURTH PRACTICE.

To visit our Lord in a Spirit of Zeal.

ONE of the most excellent ends you can propose to yourself in visiting our Lord is, no doubt, to enkindle in your heart an ardent zeal for the interests of his glory. For that purpose, consider in his presence the enormous ingratitude with which men in general repay his inestimable benefits. It is through love for them, that he dwells and offers himself continually to the Divine Justice on our altars; and yet mankind, ungrateful to excess, insult, despise, and dishonour him, and renew all the injuries he suffered on Calvary. How many impious wretches who blaspheme him, and heretics who disown and trample him under foot; how many Catholics who render him an object of derision, and crucify him anew in themselves, by receiving him into a heart defiled with crimes! At the remembrance of so many irreverences, profanations, and sacrileges, committed against the adorable Heart of your Saviour, even in the sacrament of his love, surrender your heart to the most lively sorrow, the bitterest lamentations, the most piercing anguish, to sighs and tears. Ardently desire, and fervently conjure the Eternal Father, to vouchsafe, through his infinite mercy and almighty power, to put a stop to these evils, and to infuse into all hearts the sentiments of respect and love which they owe to their Saviour, continually sacrificed for the love of them. Conceive a generous, constant, and heroic desire to exert all your powers in procuring him true adorers; but let your prevailing sentiment be, a most sincere sorrow and true contrition, for the irreverences and infidelities which you yourself are perhaps guilty of towards this amiable Saviour, for whom you ought to burn with love, and to immolate your life a thousand times.

FIFTH PRACTICE.

To visit our Lord in a Spirit of Penance.

CONSIDER, that from this sacred sanctuary, now his tribunal, Jesus fixes his eyes on you; he beholds you, he reads your heart, he knows all its thoughts, he discovers all its views, he weighs all its intentions. Men see only your exterior; but under this exterior, which perhaps deceives them, you do not deceive him: he knows the whole state of your soul, without any other examination than a look. Now, what defects, what infidelities, what sins does he not discover in your soul? Reflect, that he exhibits them to your view, reproaches you interiorly for them, and threatens to punish you unless you amend your conduct.—Yet this amiable Saviour still offers you pardon, and his Heart inflamed with love, is still open, that you may find a remedy for all your spiritual disorders and perfect reconciliation. Do not, therefore, defer going with confidence to this throne of grace, that you may obtain mercy while it is still time. Thus, with sentiments of the most sincere regret, lament in his presence your ingratitude to him, after having presented you with so many graces, illuminations, and interior excitements, to induce you to love and serve him with fervour. Beg his pardon for your negligence and sluggishness in his service, for your habitual self-seeking, your immoderate desire of esteem and admiration, for your attachment to all your conveniencies, your impatience, your anger, secret pride, and many other defects, which your levity and distraction of mind prevent you from perceiving in yourself, and which are offensive to your heavenly Master. Sometimes cast yourself at his feet, like the publican who prayed in the temple, and say with him: "O God be merciful to me a sinner!"—*Luke*, xviii. 13. Sometimes like the leper in the gospel, beg of him " to cure the wounds of your soul."—*Matth.* viii. 2. Sometimes, with Magdalen, pour forth your heart with feelings of the most bitter sorrow and ardent love; many sins were forgiven her, because she loved much. Finally, think that he asks you, as he formerly did St. Peter, whether you love him or not; and reply to him, like this apostle, with all the ardour of which your heart is capable: "Lord thou knowest that I love thee."—*John*, xxi. 17.

SIXTH PRACTICE.

To visit our Lord in a Spirit of imitating the Virtues of which he gives us Examples in the Eucharist

OUR Lord has given us, during his mortal life, and gives us still in the Sacrament of the Altar, the examples of all virtues: meditate on these admirable virtues at his feet, and beg his grace to imitate them; in particular, the four following:

The first is Humility. For what is the life of your Saviour in this Sacrament?—It is a debased, despised, and unknown life. "He is verily a hidden God," (*Isa.* xlv. 15,) since all his grandeur and the splendour of his glory are entirely veiled in this Sacrament. His amiable Heart has deigned to reduce him to this state of humiliation, to teach you the love of humility. Do you love this virtue, so pleasing to your divine Master? Do you not love, on the contrary, splendour, elevation, the esteem of men, and whatever flatters your pride and vanity? Reflect, that Jesus tells you, that if you wish to please him to a greater degree, you should "love to be unknown, and to be deemed as nothing."—*Imit. of Christ*, b. i. c. 2.

The second is Obedience. Jesus renders himself present on our altars at all times, in all places, every time that the priests consecrate, however wicked they may be, how evil soever the intentions they may have; and he abandons himself to their disposition, nor can all the sacrileges that shall ever be committed, induce him to withdraw himself from us. Reflect that this divine Saviour tells you: "I came down from Heaven, not to do my own will, but the will of him that sent me."—*John*, vi. 38. Learn then, from this example, to follow eagerly, in all things, the will of God, and to obey promptly, exactly, and with constancy, all superiors, in every thing they command you to do that is good and just.

The third is Meekness, and invincible Patience, amidst the many outrages done him by separatists, whose impiety leads them to trample him under foot; by sinners who receive him in hearts defiled with crimes; by persons who, while they even profess their attachment to him, sometimes treat him with reserve and indifference. Yet this divine Heart suffers all these indignities with unalterable calmness and patience; and as if he was insensible of them, he is always ready to load with his graces his enemies themselves. How little do you imitate your heavenly Master! Where is your patience in bearing the contempt and injuries you may have to suffer?—Learn, at last from your God, " to be meek and humble of heart."—*Matth*. xi. 29.

The fourth, in fine, is extreme Charity, which makes him exercise towards us all the works of the greatest mercy. He satiates those who hunger and thirst for justice, and makes them partakers of abundant celestial delights. There he clothes and adorns us with the gifts of grace and the riches of his merits; there he delivers us from the slavery of our passions, and heals the wounds and infirmities of our souls. He instructs, strengthens, and comforts us. In a word, he fulfils towards us the duties of Father, of Friend, of Master, of Physician, of Saviour, and Redeemer. How often have not you yourself experienced the precious effects of your Redeemer's liberal charity? He requires from your gratitude, in return, to practice works of charity towards your neighbour: how do you acquit yourself of them?

SEVENTH PRACTICE.

To Visit our Lord in a Spirit of Sacrifice.

THE whole life of Jesus on earth was a continual sacrifice.—*Imit. of Christ*, b. ii. c. 12. He commenced it from the first moment of his incarnation, and his death on the cross was, to use the expression, but the consummation of this long and painful sacrifice. The sacrifice of Jesus Christ still continues, and shall continue till the end of the world; because this divine Saviour is without intermission on our altars as a victim, and represented as slain. He retains the precious wounds of his passion, which he incessantly presents to his Father in our favour; and he continues to humble, to offer himself, to pray, to immolate himself, for the same ends for which he humbled, he offered himself, he prayed, he immolated himself on the altar of the cross.

But if Jesus sacrifices himself, it is in order that you may sacrifice yourself with him. It is in order that you may learn to know the infinite majesty of his Father, and how you ought to honour him by continual sacrifices.—Endeavour, then, to fulfil the designs of this divine Saviour. Correspond with the dispositions and sentiments of his adorable Heart, and in union with this Sacred Heart, offer yourself to God in a spirit of sacrifice. Immolate yourself by an entire and perfect devoting of your soul, your body, and all your actions. Sacrifice to him your passions, your inclinations, your dearest interests, and whatever can be displeasing in you, to his infinite Majesty, that you may be henceforth a victim continually immolated to the glory of the Lord; a victim of expiation, to appease his wrath and satisfy his justice; a victim of thanksgiving, to acknowledge his benefits and to obtain additional graces; a victim of the most perfect holocaust, burning with the fire of his love, dead to the world and to yourself, and living for God alone, in Jesus Christ and as Jesus Christ. *Amen.*

SECOND EXERCISE.

FOR VISITING THE MOST HOLY SACRAMENT;

Taken from the Seven Petitions of the Lord's Prayer.

I.—*Hallowed be thy Name.*

CONSIDER that Jesus present on this altar, is the model of all sanctity; he is sanctity himself. It is in him, by him, and with him, that all honour and glory are rendered to the infinite Majesty. It is only forming yourself on this divine model, that you can sanctify the name of the Lord: but, alas! how little do you resemble him! Far from glorifying your God, you have too often dishonoured him, and preferred your pride and satisfaction to his glory and will. Blush at the enormity of such conduct, and entreat the most holy Heart of Jesus, debased by the most profound humiliations, to grant you the grace of true and sincere humility, which may become the basis of your satisfaction, by teaching you to sacrifice your dearest interests to the honour and glory of your God.

II.—*Thy Kingdom come.*

CONSIDER that Jesus, present on this altar, is the Sovereign King of the world and of all beings. He is the King of all ages, the King of Kings, the Lord of Lords. Heaven is his palace, the highest seraphim are his servants, the earth his foot-stool; and yet this King, infinitely great, rich, and powerful, comes from the throne of his glory, to dwell, hidden and debased, in the midst of us, with a view to reign over our hearts by the charms of his love, and to render them afterwards partakers of the kingdom of of his glory.—Are you of the number of his obedient and faithful subjects? Alas! instead of obeying him as your King, you have often revolted against him, and allowing yourself to be carried away by the false splendour of sensible objects, you have been indifferent to the eternal kingdom to which he destines you. Detest your folly and blindness; conjure the Sacred Heart of your amiable King to establish his empire in your heart, to reign in it alone, and, in particular, to inspire you with a perfect disengagement from all the goods of this world, that you may sigh only for those of Heaven.

III.—*Thy will be Done on Earth as it is in Heaven.*

CONSIDER that Jesus, present on this altar, is your Father, the best and most tender of Fathers, who by his death has given you the life of grace, and promised you eternal happines for your inheritance, if you fulfil towards him the duties of a submissive and obedient son. Have you fulfilled these duties so just, so glorious, so advantageous to yourself? You have quite forgotten them. Ungrateful and unnatural child, you have despised, abandoned, and dishonoured this amiable Father, and basely squandered the inestimable treasures with which he enriched you. Yet this indulgent and merciful Heart is still inclined to forgive, you. Return, therefore, to him without delay. Confused, humbled, penetrated with sorrow, rush into his arms, and promise him an inviolable fidelity, an entire and perfect conformity to his will in all things.

IV.—*Give us this day our Daily Bread.*

CONSIDER that Jesus, present on this altar, is the good Shepherd, who gave his life for his sheep, and who sacrifices himself every day to feed them with his Flesh and Blood. He has enrolled you amongst his flock, provided for all your wants, assisted you in your infirmity, revived you in your languor, sought you in your wanderings; he has carried you on his shoulders and in his Heart. Have you been sensible to so many benefits, corresponded to so may cares? You have resisted him. Deaf to his voice, you have obstinately refused to follow him, and to return to him when he called you. Acknowledge your blindness and ingratitude. Tell him with the prophet: "I have gone astray like a sheep that is lost; seek thy servant," O my God.—*Ps.* cxviii. 176. And to render yourself worthy of his favours, promise an entire resignation to his amiable guidance, a perfect conformity of mind and heart to whatever he shall please to command you.—Are not your interests secure, when the Lord takes charge of them?

V.—*Forgive us our Trespasses, as we forgive them that trespass against us.*

CONSIDER that Jesus, present on this altar, is your Judge, the same judge, before whom you shall one day appear, to give an account of your past life; a judge, then severe and inexorable, but at present, a judge filled with goodness and mercy. His amiable Heart is still open to you; it rests with yourself to have recourse to him. He offers pardon to contrite and humble hearts, and extends his mercy to us in the same degree that we extend our mercy to others. Thus, prostrate before him, conceive the most lively sorrow for having so often and so greviously insulted him; sacrifice to him, with all your heart, your resentments, your aversions, your coldness towards all those who may have offended you; and promise him to fulfil all the duties of the most extensive and perfect charity.

VI—*Lead us not into Temptation.*

CONSIDER that Jesus, present on this altar, is that amiable Saviour, that generous Deliverer, who vanquished the powers of hell, destroyed the dominion of sin and death, and who, delivering you from the most shameful servitude, made you worthy to participate in the inheritance of the saints: but to attain it, you must give combat, and it is only by combating with and like Jesus Christ, that you can come off victorious. Now, it is by the cross that Jesus has vanquished; it is only, then by the cross that you can subdue these formidable enemies. Yet you fly from the cross, and seek, on the contrary, what favours your inclinations, what flatters your senses and self-love. Consider to what dangers such conduct exposes you; and beg of the Sacred Heart of Jesus, the necessary strength to embrace and practise self-denial and christian mortification.

VII.—*But deliver us from Evil. Amen.*

CONSIDER that Jesus, present on this altar is the inexhaustible source of all treasures. His liberal Heart diffuses them abundantly on all those who invoke him: why have you not constant recourse to it? You would find in it the alleviation of all your pains, because it would give you patience to assuage and render them advantageous to you; but what is still more, you would find in it a remedy for all the evils with which your soul is oppressed, a cure for your inordinate passions, your vicious habits, and the fatal wounds which you have received by sin. Address yourself, then, to this tender and all-powerful Heart, and beg, in particular, the grace to subdue your predominant passion, and the inestimable gift of final perseverance. *Amen.*

THE HOLY EXERCISE

OF

THE LOVE OF GOD.

AN INVITATION

To the frequent Use of Acts of the Love of God, in Imitation of the Sacred Heart of Jesus.

IT is certain, that the Sacred Heart of Jesus, during the mortal life of this Man-God, was incessantly inflamed with the most pure, perfect, and most ardent love for God! This Sacred Heart still burns with the same love in the sacrament of the Eucharist, and will burn with this love for ever in Heaven. Now there is nothing in which the soul devoted to the Sacred Heart of Jesus, should endeavour more to imitate him, than in loving God with as much perfection as possible: this adorable Heart desires nothing so much as to see our hearts quite burning with divine love, and we have the most urgent motives to yield to his desires and examples.

1. Nothing is more reasonable than to love God, who is infinitely kind and perfect, who has conferred on us so many benefits, who does not cease to do so, and who wishes to render us eternally happy.

2. Nothing is more just than to obey the express command which God has given us, to love and serve him.

3. Nothing is more honourable for us, than to raise our hearts and love above all created objects, to consecrate them solely to God, to unite ourselves with his infinite Majesty by mutual love, and to contract a holy familiarity with the God of the universe and the Creator of all things. We may judge of it by the comparison of a king, with whom we should be connected by the most tender bonds of friendship.

4. Nothing is more excellent—since all we can do is less than an atom, when compared to one single act of the love of God: nothing makes us approach so near the life of the blessed, and the life even of God, which is a life of love.

5. Nothing is so useful—since these repeated acts of the love of God cause us to accumulate, incessantly, merits upon merits, and procure us the possession even of God,

and all the blessings which accompany him for eternity.

6. Nothing is so easy—since nothing is required but to love, and to love him who is infinitely amiable and good, who gave us a heart capable of loving him, and gives us all the graces necessary for loving him.

7. Nothing is so necessary—since we must either love God or be lost. The condition is absolute: you must burn with the fire of divine love in this world, or be burned in the fire of hell in the next.

8. Nothing is more important for all eternity; and that you may conceive it the better, ask yourself the following questions:

Who does not regret having hitherto omitted thousands and thousands of acts of the love of God? and who would not wish to make as many such acts in future, as he has omitted for the past? who would not wish it with all his heart?

Who is it that would not wish to make as many acts of the love of God, as were made by the holy Magdalen after her conversion, and as have been made by many virtuous persons during their lives?

Who is it that would not wish to make as many as has have been made, as are made, and as shall be made to the end of the world?

You acknowledge, that a man must be devoid of feeling, who does not desire this with all the powers of his soul.—What! that I alone should be able to make as many acts of the love of God, as have been made, and as shall be made by all the virtuous and just in this world!—Ah! were it in my power, what would I not do to obtain so great a blessing?

But who, on the contrary, would wish to omit, in future, as many acts of the love of God, as he has omitted during the past?

Who is it that would wish to prevent as many acts of the love of God, as were made by the holy Magdalene from the period of her conversion, and by so many other saints during their lives?

Who would wish to prevent, if he could, as many acts of the love of God, as have been made, and shall be made to the end of the world?

You acknowledge that a man must have the malice of a demon to entertain such a desire. What? that I alone should prevent as many acts of the love of God, as there have been made, and as shall be made by all the just souls in this world! Ah! were I reduced to the alternative, what would I not suffer, rather than prevent so much good?

Consider now these two truths: the one, that the saints love God more or less perfectly in Heaven, according as they loved him in this world; the other, that the love of every saint for eternity, is more considerable, by its duration, than all the acts of the love of God could be, by their number, which all the saints have been able to produce during their mortal lives; since the number of the latter is limited, and the duration of the former infinite.

It is then certain, that those who have not loved God in this life, will not love him in the next; and, consequently dying in sin, they will deprive God of more glory, in some manner, than if they really prevented all the acts of the love of God that the saints could have made on earth.

It is certain, moreover, that those who neglect now to make an act of the love of God, even though they should not be obliged to it, and might omit it without sin, expose themselves, nevertheless, to love God less perfectly for all eternity; and consequently, if they do not repair this negligence by their fervour, they will deprive God, in some manner, of more glory than can be expressed.

After that, do you conceive all the evil which results from the sole omissions of your past life? how often have you omitted acts of the love of God? And, if you do not repair these faults, how much have you wrested, ravished from the glory of God? He alone knows it, since it is infinite, because he alone knows what is infinite.

And of what treasures, of what riches, O christian soul, have you not deprived yourself by your negligence? What sorrow at the hour of your death, when you think of these moments! What? I could have loved God a thousand times, a million of times more than I have; and if I had loved him in this manner, I should love him to a greater degree for eternity!—How wretched am I! I have deprived myself of this great happiness.

Let us, therefore, increase in love, while it is in our power; let us suffer no vacuities in the days and hours of our life; life passes like a shadow, and will soon disappear: let us not expose ourselves to the risk of weeping in vain, for our sloth and negligence; let us strive to repair the past, and make, during the short time we have to live, many acts of the love of God, with as much perfection as possible. It was thus the Francis's of Assisium, the Xaviers, the Teresas, the Gertrudes, and many other fervent souls, were actuated, who made several hundred of them in the course of the day; and there have been servants of God who made several thousand of them in the same space of time. Let us imitate them as much as possible, and consider all the moments of the day as so many signal favours from Heaven, since there is not a moment of these in which we cannot increase our treasure by increasing our love; and were we to increase it only by one degree, this degree of love that we have on earth, will remain for ever in Heaven.

What value, what advantage, is contained in a single act of the love of God, formed during this life! Were it even true that we gained but little by every act of love, this little is, in some manner, infinite, because it is eternal. What loss does not a soul sustain by its supineness and negligence, in omitting to make an act of the love of God! Of what blessings, of what treasures, does it not deprive itself!

Raise up then, as often as you can, O christian reader, raise up your heart by acts of the love of God, as ardent as you are capable of forming; and remember, that according to St. Teresa, "it is with the love of God as it is with a great fire; to keep it burning, it must be continually supplied with wood." Remember, also, what St. Augustin says, speaking on the love of God, that "charity cools, when the heart is silent."—*Aug. in Ps.* 37.

Thus contract the holy habit of elicting, from both heart and mouth, repeated acts of the love of God. Your heart is your constant companion, and it is from the abundance of the heart, that glowing ejaculations should proceed, which express those acts of love.

Commence, by forming one act every hour; then you can make one every half-hour; you may afterwards make one every quarter of an hour, or you can form a certain number from noon to evening. It is by this means that you will gradually come, like the saints, to make every day a great number of these acts. It is thus you will be able to say, in some manner like the saints: *We live by love; the practice of the love of God is our most ordinary practice.* But if you spend your time in this manner, forming acts of the love of God during your life, will you not have reason to hope from his mercy, that he will grant you the grace to die, like many of the saints, in the actual exercise of divine love? Oh! what a grace, to die in the actual love of our God, so that the last breath of life should be a breathing of love, and the rapture of a soul which flies towards God! Ah! how precious is this death! All that we shall ever be able to do to obtain it, is inadequate to the purchase of a blessing so great and so inestimable.

Let not disgust induce us to give up or neglect so great and holy an exercise. We must remember, that notwithstanding our disgust;—

1. We are not less pleasing to God, in making these acts of love, though we may experience no pleasure in them.

2. That consequently we do not cease to increase our merits, and the love of God, which we shall have for ever in Heaven.

3. That our sloth and negligence would cause us incalculable losses.

Since the practice of which we speak is so glorious to God, and of such advantage to our souls, let us no longer fear the trifling difficulty we may feel in making these acts of divine love. Great fatigues and mental exertions are not necessary: let us have a good heart and a good will, and this will be sufficient to please God and to enrich ourselves. The saints, far from finding this practice troublesome, considered it as a source of delight. St. Gertrude repeated, with inexplicable delight, two hundred and twenty-five times in the day: "*I adore, praise, and bless the most Holy Trinity!*" St. Francis of Assisium repeated nothing during an entire night but these few words: "*My God and my All!* The lives of St. Catherine of Sienna, St. Catherine of Genoa, St. Teresa, St. Magdalene of Pazzi, to omit many others, furnish us with the like examples.

Do not be afraid, that your application to form acts of this sort, from time to time, will take off your attention from your other employments: it will, on the contrary, be a means to make you discharge them better; because you will perform them through a motive of love, and in the presence of your beloved, and, as it were, under his eyes. And what can you gain that is equal in value to what you would lose? For whom do you labour? Why do you deprive your soul of its true riches? Desire what is of most consequence. Can you not from time to time exclaim, addressing yourself to the Almighty: *I love you.* What! is it a troublesome matter, or capable of making you neglect the duties of your state of life, to say from time to time: *My God I love you?* No, no; the saints did not think so; they even acquired new strength in that practice, and additional courage to acquit themselves better of their respective duties.

We daily see persons who do not complain of hours spent at games, amusements, and in useless conversation; and we complain of the moments which God requires from us, to form a few acts of divine love. Ah! if we had a little faith, we should regard as nothing, all the gifts of the world and of nature, when compared to the gifts of grace and glory, when compared to one single act of the love of God.

Do not look on this practice as too difficult, and above your strength. You aspire to the bliss of the saints: you will be what they are, if you do what they have done. Divine love increases, like other habits, by repeated acts: the greater number of these acts you make, the more familiar will the habit become. Suppose you should form but six every day, three in the forenoon and three in the afternoon, this will be more than two thousand acts of love in one year, more than twenty thousand in ten years; that is, more than twenty thousand degrees of glory for the next life. If you make six of these acts in the forenoon and six in the afternoon, there are more than forty thousand in ten years. Reason thus, by a similar proportion, on the losses you would sustain by neglecting to make these acts of divine love.

What merits should we not require, what perfection should we not soon attain to, were we faithful to this holy practice in question! Why is there so much difference between persons of the same condition and the same state of life, who perform the same exterior actions and the same exercises of piety?— Because the heart and the love are not the same. Whence comes it, that some saints who died very young, are so highly exalted in glory, and have acquired more merit in a few years, than others who have lived sixty or eighty years?—The reason is, that in this short time they produced more acts of divine love, these acts were more excellent and more fervent, and because, in a word, they loved God more intensely.

If the little hardship which is felt in the practice of this holy exercise affrights you, reflect on the glory which will result to God from it, and the inestimable recompense which you will acquire.

To avoid disgust, which the devil may perhaps endeavour to suggest, you may diversify these acts, and perform them sometimes in one way, sometimes in another, according to the attractions of grace and the inward dispositions of joy, sorrow, peace, trouble, or temptation, in which you may find yourself. You may likewise occupy yourself in forming acts of love, pious affection, or preference, &c.—we shall give some examples of them in the sequel. But you must remember;—

1. That is not sufficient to pronounce them with the mouth, nor even to express them in thought; but the heart must pronounce them.

2. As it is certain that we cannot form any act of the love of God, without supernatural grace, we have also reason to think, when we do what lies in our power, and use these forms with care and application, that God will grant that grace with which we can really make an act of love, since he is always at the door of our hearts, and desires nothing so much from us as our love.

Let us not neglect to beg this sacred love

most particularly from him: he never refused it to fervent and persevering prayer. It is by our works and conduct that we should prove to this infinitely amiable God, the sincerity and extent of our love for him.

We have rather enlarged on this practice, as it appeared to us of the greatest importance; besides, nothing is more conformable to the desires and example of the adorable Heart of Jesus; nothing better calculated to render us agreeable to this Sacred Heart, and to draw down on us that abundance of graces which it seeks to diffuse, and of which it is the source.

A PRAYER.

THAT I could, my God, for the remainder of my life, multiply the acts of my contrition and love, to a still greater number than that of my past infidelities! O that I could form acts of contrition and of love, so vehement, that their vehemence may repair the glory of which I have deprived thee, and the losses I have suffered, by my tepid and negligent manner of loving thee, my only good.

At least, O my God, since one single act of love procures thee so much glory on earth; since, after my death, it will hasten the happy moment which shall unite me to thee; since, in Heaven, it shall add to thy glory for all eternity; I desire, (the resolution is taken through thy grace, and with the help of that same grace I will execute it,) I desire I say, to do and suffer every thing through love for thee. I wish to speak only by love, to act only by love, to be all love; not to live, not to breath, but in love, through love, and for love. *Amen.* My God! *Amen.*

CONSIDERATIONS,

On the Love of God.

[The following considerations contain the most proper motives to enkindle in our hearts an ardent love of God: try, then, to penetrate them in their fullest extent. To effect this, there are two extremes to be avoided, spiritual sloth and curiosity. The effect of spiritual sloth is, to reap with indifference these considerations, to make no effort to examine or search into them. The effect of curiosity is, to pass lightly over all these truths, to fly from one article to another with precipitation. To remedy this, we must read, with a reasonable application, each of these propositions, and dwell on them as long as we feel ourselves devoutly affected, without passing to another, or even reading it entirely, unless we perceive our devotion abated, our minds distracted, and that it is time to proceed to another.]

I.

GOD is good; yes, without doubt; he is good, and infinitely good. God is essentially good, and his goodness is neither limited nor transient, but infinite, unchangeable, and eternal.

Is not such goodness deserving of love, and of infinite love?

Yes, without doubt, it deserves it!—But, O my God since I cannot love thee infinitely, I desire, at least, to increase in thy love without limit and measure.

II. God loves me; this is most certain: God loves me. What an honour, what consolation! And his love for me is so great, so perfect, that it is equal to him who is infinite, and eternal; for all that is in God, is God; great, immense, eternal, infinite, like God.

God loves me then with infinite love. Ah! how great is the love of God for me! and what should be my love for him?—I ought to love him with infinite love.

But I am inadequate to such great love; my heart is not capable of it; it belongs only to God to love himself in that manner. Love thyself, then, O my God; love thyself as thou meritest: and because thou lovest thyself thus, I rejoice for it, and I honour, with all my heart, the love which thou bearest thyself.

But, that I may not be ungrateful, I desire to render thee, as far as I possibly can, love for love. Thou lovest me in the highest degree, and I desire to love thee in the same manner. Thou art infinite, and as for me, I am very little and limited; but he that gives all, gives what he can, and thou art satisfied with it. I give thee, then, O my God, all for all. Thou lovest me in the highest degree, and I desire to love thee in the same manner.

III. God desires I should love him: he desires it, no doubt, and commands it.

Does he not confer a great honour on me, by asking my love? and is it not just I should grant it to him?

Yet how many times has he not asked it? O what goodness! And how often have I refused it? O what ingratitude! I beseech thee, now, O my God to accept of my heart, my will, my love, which thou hast desired so long. Ask me no more, O my God; but possess my heart; inflame, transform it all into love for thee.

IV. God gives me his grace to love him. This is true; as true as it is, that he desires me to love him; for, without his grace, I could not love him with a love of charity such as he requires from me

He gives me, therefore, his grace to love him: why should I not receive it? I receive it with all my heart.

But having received it, and being enabled by it to love God, why should I not love him?

My God, I receive thy grace as thou offerest it to me, and I will employ it entirely, with all my heart, in loving thee. Yes, my God, I love thee with gratitude, and I desire to employ myself wholly in loving thee.

V. When God offers me his grace to love him, he offers me what is more beautiful, without comparison, than the stars, the sun, and even the angels in their natural state.

And when, with his grace, I make an act of the love of God, I do the most beautiful and useful act in the world.

Why, then, should I not henceforth love my God? All my employment shall be, to love God and and to do his holy will.

VI. O my soul! of what thinkest thou, when thou dost not think of God? Alas! of what dost thou think? Thou thinkest of thyself, and of a thousand superfluous things.

Thou thinkest, then, more of the world than of God himself; and yet, should any thing in the world occupy thee like God?

O my soul! what lovest thou, when thou lovest not God? Is there any thing, except God, that is not infinitely inferior to God, less beautiful than God, less good than God?

And thou lovest that more than God; at least thou hast loved it more; but at present............but in future............ Ah! My God, my God, it is thou whom I love at present; it is thou whom I shall love in future, more than all other things in the world.

God takes care of me, as if there was no other but I in the world;—yes, he takes care of me, as if there was no other but I: and all he does for others, neither distracts him nor takes off his attention from the care he takes of me. Should I not, then, endeavour to serve him, as if there was no world at all? God alone in my mind; God alone in my heart; God alone my life; God alone my treasure; God alone my all.

VII. Of all occupations, not only there is none that can be compared to that of loving God, but all others together could not be equal to it. Why, then should I not devote myself to it?

O precious occupation! whoever devotes and applies himself to it, has no reason to envy any other; and those who devote themselves to other pursuits, may be tempted to envy those who apply themselves to this holy practice. To love God is the most delightful occupation of the angels, the saints, and of God himself.

VIII. A God of infinite Majesty occupies himself, through his infinite goodness, with me, and communicates to me his graces, that I may occupy myself with him, and love him; and I will not submit to him!

Behold, I submit, O my God; I submit to thee, with all my heart, and for ever.

IX. O my God, how faithless have I been in my promises and best resolutions! I told thee, in mind or expressions, that I gave thee my heart; and this heart was still my own, though I said it was thine.

But now, I say, O my God, (and I sincerely desire to fulfil what I say,) that I give thee my heart; yes, I give it to thee; it is thine; I have no further claim to it; dispose of it as thou pleasest.

X. God does not act towards me at intervals, offering me one day his grace, and offering me none on the other: no, he does not treat me in this manner; as without intermission he gives me existence, so without intermission he offers me his grace: it is always in my power to receive his grace, and always to love him. How many times, then, having it in my power to love God, have I not failed to love him? It was in my power: why have I not loved him? Ah! my God, thou hast desired it—and, wretch that I am, I desired it not.

But, now, O my God, I desire it; yes, without doubt, I desire it. Love, O my God, love, love.

XI. My interior occupation shall be, to keep my heart so disengaged, so peaceable and submissive, that I may not prevent, in any way, either the produce or increase of the divine love in my heart: and from this moment, O my God, I present myself to thy divine Majesty, as disengaged, peaceable, and submissive, as I possibly can be. Give me thy love, and augment it, until it be such as thou desirest.

XII. I desire no longer to look on my heart as my own property: it is thine, O my God; it is just that thou shouldest be its Master. I leave and surrender it to thee; govern it as thou pleasest.

This heart within me is no longer mine; it is my heart no longer, it belongs to God. I must leave it, and I leave it to my God; it is his domain, his abode, his temple. I consent that he may shed his lights on it, or leave it in darkness; do in it whatever he pleases.

XIII. What advantages shall I not discover in loving God? My sins shall be effaced, grace will be granted me, my enemies will be subdued, my salvation will be secured, God will be satisfied.—From this moment, without further delay, I am resolved to love my God, and to love him for ever. I wish to do whatever his love requires—for his love requires nothing but what I am willing to do and suffer for him, were it necessary.

XIV. How badly is our time employed, when we employ it in any thing else but in loving God! since all the time, not employed in loving him and in doing his will, is an eternity of love entirely lost, which we should have gained had we employed this time in loving God. Ah! my God, how great an increase of thy love have I lost for eternity!— Ah! how much have I lost! But that I may lose no more, from this moment I love thee and I wish to love thee as much as I can, without ceasing, from this moment to the last of my life; I wish to live and to love at the same time; and, at the instant even of my death, I desire to die in loving thee, and to love thee in dying.

XV. Should we reject, so long, the most precious thing in the world, the possession of which is in our own power; that is, the love of God? What can be more glorious, beneficial, delightful, or excellent? Why, then, do I resist the divine love; why defer to love a God, who has loved me for all eternity? Ah! my God, pardon all my past resistance.—Divine love, I resist thee no longer; on the contrary, I desire thee with all my heart. It is through thee, O my God, I exist; for thee I exist, and to thee I belong. Thou art my all; and all that is in me is not mine but thine, all thine, and for ever.

ACTS OF THE LOVE OF GOD.

Acts of Love and Complacency.

HOW much do I rejoice, O my God, for the infinite glory which thou dost enjoy, and the infinite perfections which thou possessest! I rejoice, for the love of thee, that thou art immense, infinite, almighty, eternal, and the source of all good. I rejoice that thou lovest thyself as much as thou meritest, and thou lovest thyself infinitely; and it is a subject of infinite joy to me, to know the love which the angels and saints have for thee, and shall have for eternity.

"I will rejoice in the Lord, and I will joy in God my Jesus."—*Habac.* iii. 18.

"O Lord God, Creator of all things, dreadful and strong, just and merciful, who alone art gracious, who alone art just, and almighty, and eternal."—2 *Machab.* i. 24, 25.

"Great is the Lord, and greatly to be praised: and of his greatness there is no end."—*Ps.* cxliv. 3.

Acts of Love and Desire of the Glory of God.

O THAT I could, O my God, make thee loved by all mankind! I could wish for a moment to be the master of all hearts; I would, without delay, consecrate them to thee, and sacrifice them to thy love. I would wish, O my God, to be able to erect temples in all places to thine honour; to overthrow all idols; to convert infidels and sinners; finally, to make thee known and loved by all the nations of the earth.

O God of my heart, how much would I rejoice to see thy name glorified, and "thy will done on earth as it is in Heaven!"

Blessed be the Lord for evermore. So be it, so be it."—*Ps.* lxxxviii. 53.

"To the King of ages, immortal and invisible, the only God, be honour and Glory for ever and ever."—1 *Tim.* i. 17.

Glory be to the Father, and to the Son, and to the Holy Ghost; as it was in the beginning, is now, and ever shall be, world without end. *Amen.*

Acts of the Love of Preference.

MY God, I prefer thee to all, and I love thee more than all that is not thyself. Henceforth thou wilt be all things to me, and all other things will be as nothing to me.

Reign in my heart, O my God, and possess it alone and for ever. I desire to be entirely thine, O my God and my love, and nothing but thine, and for ever.

"The God of my heart, and the God that is my portion for ever."—*Ps.* lxxii. 26.

"What have I in Heaven? and, besides thee, what do I desire upon earth?"—*Ibid.* 25.

"My God and my All."—*St. Francis.*

Acts of dolorous Love or Contrition.

AH! how sorry am I, O my God, for having delayed so long to love thee! How I grieve for having still loved thee so little!

O my God, I am pierced with sorrow for having offended thee because thou art infinitely amiable and infinitely perfect. How happy are those who have, in early life, devoted themselves to thee, and who have never ceased to be thine!

Ah! could I redeem the precious moments I have lost! If I could now make the thousands of acts of love, which I might have made during all the hours employed so badly!

"Father, I have sinned against Heaven, and before thee."*Luke*, xv. 21.

"Turn away thy face from my sins, and blot out all my iniquities."—*Ps.* l. 11.

"Be merciful to me, a sinner,"—*Luke,* xviii. 13.

Acts of the Love of Conformity.

MY God, do in me, with me, and by me, in all that concerns me, in all that belongs to me, and in all things, for time and eternity, whatever thou pleasest. I desire to do, for the love of thee, whatever thou wouldst have me to do.

My sole desire is to please thee, my God! and all my joy, my peace, and my happiness consists in doing thy will.

My heart, O my God, desires most ardently to see thy holy will accomplished for ever. I desire all thou desirest, and because it is thy desire.

"Not my will, but thine be done."—*Luke*, xxii. 42.

"Lord, what wilt thou have me to do?"—*Acts*, ix. 6.

"My heart is ready, O God, my heart is ready."—*Ps.* cvii. 1.

Acts of Desire to Love God.

O MY Lord and my God, when shall I love thee with all my heart, and as thou desirest I should love thee?

Ah! how happy should I be, O my God, if I alone could love thee, as much as the angels and the saints love thee in Heaven!

O goodness, O infinite love, who would not desire to love thee daily more and more? My heart sighs, without ceasing, after the precious gift of increasing love. Deign, I beseech thee, to fulfil its desires.

"O life, by which I live, without which I die, where art thou? where shall I find thee? Be thou always present to my soul, present in my heart, present in my mouth, present to my ears, present to assist me; because I languish with love, because without thee I die."—*St. Aug. Solil.* c. 1.

"Let the glowing and delicious force of thy love swallow up my soul, and in it consume all earthly affections, that I may cleave to thee alone, and feast on the sole recollection of thine inexpressible sweetness.—*St. Aug. Medit.* c. 35.

"O fire which ever burnest, and art never quenched, do thou inflame me!"—*St. Aug. Solil.* c. 19.

Acts of Desire to see God.

MY God, who art the delight of my soul, when shall I see and possess thee? O when shall I contemplate thee on the throne of thy glory? When shall I love thee ardently, solely, eternally?

What happiness in Heaven, O my God, to see that all shall praise thee, bless thee, sanctify thy holy name! to see that all shall love thee, and none offend thee!—When shall I dwell in that mansion of peace, to bless and to love thee for ever? O the unfortunate world I inhabit, where God is loved so little, and so often offended! O My God, I desire with ardour, and expect with submission, the happy moment when I shall begin to love thee with a pure and perfect love, never to cease burning with that love for all eternity!

"The mercies of the Lord I will sing for ever."—*Ps.* lxxxviii. 1.

"When shall I come and appear before the face of God?"—*Ps.* xli. 3.

"I desire to be dissolved, and to be with Christ."—*Phil.* i. 23.

An Abridgement of the Acts of the Love of God.

1.

I rejoice, my God, that thou art sovereignly perfect.

2. I desire that thou mayest enjoy all the glory which thou canst receive from thy creatures.

3. I love thee more than all which is not thyself.

4. I detest all my sins for the love of thee. Ah! may I die a thousand times, rather than displease thee.

5. O my God! who art all love, inflame my heart for ever with the fire of thy divine love.

6. Oh! when shall I see thee, when shall

I possess thee, when shall I love thee only, O infinite goodness?

7. How sorry am I, O my God, to see thee so often offended, and loved so little!

8. Thy will be done.

9. I desire to express all these sentiments, when I say with heart or mouth: *My God I love thee!*

[Adopt the saintly habit of repeating often in the day some of these short acts which we have given;—have the intention pointed out in No. 9, or you may apply this intention to the form of the act which you shall have chosen.]

ASPIRATIONS.

By way of Prayer, to beg the divine Love from the Holy Ghost.

DIVINE Spirit who art all spirit and love,—Love of the Father and the Son,—personal, substantial, eternal, and infinite Love, draw us to thee, that we may be transformed into love.

Come to us, O divine love, descend upon us; behold our hearts, which thou hast sought so long, and the access to which has been so often shut against thee; behold they are, at length, entirely disposed and open to receive thee.

Divine love, thou hast sought us when we withdrew from thee: wilt thou quit us now when we seek thee? Ah! thou lovest and seekest us even now; and it is thyself who dost excite us to desire and seek thee. Alas! without thee we should still go astray. Come, then, O divine love; come, we conjure thee: replenish our hearts, which pant after thee. Enter, thyself, with thy graces; deign, thyself, to become master of them. They emplore only thee, desire only thee, thirst only after thee.

Thou camest on earth, O Spirit of love, thou camest for us, as well as for all the saints. Thou art for us, as well as for them, the Spirit of love. Come, then, O creating Spirit of love; O divine and heavenly fire, light up in our hearts the flames of ardent love with which the saints burned upon earth, and with which they are inflamed in heaven.

Come, with all thy inflamed affections, to burn and consume our hearts. They are thy victims: let them burn with generous and undivided love, with ardent and uninterupted love, with consuming love, which may destroy in us, generally, all that could offend thine infinite sanctity; with a suffering love, which delights in suffering for God, in expecting the happy moment to enjoy him for eternity.

Holy Spirit, Spirit of love, dilate our hearts by thy chaste flames, and replenish them with an intoxicating and panting love; ever confused for having offended a God infinitely amiable, and so imperfectly loved; ever sighing, ever thirsting to love him more and more. Ah! may the measure of our love be, in future, to know no measure. The more we shall possess thee, O divine love, the more ardently shall we desire thee; and the ardour of these new desires will induce thee to descend upon us with greater abundance. Thus shall we live in desiring thee always, and always receiving thee.

Ah! come, come, O divine fire, O pure and infinite charity, that having possessed thee during our lives, thou mayest possess us after our death. By this means we shall pass from love to love; from the love which is here below inspired by grace, to the love which thy presence renders fixed and immutable in Heaven. There we shall no longer exist but in the ardent flames of thy holy love; there we shall be all love, enraptured with the sweets and eternal joys and Paradise.

Ah! when, O divine love, ah! when shall we possess this incomparable happiness? In the mean time we shall desire, with new ardour, to possess thee more perfectly. We shall love thee with such fervour and perseverance, with the help of thy grace, that, at the hour of our death, nothing shall deprive us of the love and beatific sight of the adorable Trinity. *Amen.*

THE HOLY MASS

FOR THE

FEAST OF THE SACRED HEART OF JESUS.

PART I.

The Preparation of the Offerers, by Acts of Humility, Praise, Faith, &c.

The Priest at the foot of the Altar, beginning, says,

IN Nomine Patris, et Filii, et Spiritus Sancti. *Amen.*

Ant. Introibo ad altare Dei.

R. Ad Deum qui lætificat juventutem meam.

IN the name of the Father, &c. *Amen.*

Ant. I will go unto the altar of God.

R. To God, who rejoiceth my youth.

Psalm 42.

JUDICA me, Deus, et discerne causam meam de gente non sancta: ab homine iniquo et doloso erue me.

JUDGE me, O God, and distinguish my cause from the nation that is not holy: from the unjust and deceitful man deliver me.

R. Quia tu es, Deus, fortitudo mea, quare me repulisti? et quare tristis incedo, dum affligit me inimicus?

P. Emitte lucem tuam et veritatem tuam: ipsa me deduxerunt et adduxerunt in montem sanctum tuum, et in tabernacula tua.

R. Et introibo ad altare Dei : ad Deum qui lætificat juventutem meam.

P. Confitebor tibi in cithara, Deus, Deus meus : quare tristis es, anima mea; et quare conturbas me?

R. Spera in Deo, quoniam adhuc confitebor illi : salutare vultus mei, et Deus meus.

P. Gloria Patri, et Filio, et Spiritui Sancto :

R. Since thou, O God, art my strength, why hast thou cast me off? and why do I go sorrowful, while the enemy afflicteth me?

P. Send forth thy light and truth : they have conducted and brought me to thy holy mount, and into thy tabernacles.

R. And I will go unto the altar of God: to God who rejoiceth my youth.

P. I will praise thee on the harp, O God, my God: why art thou sorrowful, O my soul; and why dost thou disturb me?

R. Hope in God, for I will yet praise him; the salvation of my countenance, and my God.

P. Glory be to the Father, and to the Son, &c.

R. Sicut erat in principo, et nunc, et semper, et in sæcula sæculorum. *Amen.*

P. Introibo ad altare Dei.

R. Ad Deum qui lætificat juventutem meam.

P. Adjutorium nostrum in nomine Domini.

R. Qui fecit cœlum et terram.

P. Confiteor Deo omnipotenti, &c.

R. Misereatur tui omnipotens Deus, et dimissis peccatis tuis, perducat te ad vitam æternam.

P. *Amen.*

R. Confiteor Deo omnipotenti, beatæ Mariæ semper virgini, beato Michaeli archangelo, beato Joanni baptistæ, sanctis apostolis Petro et Paulo, omnibus Sanctis, et tibi, Pater, quia pec-

R. As it was in the beginning, is now and ever shall be, world without end. *Amen.*

P. I will go unto the altar of God.

R. To God who rejoiceth my youth.

P. Our help is in the name of the Lord.

R. Who made heaven and earth.

P. I confess to Almighty God, &c.

R. May Almighty God be merciful to thee, forgive thee thy sins and bring thee to life everlasting.

P. *Amen.*

R. I confess to Almighty God, to the blessed Mary ever a virgin, to blessed Michael the archangel, to blessed John the baptist, to the holy apostles Peter and Paul, to all the Saints,

cavi nimis cogitatione, verbo, et opere, *mea culpa, mea culpa, mea maxima culpa*. Ideo precor beatam Mariam semper virginem, beatum Michaelem archangelum, beatum Joannem baptistam, sanctos apostolos Petrum et Paulum, omnes Sanctos et te, Pater, orare pro me ad Dominum Deum nostrum.

P. Misereatur vestri omnipotens Deus, et dimissis peccatis vestris, perducat vos ad vitam æternam.

R. Amen.

P. Indulgentiam, absolutionem, et remissionem peccatorum nostrorum, tribuat nobis omnipotens et misericors Dominus.

R. Amen.

and to thee, O Father, that I have grievously sinned in thought, word, and deed, *through my fault, through my fault, through my exceeding great fault*. Therefore I beseech the blessed Mary ever a virgin, blessed Michael the archangel, blessed John baptist, the holy apostles Peter and Paul, and all the Saints, and thee, O Father, to pray to the Lord our God for me.

P. May almighty God have mercy on you, forgive you your sins, and bring you to life everlasting.

R. *Amen.*

P. May the almighty and merciful Lord grant us pardon, absolution, and remission of our sins.

R. *Amen.*

P. Deus, tu conversus vivificabis nos.

R. Et plebs tua lætabitur in te.

P. Ostende nobis, Domine, misericordiam tuam.

R. Et salutem tuam da nobis.

P. Domine, exaudi orationem meam.

R. Et clamor meus ad te veniat.

P. Dominus vobiscum:

R. Et cum spiritu tuo.

P. O God thou being turned towards us, wilt revive us.

R. And thy people shall rejoice in thee.

P. Show us thy mercy, O Lord.

R. And grant us thy salvation.

P. O Lord, hear my prayer.

R. And let my cry come unto thee.

P. The Lord be with you:

R. And with thy spirit.

Then the Priest going up to the Altar, says,

TAKE away from us our iniquities, we beseech thee, O Lord, that we may be worthy to assist with pure minds at the celebration of these tremendous mysteries: through Christ our Lord. *Amen.*

When he bows down before the Altar, he says,

WE beseech thee, O Lord, by the merits of thy Saints, whose relics are enclosed in this altar, and of all the Saints, that thou wouldst vouchsafe to forgive us all our sins. *Amen.*

Then turning to the Book, he reads the INTROIT.

Cant. iii.

GO forth, ye daughters of Sion, and see King Solomon in the diadem, wherwith his mother crowned him in the day of his espousals, and in the day of the joy of his heart.—*Ps.* xliv. My heart hath uttered a good word: I speak my works to the king. Glory, &c. Go forth, &c.

After which follows:

P. Kyrie eleison.	P. Lord have mercy on us.
R. Kyrie eleison.	R. Lord have, &c.
P. Kyrie eleison.	P. Lord have, &c.
R. Christe eleison.	R. Christ, have &c.
P. Christe eleison.	P. Christ have, &c.
R. Christe eleison.	R. Christ have, &c.
P. Kyrie eleison.	P. Lord have, &c.
R. Kyrie eleison.	R. Lord have, &c.
P. Kyrie eleison.	P. Lord have, &c.

Then, if it be neither Lent nor Advent, is said or sung the angelical hymn, GLORIA IN EXCELSIS.

GLORIA in excelsis Deo, et in terra pax hominibus

GLORY be to God on high, and on earth peace to men of good

bonæ voluntatis. Laudamus te, benedicimus te, adoramus te, glorificamus te. Gratias agimus tibi propter magnam gloriam tuam, Domine Deus, Rex cœlestis, Deus Pater omnipotens. Domine Fili unigenite Jesu Christe. Domine Deus, Agnus Dei, Filius Patris, qui tollis peccata mundi, miserere nobis; qui tollis peccata mundi, suscipe deprecationem nostram; qui sedes ad dexteram Patris miserere nobis. Quoniam tu solus sanctus, tu solus Dominus, tu solus altissimus, Jesu Christe, cum Sancto Spiritu, in gloria Dei Patris. *Amen.*

will. We praise thee, we bless thee, we adore thee, we glorify thee. We give thanks to thee for thy great glory, O Lord God, heavenly King, God the Father Almighty. O Lord Jesus Christ, the only begotten Son. O Lord God, Lamb of God, Son of the Father, who takest away the sins of the world, have mercy on us; who takest away the sins of the world, receive our prayer; who sittest at the right hand of the Father, have mercy on us. For thou only art holy, thou only art the Lord, thou only, O Jesus Christ together with the Holy Ghost, art most high, in the glory of God the Father. *Amen.*

2 M

The Priest turning towards the People, says,

P. Dominus vobiscum:

R. Et cum spiritu tuo.

P. The Lord be with you:

R. And with thy spirit.

Going to the Book he reads the COLLECTS.

CLOTHE us, O Lord Jesus, with the virtues of thy Sacred Heart, and inflame our souls with the fire of thy divine love; that we may be conformed to the image of thy goodness, and be worthy of participating in thy redemption; who livest, &c.

The Clerk having answered, Amen, *the Priest then reads the* EPISTLE.

St. Paul to the Ephesians *Chap.* iii. v. 8.

BRETHREN, to me, the least of all the Saints, is given this grace, to preach among the Gentiles the unsearchable riches of Christ, and to enlighten all men, that they may see what is the dispensation of the mystery which hath been hidden from eternity in God, who created all things. For this cause I bow my knees to the Father of our Lord Jesus Christ, of whom all paternity in heaven and earth is named; that he would grant you according to the riches of his glory, to be strengthened with might by his spirit unto the inward man; that Christ may dwell, by faith, in your hearts; that being rooted and founded in charity, you may be able to comprehend with all the Saints, what is the breadth, and length, and height, and depth: to know also the charity of Christ, which surpasseth knowledge, that you may be filled unto all the fullness of God.

At the end of the Epistle the Clerk answers,

R. Deo gratias.   R. Thanks be to God.

Then follows the GRADUAL.

Matt: xxi. 5.

TELL ye the daughters of Sion: Behold thy king cometh to thee, meek.—*Is.* xlii. He shall not be sad, nor troublesome: he shall not cry, neither shall his voice be heard abroad. Alleluia, Alleluia.

Math. xi.—Learn of me, because I am meek and humble of heart: and you shall find rest to your souls. Alleluia.

After Septuagesima.

GRADUAL. *Ps.* lxvii.—My heart hath expected reproach and misery: and I looked for one that would grieve together with me, but there was none; and for one that would comfort me, and I found none.

TRACT. *Ps.* xxi.—But I am a worm and no man: the reproach of men and the outcast of the people. All they that saw me have laughed me to scorn: they have spoken with the lips and wagged the head. I am poured out like water, and all my bones are scattered. My heart is become like wax melting in the midst of my bowels.

After Easter.

ALLELUIA, Alleluia. *Ps.* 19.—Lord, my God, I have cried out to thee, and thou hast healed me: thou hast led my soul out of hell. Alleluia.

Thou hast turned for me my mourning into joy: thou hast cut my sackcloth, and hast compassed me with gladness. Alleluia.

The Prayer before the Gospel.

CLEANSE my heart and my lips, O Almighty God, who didst cleanse the lips of the Prophet Isaiah with a burning coal; and vouchsafe, through thy gracious mercy, so to purify me, that I may worthily attend to thy holy Gospel: through Christ our Lord. *Amen.*

Bless me, O Lord.

May the Lord be in my heart and on my lips, that I may worthily and in a becoming manner attend to his holy Gospel. *Amen.*

P. Dominus vobiscum:

R. Et cum spiritu tuo.

P. Sequentia sancti Evangelii secundum Joannem.

R. Gloria tibi, Domine.

P. The Lord be with you:

R. And with thy Spirit.

P. The continuation of the holy Gospel according to St. John.

Glory be to thee, O Lord.

THE GOSPEL.

John. xv. 9.

AT that time: Jesus said to his disciples: As the Father hath loved me, I also have loved you. Abide in my love. If you keep my commandments you shall abide in my love, as I also have kept my Father's commandments, and abide in his love. These things I have spoken to you, that my joy may be in you, and your joy may be filled. This is my commandment, that you love one another as I have loved you. Greater love than this no man hath, that a man lay down his life for his friends. You are my friends, if you do the things that I command you. I will not now call you servants: for the servant knoweth not what his Lord doth. But I have called you friends: because all things whatsoever I have heard of my Father, I have made known to you. You have not chosen me; but I have chosen you, and have apppointed you that you should go, and should bring forth fruit: and your fruit should remain: that whatsoever you shall ask of the Father in my name, he may give it you.

At the end of the Gospel the Clerk answers.

R. Laus tibi Christe.   R. Praise be to thee O Christ.

Then the Priest says, in a low voice, 'May our sins be blotted out by the vows of the gospel.'

The NICENE CREED.

CREDO in unum Deum, Patrem omnipotentem, factorem cœli et terræ, visibilium omnium et invisibilium.

Et in unum Dominum Jesum Christum, Filium Dei unigenitum; et ex Patre natum ante omnia sæcula: Deum de Deo; Lumen de Lumine; Deum verum de Deo vero; genitum non factum;

I BELIEVE in one God, the Father almighty, maker of heaven and earth, and of all things visible and invisible.

And in one Lord Jesus Christ, the only begotten Son of God; and born of the Father before all ages: God of God; Light of Light; true God of true God; begotten, not made; consubstantial to the Father.

consubstantialem Patri, per quem omnia facta sunt. Qui propter nos homines, et propter nostram salutem, descendit de cœlis, et incarnatus est de Spiritu Sancto, ex Maria Virgine, * ET HOMO FACTUTS EST. Crucifixus etiam pro nobis, sub Pontio Pilato passus, et sepultus est; et resurrexit tertia die, secundum scripturas. Et ascendit in cœlum, sedet ad dexteram Patris, et iterum venturus est cum gloria judicare vivos et mortuos; cujus regni non erit finis.

Et in Spiritum Sanctum, Dominum et vivificantem, qui ex Patre Fillioque procedit; qui cum

by whom all things were made. Who for us men, and for our salvation, came down from heaven, and was incarnate by the Holy Ghost, of the Virgin Mary, * AND WAS MADE MAN. Was crucified also for us, suffered under Pontius Pilate, and was buried; and the third day he rose again, according to the scriptures. And ascended into heaven, sitteth at the right hand of the Father, and shall come again with glory to judge both the living and the dead; of whose kingdom there shall be no end.

And in the Holy Ghost, the Lord and Giver of Life, who proceedeth from the Father and the Son;

* At those words the people kneel down to adore God for the ineffable mystery of the Incarnation.

Patre et Filio simul adoratur et conglorificatur; qui locutus est per Prophetas. Et unam sanctam Catholicam et Apostolicam Ecclesiam. Confiteor unum Baptisma in remissionem peccatorum. Et expecto resurrectionem mortuorum, et vitam venturi sæculi. *Amen.*	who together with the Father and the Son, is adored and glorified; who spake by the Prophets. And one holy Catholic and Apostolic Church. I confess one baptism for the remission of sins. And I expect the resurrection of the dead, and the life of the world to come. *Amen.*

PART II.

The Preparation and Sanctification of the Bread and Wine for the use of the Sacrifice.

P. Dominus vobiscum:	P. The Lord be with you:
R. Et cum spiritu tuo.	R. And with thy spirit.
P. Oremus.	P. Let us Pray.

Then is said the OFFERTORY.

1 Paralip. xxix.

LORD God, I, in the simplicity of my heart, have joyfully offered all these things, and I have seen with great joy, thy people which are here present, offer thee their offerings. God of Isarel, keep for ever this will of their hearts. Alleluia.

The Priest offering up the Host says,

ACCEPT, O holy Father, almighty and eternal God, this unspotted Host, which I thy unworthy servant offer unto thee, my living and true God, for my own innumerable sins, offences, and negligences, and for all here present, as also for all faithful, Christians both living and dead, that it may avail both me and then unto eternal life. *Amen.*

Putting the Wine and Water into the Chalice, he says,

O God, who in creating human nature, didst wonderfully dignify it and afterwards more wonderfully reform it, grant that by the mystery of this Water and Wine, we may be made partakers of this divine nature, who vouchsafed to become partaker of our human nature, Jesus Christ our Lord, thy Son, who, with thee, in the unity of the Holy Ghost, liveth and reigneth God, for ever and ever. *Amen.*

At Offering the Chalice, he says,

WE offer thee, O Lord, the Chalice of Salvation, beseeching thy clemency, that it may ascend before thy divine Majesty as a most sweet odour, for our salvation, and for that of the whole world. *Amen*

The Priest humbly bowing himself, says,

ACCEPT us, O Lord, who come in the spirit of humility, and with a contrite and humble heart; and grant that the Sacrifice which we offer this day in thy sight, may be pleasing to thee, O Lord God.

At blessing the Bread and Wine, he says,

COME, O Almighty and Eternal God, the Sanctifier, and bless this Sacrifice, prepared for the glory of thy holy name.

At Washing his Hands, he says, Psalm. xxv. 6.

I WILL wash my hands among the innocent; and go up to thy altar, O Lord.

That I May hear the voice of praise: and publish all thy wonderful works.

O Lord I have loved the beauty of thy house: and the place where thy glory dwelleth.

Destroy not my soul with the impious: and my life with men of blood.

In whose hands are iniquities: their right hands are filled with bribes.

But I have walked in mine innocency: **redeem me, and have mercy on me.**

My feet have stood in the right path: in the assembly of the Faithful I will bless thee, O Lord.

Glory, &c.

Bowing in the midst of the Altar, he says,

ACCEPT, O holy Trinity, this Oblation which we make thee, in memory of the passion, resurrection, and ascension of our Lord Jesus Christ; and in honour of the ever blessed Virgin Mary, the blessed John Baptist, the holy Apostles Peter and Paul, and of all the Saints; that it may be available to their honour and to our salvation. And may they vouchsafe to interceed for us in heaven, whose memory we celebrate on earth: through the same Christ our Lord. *Amen.*

Turning himself towards the People, he says,

BRETHREN, pray that my Sacrifice and yours may be acceptable in the sight of God the Father Almighty.

R. May the Lord receive the Sacrifice from thy hands, to the praise and glory of his own name, and to our benefit, and that of all his holy Church.

Then the Priest says the SECRET PRAYER.

WE beseech thee, O Lord, to inflame our souls with the fire of the Holy Ghost;

which our Lord Jesus Christ has sent on earth, from the secret recesses of his Heart, to enkindle in us his love: who liveth, &c.

P. Per omnia sæcula sæculorum.

R. Amen.

P. World without end.

R. Amen.

THE PREFACE.

P. Dominus vobiscum:

R. Et cum spiritu tuo.

P. Sursum corda.

R. Habemus ad Dominum.

P. Gratias agamus Domino Deo nostro.

R. Dignum et justum est.

P. The Lord be with you:

R. And with thy spirit.

P. Raise up your hearts on high.

R. We have raised them to the Lord.

P. Let us give thanks to the Lord our God.

R. It is meet and just.

From Trinity Sunday to Septuagesima is said the Preface of the Nativity—as follows:

IT is truly meet and just, right and available to salvation, that we should always and in all places, give thanks to thee, O holy Lord, Father Almighty, eternal God; since by the mystery of the Word made Flesh, a new ray of thy glory has appeared to the eyes of our souls; that whilst we behold God visibly, we may be carried by him to the love of things invisible. And therefore with the Angels and Archangels, with the Thrones and Dominations, and with all the heavenly Host, we sing an everlasting hymn to thy glory. saying, Holy, Holy, Holy, Lord God of Sabaoth Heaven and earth are full of thy glory. Hosanna in the highest. Blessed is he that cometh in the name of the Lord. Hosanna in the highest.

From Septuagesima to Pentecost is said the Preface of the Holy Cross—as follows:

IT is truly meet and just, right and available to salvation, that we should always and in all places, give thanks to thee, O holy Lord, Father Almighty, eternal God; who hast appointed that the salvation of mankind should be wrought on the wood of the Cross; that whence death came, thence life might arise; and that he who overcame by the tree, might also by the tree be overcome. Through Christ our Lord; by whom the Angels praise thy Majesty, the Dominations adore it, the Powers tremble before it, the Heavens and the heavenly Virtues, and blessed Seraphim, with common jubilee, glorify it. Together with whom we beseech thee, that we may be admitted to join our humble voices, saying: Holy, holy, holy, &c.

PART III.

Th: CANON of the Mass, or the mean Action of the Sacrifice.

WE therefore beseech thee, most merciful Father, thro' Jesus Christ thy Son, our Lord, that thou wouldst vouchsafe to accept and bless these gifts and offerings, this holy and unspotted Sacrifice, which in the first place we offer unto thee for thy holy Catholic Church, to which we beseech thee that thou wouldst vouchsafe to grant peace; as also to preserve, unite, and govern it, throughout the world; together with thy servant N. our chief bishop, N. the bishop of this district, [*name then,*] as also all orthodox believers and professors of the Catholic and Apostolic faith.

A Commemoration of the Living.

BE mindful, O Lord, of thy servants, men and women.—N.N.—[*Here the Priest prays awhile for those he intends to pray for.*] And of all here present whose faith and devotion are known unto thee; for whom we offer, or who offer up to thee this Sacrifice of praise for themselves, and for all that belong to them; for the redemption of their own souls; for the safety and salvation they hope for; and who now pay their vows to thee, the eternal, living, and true God.

SACRED HEART OF JESUS.

Being united in communion with the Saints, and honouring, in the first place, the memory of the glorious Mary, ever a virgin, the mother of our Lord Jesus Christ, as also of the blessed apostles and martyrs. Peter and Paul, Andrew, James, John, Thomas, James, Philip, Bartholomew, Mathew, Simon, and Thaddeus Linus, Cletus, Clement, Xystus, Cornelius, Cyprian, Laurence, Chrysogonus, John and Paul, Cosmas and Damian, and of all thy Saints; by whose merits and prayers, grant that we may on all occasions be defended by the help of thy protection: through the same Christ our Lord. *Amen.*

Spreading his hands over the Oblation, he says,

WE therefore beseech thee, O Lord, graciously to accept this offering of our homage, as also of thy whole family: dispose our days in thy peace, preserve us from eternal damnation, and rank us in the number of thine elect: through Christ our Lord. *Amen.*

Which oblation do thou, O God, vouchsafe, we beseech thee, in all respects to bless, approve, ratify, and accept; that by the descent of the Holy Ghost, whose power is almighty, it may be made to us the body and blood of thy most beloved Son, our Lord Jesus Christ:

Who, the day before he suffered, took bread into his sacred and venerable hands, and with his eyes lifted up towards heaven, giving thanks to thee Almighty God, his Father, he blessed it, brake it, and gave it to his Disciples, saying: 'Take, and eat ye all of this, for THIS IS MY BODY.'

After the Priest has adored and elevated the sacred Host, he proceeds:

IN like manner after he had supped taking this most excellent Chalice into his sacred and venerable hands, and giving thanks also unto thee, he blessed it, and gave it to his Disciples, saying: 'Take, and drink ye all of this, for THIS IS THE CHALICE OF MY BLOOD, of the new and eternal Testament: the mystery of Faith: which shall be shed for you, and for many, to the remission of sins,

'As often as ye do these things, ye shall do them in remembrance of me.'

Here, after he has adored and elevated the Chalice, he goes on:

THEREFORE, we thy servants, O Lord, as also thy holy people, being mindful, as well of the blessed passion of the same Christ thy Son, our Lord, as of his resurrection from the dead, and his glorious ascension into heaven, offer unto thy most excellent Majesty, of thy gifts bestowed upon us a pure Host, a holy Host, an immaculate Host; the holy bread of eternal life, and Chalice of everlasting salvation.

Upon which vouchsafe, we beseech thee, to look with a propitious and pleasing countenance, and to accept them, as thou wert pleased graciously to accept the gifts of thy just servant Abel, and the sacrifice of our Patriarch Abraham, and that which thy High Priest Melchisedech offered unto thee, a holy Sacrifice, and spotless Victim.

We most humbly beseech thee, O Almighty God, that thou wouldst command these offerings to be carried by the hands of thy holy Angel unto thine altar on high, in the sight of thy divine Majesty, that as many of us as *assist at this oblation*, or partake of the sacred body and blood of thy Son, may be filled with every heavenly grace and blessing; through the same Christ our Lord. *Amen.*

The Commemoration of the Dead.

BE mindful, O Lord, of thy servants, men and women, who are gone before us with the sign of Faith, and rest in the sleep of peace.—[*Here such Dead as are prayed for, should be particularly mentioned.*] To these,

O Lord, and to all who sleep in Christ, grant we beseech thee, a place of refreshment, light, and peace: through the same Christ our Lord. *Amen.*

The Priest striking his breast, says,

AND to us also, thy unworthy servants, who hope iu the multitude of thy mercies, vouchsafe to grant some part and fellowship with thy holy Apostles and Martyrs, with John, Stephen, Matthias, Barnabas, Ignatius, Alexander, Marcelline, Peter, Felicitas, Perpetua, Agatha, Lucy. Agnes, Cecily, Anastatia, and all thy saints: into whose company we beseech thee to admit us, not in confidence of any merit of our own, but of thine own gracious mercy and pardon. Through Jesus Christ our Lord.

By whom, O Lord, thou dost always create, sanctify, quicken, bless, and give us those good gifts: so, by him, with him, and in him is, to thee, O God the Father Almighty, in the unity of the Holy Ghost, all honour and glory.

P. Per omnia sæcula sæculorum.
R. *Amen.*

P. For ever and ever.
R. *Amen.*

PART IV.

The COMMUNION, or Sacramental Part of the Canon.
Let us Pray.

INSTRUCTED in thy saving precepts, and following thy divine directions, we presume to say:

Pater noster, &c.	Our Father, &c.
R. Sed libera nos a malo. P. *Amen.*	R. But deliver us from evil. P. *Amen.*

Deliver us, we beseech thee, O Lord, from all evils, past, present, and to come: and by the intercession of the blessed and ever glorious Virgin Mary, Mother of God, of the holy Apostles Peter and Paul, of Andrew, and of all the Saints, mercifully grant peace in our days, that through the assistance of thy mercy, we may be always free from sin, and secure from all disturbance. Through the same Lord Jesus Christ thy Son, who liveth and reigneth with thee God, in unity with the Holy Ghost.

P. Per omnia sæcula sæculorum R. *Amen,*	P. World without end. R. *Amen.*
P. Pax Domini sit	P. May the peace

semper vobiscum: of the Lord be always with you:

R. Et cum spiritu tuo. R. And with thy spirit.

Breaking the Host, he puts a particle thereof into the Chalice, saying,

MAY this mixture together, and consecration of the Body and Blood of our Lord Jesus, be to us that receive it, *or assist thereat*, effectual to eternal life. *Amen.*

Then bowing and striking his breast, he says, thrice,

LAMB of God, who takest away the sins of the world, have mercy on us.

Lamb of God, who takest away the sins of the world, have mercy on us.

Lamb of God, who takest away the sins of the world, give us peace.

LORD Jesus Christ, who saidst to thy Apostles, I leave you peace, I give you my peace,' regard not my sins, but the faith of thy Church; and vouchsafe to grant her that peace and unity which is agreeable to thy will; who livest and reignest for ever and ever. *Amen.*

O LORD Jesus Christ, Son of the living God, who, according to the will of thy Father, with the co-operation of the Holy Ghost, hast, by thy death, given life to the world, deliver me by this thy most sacred Body and Blood, from all my iniquities, and from all evils; make me always live up to thy commandments; and never suffer me to be separated from thee: who livest and reignest with God the Father, in the unity of the Holy Ghost, world without end. *Amen.*

LET not the participation of thy body, O Lord Jesus Christ, which I, though unworthy, presume to receive, turn to my judgment and condemnation; but let it, through thy mercy, become a safeguard and remedy, both of soul and body: who with God the Father, in the unity of the Holy Ghost, livest and reignest God for ever and ever. *Amen.*

Kneeling, rising, and taking the Host in his hands, he says,

I WILL partake of this heavenly Bread, and call upon the name of the Lord.

He strikes his breast, saying devoutly, thrice,

LORD, I am not worthy that thou shouldst enter under my roof; speak only the word and my soul shall be healed.

(*During the time of the Priest's Communicating, it would be profitable for persons who are not then in a state of actually communicating, to communicate spiritually or in desire: for this purpose, say the following prayer:*)

O THAT I were among the number of those whose sanctity allows them to communicate daily? What a happiness, O my God? could I at this moment erect a throne for thee in my heart, pay thee my homage, lay open to thee my wants, and participate in the favours thou grantest to those who *really and worthily receive* thee. But since I am unworthy, do thou, O Lord, supply my want of the proper dispositions. Grant the pardon of my manifold sins, which I detest from the bottom of my heart, because they displease thee. Cast thy compassionate eye upon me, and purify my soul, that the ardent wish I now conceive to be united to thee, by a worthy communion, may be speedily accomplished. But until the arrival of so happy a moment, I earnestly entreat thee, O dearest Lord, that thou wouldst make me partaker of all these advantages which the communion of the Priest may produce in those thy people. By the efficacy of this enlivening sacrament, increase my faith;

strengthen my hope; revive in my soul the rays of divine charity; inflame my heart with thy love, that it may pant only for thee. and live for thee alone. *Amen.*

Receiving reverently both parts of the Host, he says,

MAY the body of our Lord Jesus Christ preserve my soul to life everlasting *Amen.*

Taking the Chalice, he says,

WHAT return shall I make to the Lord, for all the things that he hath given unto me? I will partake of the Chalice of salvation, and call upon the name of the Lord. Praising I will call upon the Lord, and I shall be saved from mine enemies.

Receiving the Blood of our Saviour, he says,

MAY the Blood of our Lord Jesus Christ preserve my soul to life everlasting. *Amen.*

Taking the first Ablution, he says,

GRANT, Lord, that what we have partaken of with our mouth, we may receive with purity of mind; and that of a temporal gift it may become unto us an everlasting remedy. *Amen.*

Taking the second Ablution, he says,

MAY thy body, O Lord, which I have received, and thy Blood, which I have drank, cleave to my soul; and grant, that no stain of sin remain within me, who have been fed with this pure and holy Sacrament. Who livest and reignest for ever and ever. *Amen.*

Having wiped his Mouth, Fingers, and the Chalice, he then says the COMMUNION.

O TASTE, and see that the Lord is sweet; his mercy is eternal. Alleluia.

PART V.

The public Thanksgiving after Communion.

P. Dominus vobiscum:

R. Et cum spiritu tuo.

P. Oremus,

P. The Lord be with you:

R. And with thy spirit,

P. Let us Pray.

The POST COMMUNION

MAY thy grace, O Lord Jesus, we beseech thee, afford us divine favour, in order that, being sensible of the sweetness of thy most loving Heart, we may learn to despise earthly things, and love such as are heavenly; who livest and reignest, &c.

P. Dominus vobiscum:	P. May the Lord be with you:
R. Et cum spiritu tuo.	R. And with thy spirit.
P. Ite, Missa est.	P. Depart the Mass is finished.

Or, if "The Gloria in excelsis" *has not been said,*

P. Benedicamus Domino.	P. Let us bless the Lord.
R. Deo gratias.	R. Thanks be to God.

MAY the performance of this my homage be pleasing to thee, O Holy Trinity; and grant that the sacrifice which I, though unworthy, have offered up in the sight of thy Divine Majesty, may be acceptable to thee, and, through thy mercy, become a propitiation for me, and all those for whom it hath been offered. Through Christ our Lord. *Amen.*

The Priest turning himself towards the people, says,

MAY Almighty God, Father, Son, and Holy Ghost, bless you. *Amen.*

P. Dominus vobiscum:

R. Et oum spiritu tuo.

P. Initium sancti Evangelii secundum Joannem.

R. Gloria tibi, Domine.

P. May the Lord be with you:

R. And with thy spirit.

P. The beginning of the Gospel according to St. John.

R. Glory be to thee O Lord.

The Gospel according to St. John.

IN the begining was the Word, and the Word was with God, and God was the Word; the same was in the beginning with God. And all things were made by him; and without him was nothing made that was made; In him was life, and the life was the light of men; and the light shined in darkness, and the darkness did not comprehend it.

There was a man sent from God, whose name was John. This man came for a witness to bear testimony of the light, that all men might believe through him. He was not the light, but was to give testimony of the light. It was the true light, which enlighteneth every man that cometh into this world.

He was in the world, and the world was made by him, and the world knew him not. He came unto his own, and his own received him not. But as many as received him, to them he gave power to be made the sons of God, to those that believe in his Name; who are born, not of blood, nor of the will of the flesh, nor of the will of man, but of God. And *the Word was made Flesh,* and dwelt amongst us. And we saw his glory, the glory as it were of the only begotten Son of the Father, full of grace and truth.

R. Deo gratias.   R. Thanks be to God.

ACTS OF ADORATION
TO THE
SACRED HEART OF JESUS.

Which may be practised on every Friday, during the NOVENA, or nine days previous to the Feast of the Sacred Heart; within its Octave, or at any other time devotion may suggest.

N. B.—Where the Sodality of the Sacred Heart is established, this prayer may be publicly recited immediately after Mass, with Benediction of the most blessed Sacrament, on the first Friday of every month.

IN the name of the Father, and of the Son, and of the Holy Ghost. *Amen.*

Come, O Holy Ghost, replenish the hearts of thy faithful, and kindle in them the fire of thy divine love.

V. Send forth thy Spirit, and they shall be created.

R. And thou wilt renew the face of the earth.

Let us pray.

O LORD God of infinite goodness and mercy, grant us, we beseech thee, the grace to be always directed and comforted by thy holy Spirit, through Christ our Lord. *Amen.*

SACRED HEART OF JESUS.

Soliloquy of the Soul.

MY soul, enliven thy faith, and consider that in the most adorable Sacrament of the altar, Jesus Christ is really present, true God and true Man, with his Sacred Heart inflamed with most ardent love for thee. Recall thy wandering thoughts, and reflect that thou speakest to the King of heaven and earth to thy most loving Lord, Brother, Saviour, and Spouse, Oh! how many seraphim stand round the altar, and with awful reverence adore his divine Majesty in the most holy Eucharist? O my soul, unite with them, and with profound sentiments of animated faith, firm confidence, ardent love, and humble homage, adore and bless thy God, whose presence constitutes the bliss of Paradise, and whose most sweet Heart is open to enrich thee with those precious graces, of which he is the inexhaustible and eternal source.

Five devout Prayers in honour of the most Sacred Heart of Jesus.

I ADORE you, O Sacred Heart of Jesus, in the most august Sacrament of the altar, where you show the wonderful excess of your tender love. I thank your infinite goodness, by which you have instituted this divine Sacrament, and have prepared for us a sacred banquet, wherein we are nourished with your own most precious body and blood. O most adorable Heart of Jesus, receive, I beseech you, my soul with all its faculties; inflame it with the fire of your divine love, and increase its ardour daily more and more.

Our Father, &c. Hail Mary, &c. Glory be to the Father, &c.

I ADORE you, O Sacred Heart of Jesus, in the most august Sacrament of the altar, where you continue to dwell, inflamed with desire that the hearts of all creatures should be united to yours, thereby to be replenished with your most precious graces. I fervently thank your incomprehensible charity for having so often visited my unworthy heart in the most holy Sacrament, and I beg you will give me an additional proof of your love, by enriching it with those graces and blessings which will render it pleasing in your sight.

Our Father, &c. Hail Mary, &c. Glory be to the Father, &c.

I ADORE you, O Sacred Heart of Jesus, in the most august Sacrament of the altar, where so many ungrateful and unbelieving Christians do not adore you, nor acknowledge your divine presence. In reparation of the injuries they commit against your divine Majesty, I come, penetrated with the most profound respect, to render you homage, and to protest with a lively faith that you are really present in the most holy Sacrament. I earnestly beseech you to enlighten those unhappy souls who are buried in the darkness of error, that they may adore and proclaim the truth of this ineffable mystery.

Our Father, &c. Hail Mary, &c. Glory be to the Father, &c,

ADORE you, O Sacred Heart of Jesus, in the most august Sacrament of the altar, where you are so little loved, and so often insulted by so many irreverent and sacrilegious communions. In reparation of such base ingratitude, I offer you the hearts of those who, with ardent love and respectful homage, entertain themselves in the presence of the blessed Sacrament, and devoutly receive you in the holy communion. In union with their oblations I offer you my poor but contrite heart, humbly begging of you to accept it, and imprint thereon, as likewise on the hearts of all Christians, that love, respect, and gratitude, with which we should be penetrated in presence of this adorable mystery.

Our Father, &c. Hail Mary, &c. Glory be to the Father, &c.

I ADORE you, O Sacred Heart of Jesus, in the most august Sacrament of the altar, where you remain day and night, without being visited by your faithful servants. Accept, O divine Heart, my poor desires to visit your divine Majesty in every temple throughout the Christian world, where you are present in the blessed Sacrament; to invite, by my humble example, all creatures to correspond by frequent visits to the excess of your love. But as I cannot effect this, I adore you here in spirit, and wherever you are in the adorable Sacrament, offering to your divine Majesty the adorations, homage, and praises of myriads of angels, who incessantly adore, honour, and glorify you, humbled for love of us, in our tabernacles.

Our Father, &c. Hail Mary, &c. Glory be to the Father, &c.

AN ACT OF REPARATION,

For the innumerable Irreverences and grievous Offences, by which we and others have insulted the Heart of Jesus.

To be made on the Feast itself, or at any other time, in presence of the Blessed Sacrament.

O MOST amiable and adorable Heart of Jesus! centre of all hearts, glowing with charity, and inflamed with zeal for the interest of thy Father and the salvation of mankind! O Heart, ever sensible of our misery, and ever ready to redress our evils; the real victim of love in the holy Eucharist, and a propitiatory sacrifice for sin on the altar of the cross; seeing that the generality of Christians make no other return for thy mercies, than contempt for thy favours, forgetfulness of their own obligation, and ingratitude to the best of Benefactors: it is just that we thy servants, penetrated with the deepest sense of the indignities offered to thee, should, as far as is in our power, make a due and satisfactory reparation of honour of thy most sacred Majesty. Prostrate therefore in body, and with humble and contrite hearts, we solemnly declare before heaven and earth, our utter detestation and abhorrence of such conduct. Inexpressible was the bitterness which our manifold sins brought on thy tender Heart; insufferable the weight of our iniquities, which pressed thy face to the earth in the garden of Olives; and inconceivable thy anguish, when expiring with love, grief, and agony, on Mount Calvary; yet thou didst with thy last breath, pray for sinners, and invite them to their duty and repentance. This we know, dear Redeemer, and would willingly redress thy sufferings, by patiently enduring our slight crosses and afflictions, and thus partake of thy bitter passion.

O merciful Jesus! ever present on our altars, with a heart open to receive all who labour and are burthened; O adorable Heart of Jesus! source of true contrition, give to our hearts the spirit of sincere penance, and to our eyes a fountain of tears, that we may bewail all our sins and the sins of the world. Pardon, O divine Jesus, all the injuries and outrages done to thee by sinners; forgive all the impieties, irreverences, and sacrileges which have been committed against thee in the holy sacrament of the Eucharist, since its institution. Graciously receive the small tribute of our sincere repentance, as an agreeable offering in thy sight, and in requital for the benefits we daily receive from the altar, where thou art a living and continued sacrifice, and in union with that bloody holocaust which thou didst present to thy eternal Father on the cross.

Sweet Jesus! give thy blessing to the ardent desire we now entertain, and the holy resolution we have taken, of ever loving and adoring thee with our whole mind, and with our whole heart, in the Sacrament of thy love; thus to repair, by a true contrition of heart, and ardent zeal for thy glory, our past negligences and infidelities. Be thou, O adorable Jesus! who knowest our frailty; be thou our mediator with thy heavenly Father, whom we have so grievously offended; strengthen our weaknesses, confirm our resolutions, and with thy charity, meekness, and patience cancel the multitude of our iniquities. Be thou our support, our refuge, and our strength, that nothing may henceforth in life or death separate us from thee. *Amen.*

LITANY OF THE SACRED HEART.

LORD, have mercy on us. Christ, have mercy on us. Lord, have mercy on us.
Christ Jesus, hear us. Christ Jesus, graciously hear us.
God the Father of heaven,
God the Son, Redeemer of the world,
God the Holy Ghost, Sanctifier of souls,
Holy Trinity, one God,
Heart of Jesus,
Heart of Jesus, formed of the Virgin Mary by the operation of the Holy Ghost,
Heart of Jesus, hypostatically united to the eternal Word,
Heart of Jesus, sanctuary of the divinity,
Heart of Jesus, tabernacle of the most holy Trinity,
Heart of Jesus, temple of all sanctity,
Heart of Jesus, fountain of divine grace,
Heart of Jesus, abode of eternal charity,
Heart of Jesus, most meek and humble,

Have mercy on us.

Heart of Jesus, most pure and chaste,
Heart of Jesus, most obedient and resigned,
Heart of Jesus, furnace of divine love,
Heart of Jesus, treasure of true wisdom,
Heart of Jesus, ocean of unfaded beauty,
Heart of Jesus, throne of bounteous mercy,
Heart of Jesus, source and model of virtues,
Heart of Jesus, fountain of waters springing to life eternal,
Heart of Jesus, our peace and reconciliation,
Heart of Jesus, the propitiatiou for our sins,
Heart of Jesus, sorrowful and agonizing in the garden,
Heart of Jesus, filled with bitterness, and replete with reproaches,
Heart of Jesus, wounded for our sins, and bruised for our iniquities,
Heart of Jesus, made obedient even unto the death of the cross,
Heart of Jesus, pierced through with a lance,
Heart of Jesus, hope of the just, and refuge of sinners,
Heart of Jesus, comfort of the afflicted, and of the tempted,
Heart of Jesus, safe port of the agonizing, and dying,
Heart of Jesus, salvation of the holy souls,
Heart of Jesus, joy and delight of the saints,
Heart of Jesus, sanctification of our hearts,

Have mercy on us.

Lamb of God, who takest away the sins of the world, spare us, O Jesus.
Lamb of God, who takest away the sins of the world, graciously hear us, O Jesus.
Lamb of God, who takest away the sins of the world, have mercy on us, O Jesus.

V. O most meek and humble Heart of Jesus, render our hearts like thine.

R. And inflame our hearts with that divine fire, which thou camest to kindle on earth.

Let us Pray.

GRANT, O Lord Jesus, that through the precious merits and inflamed love of thy most Sacred Heart, we may follow thy example, and partake of thy bountiful redemption: who livest and reignest world without end. *Amen.*

ACT OF DEDICATION,

To the Sacred Heart of Jesus.

TO promote the glory of Jesus, who for us was nailed to the cross, and of his divine Heart, glowing with love for mankind in the most blessed Eucharist, and at the same time to make reparation for the offences which are committed against his divine Majesty in this Sacrament of love, I, N.N. do freely and willingly associate myself in this pious Sodality, hoping thereby to participate in the indulgences and other spiritual benefits annexed thereto, for the expiation of my sins, and the relief of the suffering souls in purgatory. O sweetest Jesus, may the Members of this Sodality abide in thy Sacred Heart, that, observing thy saving precepts, and faithfully discharging our respective duties, we may be daily more and more inflamed with the fire of thy divine love. *Amen.*

THE DAILY PRAYERS,

To be said by the Associates of the Sacred Heart.

The Lord's Prayer, the Hail Mary, and the Creed, with the following pious Aspiration:

O sweetest Heart of Jesus, I implore,
That I may ever love thee more and more.

LITTLE OFFICE OF THE SACRED HEART.

AT MATINS.

V. O Heart of Jesus, burning with love of me, inflame my heart with the love of thee.

R. Amen.

V. Lord, open my lips.

R. And my mouth shall declare thy praise.

V. O God, incline to my aid.

R. O Lord, make haste to help me.

V. Glory be to the Father, and to the Son, and to the Holy Ghost.

R. As it was in the beginning, is now, and ever shall be, world without end. *Amen. Alleluia.*

From Septuagesima to Easter, instead of *Alleluia*, say, *Praise be to thee, O Lord! King of Eternal Glory!*

Hymn.

O Heaven's glorious King,
Who dost thy starry throne,
And its triumphant bliss postpone,
   To be our offering!

Jesus, our hearts' delight,
This faithful flock inspire
Of thy great heart to sing the fire,
   And love with praise requite.

Thy Father's only One,
Chaste Spouse of lovers pure,
Who canst no rival-love endure,
   Possess our hearts alone. *Amen.*

Anthem.

O Sacred Heart of Jesus, who didst always live in perfect submission to the will of thy Father, turn our hearts to thee, that we may ever do what is most pleasing to thee.

V. O God of my heart, my heart is ready to do thy will.

R. My God, I desire it, and to carry thy law in the midst of my heart.

Let us pray.

LOOK, we beseech thee, O God of mercy! on the Heart of thy most beloved Son, in whom thou hast been well pleased: behold the bitter afflictions he has endured for us, and the worthy satisfaction he has made to thee in our behalf; that, being thus appeased, we may obtain of thee pardon for our sins, seeing we ask it with contrite hearts. Kindle in our hearts so ardent a love of Christ, that being all inflamed with the affections of his divine Heart, we may also merit to be found according to thy Heart, through the same Jesus Christ, our Lord. *Amen.*

AT PRIME.

V. O Heart of Jesus, burning with love of me, inflame my heart with the love of thee.

R. *Amen.*

V. O God, incline to my aid.

R. O Lord, make haste to help me.

SACRED HEART OF JESUS.

V. Glory be to the Father, and to the Son, and to the Holy Ghost.

R. As it was in the beginning, is now, and ever shall be, world without end. *Amen. Alleluia.*

Hymn.

O Heart! love's victim, slain!
O Heaven's lasting joy!
To whom distressed mortals fly.
Nor fly for help in vain.

Darling of the Trinity,
The Holy Ghost is eas'd;
In thee th' Almighty Father's pleas'd,
His Son has wedded thee.

Thy Father's only One,
Chaste Spouse of lovers pure,
Who canst no rival-love endure,
Possess our hearts alone. *Amen.*

Anthem.

O Sacred Heart of Jesus, which so thirsted after our salvation, bring us sinners, by an humble and contrite heart, to a sense of ourselves, that we die not in our sins.

V. O God of my heart, my heart is ready to do thy will.

R. My God, I desire it, and to carry thy law in the midst of my heart.

Let us pray.

Look, we beseech thee, &c. *as before.*

AT TIERCE.

V. O Heart of Jesus, burning with the love of me, inflame my heart with the love of thee.
R. Amen.
V. O God, incline to my aid.
R. O Lord, make haste to help me.
V. Glory be to the Father, and to the Son, and to the Holy Ghost.
R. As it was in the beginning, is now, and ever shall be, world without end. *Amen. Alleluia*

Hymn.

 Choice Cabinet of our Lord!
No rays of light so clean,
No heaven so worthy to contain
 The treasure of his word.

 Form'd of pure virgin's blood,
Pregnant with love divine,
Thou heaven's palace dost outshine,
 A mansion fit for God.

 Thy Father's only One,
Chaste Spouse of lovers pure,
Who canst no rival-love endure,
 Possess our hearts alone. *Amen.*

SACRED HEART OF JESUS.

Anthem.

O Sacred Heart of Jesus, the most perfect pattern of purity! make us clean of heart, that we may merit to be according to thy Heart.

V. O God of my heart, my heart is ready to do thy will.

R. My God, I desire it, and to carry thy law in the midst of my heart.

Let us pray.

Look, we beseech thee, &c. *as before.*

AT SEXT.

V. O Heart of Jesus, burning with love of me, inflame my heart with the love of thee.

R. Amen.

V. O God, incline to my aid.

R. O Lord, make haste to help me.

V. Glory be to the Father, and to the Son, and to the Holy Ghost.

R. As it was in the beginning, is now, and ever shall be, world without end. *Amen. Alleluia.*

Hymn.

O may we ne'er provoke
This meek, this tender Heart,
Where love for us has fix'd his dart,
And struck the killing stroke.

When sin for vengeance calls,
This Heart, with pow'rful charm,
Glancing withholds th' Almighty's arm,
And strait his anger falls.

Thy Father's only One,
Chaste Spouse of lovers pure,
Who canst no rival-love endure,
Possess our hearts alone. *Amen.*

Anthem.

O Sacred Heart of Jesus, full of meekness towards thy enemies, let thy peace triumph in our hearts, that from the bottom of them, we may pardon all those who persecute and calumniate us.

V. O God of my heart, my heart is ready to do thy will.

R. My God, I desire it, and to carry thy law in the midst of my heart.

Let us pray.

Look, we beseech thee, &c. *as before.*

AT NONE.

V. O Heart of Jesus, burning with love of me, inflame my heart with the love of thee.

R. Amen.

V. O God, incline to my aid.

R. O Lord, make haste to help me.

V. Glory be to the Father, and to the Son, and to the Holy Ghost.

R. As it was in the beginning, is now, and ever shall be, world without end, *Amen. Alleluia.*

Hymn.

Love did this refuge win,
Love lanced our Saviour's side,
Fond love display'd the passage wide,
And bid us welcome in.

Whence blood, to wash our stain,
Gush'd out on every part;
O! take and keep us in this Heart,
For fear we sin again.

Thy Father's only One,
Chaste Spouse of lovers pure,
Who canst no rival-love endure,
Possess our hearts alone. *Amen.*

Anthem.

O Sacred Heart of Jesus, most patient in all thy sufferings! grant us, in all circumstances of life, a constant resignation to thy most blessed will. Let thy will be done in us and by us, both now and for eternity.

V. O God of my heart, my heart is ready to do thy will.

R. My God I desire it and to carry thy law in the midst of my heart.

Let us pray.

Look, we beseech thee, &c. *as before.*

AT VESPERS.

V. O Heart of Jesus, burning with love of me, inflame my heart with the love of thee.
R. Amen.
V. O God, incline to my aid.
R. O Lord, make haste to help me.
V. Glory be to the Father, and to the Son, and to the Holy Ghost.
R. As it was in the beginning, is now, and ever shall be, world without end. *Amen. Alleluia.*

Hymn.

O wond'rous power of love!
God gives himself to eat—
His blood is drink, his flesh is meat!
  And he who reigns above,

Dread Sov'reign of the skies,
Regales his mortal guest,
Himself the donor and the feast,
  Tho' hid from mortal eyes.

Thy Father's only One,
Chaste Spouse of lovers pure,
Who canst no rival-love endure,
  Possess our hearts alone. *Amen.*

Anthem.

O Sacred Heart of Jesus, most ardently in love with poverty! put thyself as a seal on my heart, that sequestered from the trifles of this earth, it may be entirely united to thee, my only treasure.

V. O God of my heart, my heart is ready to do thy will.

R. My God, I desire it, and to carry thy law in the midst of my heart.

Let us pray.

Look, we beseech thee, &c. *as before.*

AT COMPLINE.

V. O Heart of Jesus, burning with love of me, inflame my heart with the love of thee.
R. Amen.
V. Convert us, O God, our salvation.
R. And turn away thy anger from us.
V. O God, incline to my aid.
R. O Lord, make haste to help me.
V. Glory be to the Father, and to the Son, and to the Holy Ghost.
R. As it was in the beginning, is now, and ever shall be, world without end. *Amen. Alleluia.*

Hymn.

The Mother to her Son
Inclines with chaste desire,
And fans with constant sighs the fire
Which makes the couple one.

When mutually they burn,
Two hearts are but the same—
Both with each other's fire do flame,
Both equal flames return.

Thy Father's only One,
Chaste Spouse of lovers pure,
Who canst no rival-love endure,
Possess our hearts alone.

Anthem.

O Sacred Heart of Jesus, most liberal rewarder of all that love thee, let our hearts and substance be wholly consumed in thee. Be thou, my Jesus, the God of our hearts, and our portion for ever.

V. O God of my heart, my heart is ready to do thy will.

R. My God, I desire it, and to carry thy law in the midst of my heart.

Let us pray.

LOOK, we beseech thee, O God of mercy, on the Heart of thy most beloved Son, in whom thou hast been well pleased; behold the bitter afflictions he has endured for us, and the worthy satisfaction he has made to thee in our behalf: that thus being appeased, we may obtain of thee pardon for our sins, seeing we ask it with contrite hearts. Kindle in our hearts so ardent a love of Christ, that being all inflamed with the affections of his divine Heart, we may also merit to be found according to thy heart: through the same Jesus Christ our Lord. *Amen.*

REFLECTIONS,

Calculated to excite and entertain in the Soul, Gratitude and Love towards the

SACRED HEART OF JESUS.

[There have been Saints to whom the Crucifix has spoken, as St. Peter the Martyr. Place yourself at the foot of your Crucifix in a very retired place, and imagine that you have the happiness of hearing it speak to you, and that you reply to it. It will effectually speak to your heart; hear it attentively.]

FIRST COLLOQUY.
Between Jesus Christ crucified and the Sinner.

The Sinner.—Adorable Jesus, behold a miserable sinner prostrate at thy feet, imploring his conversion; but in what a situation do I behold thee, O my God. Alas! my soul is rent with sorrow at the sight. Ah! how lamentable is thy condition; I see thee mangled, torn, and bleeding; thy adorable head is pierced by a torturing crown; thy lovely countenance, the joy and delight of angels and of the blessed, is all disfigured with blood and spittle. O my God, my God! thou hast not even the form of a man. Oh! what sorrow can be like unto thy sorrow! Thy hands and feet are pierced through with gross nails; thou remainest thus suspended, and the entire weight of thy body is supported by those most acute and painful wounds. Alas! in this thy weak and exhausted state, thy sacred head has not whereon to repose; and if it lean upon the cross, the thorny crown is pressed more deeply in. O Jesus Christ, truly the man of dolours, I can no longer restrain my tears; and my heart, insensible as it is, cannot support this sight.

Jesus Christ.—My son, these exterior torments which thou beholdest, are nothing in comparison to the anguish of my soul. The impetuous torrent of the sins of men, and the wrath of my eternal Father, have fallen upon me. This immense weight of sin overwhelms my soul, and reduces it to a cruel agony. I raise my eyes to my Father to implore his assistance; but I no longer find in him a Father; I exclaim in my affliction, 'My God, my God, why hast thou forsaken me?' will not the wretched condition to which I am reduced touch the heart of a Father? What do I say? It is himself, it is my *Father*, who afflicts me; it is the mighty arm of his wrath and justice which smites me: my heart is become as wax which melts before the fire, or as water which flows upon the earth: my soul is dried up as the lime baked in the furnace. Where shall I seek consolation, or any mitigation of my sorrows? I am surrounded with enemies who bitterly insult me, and, like cruel tigers, feast upon my torments: my Apostles have forsaken me; my blessed Mother is at the foot of my cross, with my beloved disciple John, Magdalene, and some other pious souls who love me; but their sorrow serves only to increase mine. And above all, I cannot look upon my dearly beloved Mother, without that inconceivable anguish with which her heart is afflicted communicating itself entirely to mine, and piercing my soul with additional pangs. In this state I seek in vain for comfort; I cannot find, either in heaven or on earth, but that which augments my torture. It is thy heart, my son, which can adminster consolation. Dost thou wish to ameliorate my pain, or to aggravate still more the weight of my sufferings?

The Sinner.—O my God! thou piercest with a thousand darts, this miserable heart, Ah! can I be insensible to thy torments! Alas! I could not behold in that state the vilest of men, without being penetrated with compassion. O my God! that I could disengage thee from the cross, stop thy precious blood, wash thy wounds, and wipe away the filth with which thou art disfigured! O that I could at least support thy sacred head, and quench thy burning thirst! No, divine Jesus, I am not insensible to thy woes; and my tears but evince the anguish of my heart. O how ardently does this heart desire to share with thee thy sufferings, to mitigate thy pains, and to administer some consolation to thee in this sea of sorrows.

Jesus Christ.—And yet, my son, it is thou, it is thou hast caused them all! it is thou who every day renewest them; and this sensible compassion which thou dost evince, is but an illusion, whilst thy heart remains attached to sin. Ah! how canst, thou sincerely commiserate my torments, whilst thy heart is plunged in iniquity, and thou wilt, perhaps, in a few hours crucify me again? Change thy heart, my son, if thou desirest to testify a true compassion for my sufferings; renounce sin for ever, if thou wouldest administer any consolation to my bleeding heart.

The Sinner.—O my God, thy words penetrate and confound me. What a contradiction do I experience in myself; I weep over thy torments, and it is I who have been the cause of them! I wish, by partaking of them with thee, to mitigate them, and in a moment I renew them! My God, I have a horror of my miserable heart, but I cannot change it; it is thou alone, O infinite Goodness, that can effect this change, through the merits and the price of that precious blood that flows for me.

Jesus Christ.—I will change it, my son, if thou wilt attentively and frequently consider the great truths which I teach thee in my passion and death. Attend to those words which I addressed to the women who, seeing me loaded with the heavy burden of the cross, wept with compassion: 'Daughters of Jerusalem,' said I to them, 'weep not for me, but weep for yourselves, and for your children: if the green wood is treated thus, what may not the dry expect.' O sinner, what art thou in the presence of God, that he should spare thee, whilst he hath not spared his only Son! Thou art a worm of the earth; and I am the God of Heaven, equal to my Father, and partaking of the same divinity with him! thou art an object odious and abominable, and I am sanctity itself; the soul of his glory, the centre of his bliss; and yet my Father has not spared me, when actuated by the punishment of sin. Once more, sinner, what mayest thou not expect, if thou avertest not the arm of his justice, by a sincere repentance: witness how severe is his justice, how inflexible the hatred he bears to sin, when he chastises it in me, and overwhelms me beneath the arm of his wrath. It is here thou oughtest to weigh the immensity of my torments, especially of those interior pains, in comparison to which all that my body endures are nothing. Behold my Father unwearied in afflicting me; all the labours of my life have not satisfied him; the blood with which I watered the Garden of Olives, has not appeased his wrath; the insults and contempts, my cruel scourging, this crown which pierces my head, nothing could disarm his vengeance; and as long as there shall remain a drop of blood in the deepest recess of my heart, the arm of his justice shall not be restrained. What! shalt thou dare to attack so terrible a God? thou dost live in tranquillity; thou dost laugh and sport whilst in a state of sin, and under the very arm of that avenging justice.

The Sinner.—How shall I reply, O my divine Saviour? I tremble at thy words; terror and alarm freeze my blood. In what a state of blindness and stupidity have I hitherto lived: composed and insensible, I have remained in sin, as if I had nothing to apprehend from the justice of a God; from that inflexible justice, which did not spare his only Son. Thou hast opened mine eyes, O my Saviour! I see the depth of the abyss into which my sins have precipitated me; I now comprehend the frightful lot prepared for me; but do thou, who wishest not the destruction of a soul which thou hast so dearly purchased, continue to enlighten me; grant me to know why God punishes sin in so dreadful a manner.

Jesus Christ.—My Father is wisdom and equity itself, so thou must acknowledge that he does not depart from justice when he punishes; but, from the greatness of his chastisements, thou oughtest to comprehend the enormity of sin. My son, raise thine eyes and behold me! I am the victim of sin; in me thou mayest contemplate the extent of its malice, and the horrors it contains. Alas! my son, my blood alone can wash away its blackness: canst thou appreciate the value of that blood? What shouldst thou think, if God would assemble in thy presence all the men who have existed since the beginning of the world, and that in succession they should be tortured, scourged, and crucified! if afterwards, thou shouldst behold all the Angels of Heaven, crushed and annihilated? Wouldst thou not shudder? But what would be thy astonishment, on being informed that all those men and angels have been so treated, but for one single sin! Ah! thou wouldst exclaim, what must be the blackness of this crime, since it requires an expiation so tremendous? I tell thee, my son, that all this carnage, all those dreadful torments, could not atone for the smallest sin. Raise thine eyes to this cross; behold my blood, contemplate my sufferings, see the victim which sin demands. It is only the blood of a God, which can efface the smallest crime.

The Sinner.—O my God, my astonishment is such, that I cannot express, nor can I develope the sentiments of my heart. Can it be, that the smallest sin requires the blood of a God in atonement? This is a truth which I have often heard, but on which I have never seriously reflected. What a frightful monster is sin! Alas! that which I have hitherto regarded with indifference, as play and sport—that in which I delighted, is so dreadful. How incomprehensible the blindness of man; but, above all others, how great has been my blindness and my insensibility.

Jesus Christ.—This is not all, my son: judge of the malice which sin contains, by the effect which it produces on my Heart; enter into this adorable Heart; contemplate the consternation, the mortal anguish, the agony wherein it is immersed in the Garden of Olives, which appears evident in a sweat of blood; such are the sentiments of my Heart on the cross. Do not imagine that my torments are the real cause; on the contrary, I have desired and have sought those torments. The true cause of this agony is the sight of all the horrors contained in sin: it is the weight of sin that inundates, that oppresses me.

The Sinner.—O sin, thou dost agitate, thou dost alarm and oppress the Heart of God!

O infinite abyss of malice! O hateful abomination! I detest thee, I abhor thee, I renounce thee for ever. Unhappy and wretched have I been, to have so often yielded to thee; unhappy, to have so often opened my heart to thee.

SEQUEL TO THE SAME COLLOQUY.

The Sinner.—My divine Saviour, how shall I express the sentiments of my heart, in reflecting on the truths thou hast, in thy bounty, been pleased to reveal to me. I now perceive that there is no punishment, however great, which sin has not merited; since hell, and a thousand hells, are nothing, in comparison to the shedding of one drop of thy blood: but into what a state am I plunged by these reflections. Alas! I feel that I have been guilty of the most enormous crimes, and I am overwhelmed, not by one single sin, but by the immense weight of an infinite multitude of sins, more innumerable than the hairs of my head. If one single sin be so frightful, and has merited such dreadful punishments, what have I not deserved? Alas! to whom shall I have recourse? I am agitated by terror and consternation; I have rendered myself undeserving of thy compassion. Shall I dare to raise mine eyes towards thee? O! my God, wilt thou leave me in this wretched state! I have deserved it more than I can conceive or express; but, Oh! can thine adorable Heart resolve to see me perish?

Jesus Christ.—Enter, sinner, enter into this divine Heart, which is open to receive thee. It is the only asylum which thou canst find; enter into this furnace of love, and may the fire with which it is inflamed, penetrate and purify thee. O my son, canst thou be ignorant of the love with which I burn for thee! What is it that has obliged me to descend from the throne of my glory, to plunge myself into all the miseries of thy humanity? What is it that has obliged me to spend my life in labours and contradictions? What is it that has obliged me to die, surrounded by the most indignant opprobrium, and enduring the most excruciating torments. Sinner, I have loved thee; I have had compassion on the excess of miseries into which thou hast incessantly plunged thyself still deeper; I wished to screen thee from the vengeance of God; and to effect that, I have drawn it on myself! My love speaks by as many mouths as their are wounds on my body. Is it possible that thou canst be deaf to their voice, or that thou wilt not be moved by them? Thy miseries afflict me more than all the torments that I endure; I forget myself in my most extreme anguish, to remember only thee. 'Oh Father!' I exclaim, 'forgive them, for they know not what they do:' it is of all sinners that I speak; it is of them who were really my executioners: it is for thee, in particular, that I addressed this prayer to my Father. In the midst of the sorrows of death an ardent thirst devours me, and compels me to cry out, 'I thirst.' Dost thou imagine that I design to speak only of bodily thirst? Ah! that is but a figure of the burning thirst which consumes my heart, and which inflamed it during the entire course of my life: it is a thirst for thy salvation. I still experience this thirst; until now thou hast given me to drink only gall and vinegar, My son, wilt thou not satisfy my thirst? shall not such love as mine have sufficient influence to induce thee to forsake thy evil ways, and to return to me? I extend mine arms for thee; I open my heart to secure thee from the miseries thou hast deserved; I shed my blood to wash thee from all the stains of sin; I die to snatch thee from eternal death.

The Sinner.—O Jesus, victim of my sins, and of thy love for me! what dost thou discover in this miserable sinner, to merit a love such as thine? Alas! I am but a worm of the earth, an atom, a nothing! I am a sink of iniquity, that is to say, of all that is odious, abominable, and calculated to sicken the heart;

thou dost love me notwithstanding, and with a love stronger than death. Divine Heart, who can fathom this abyss of thy charity? who could measure the length and the breadth, the height and the depth of this love. O love, which doth always burn, and is never consumed, thou dost triumph over the hardness of my heart. Ah, how have I so long resisted thee? What a prodigy of insensibility! What a prodigy of ingratitude! Alas! it was not sufficient for me to be insensible to a love such as thine, but, influenced by a fury which cannot be conceived, I have outraged my God, I have persecuted my Benefactor, I have crucified my Saviour.

Jesus Christ.—My son, thou canst not too frequently meditate on thy ingratitude, since the confusion and horror thus excited shall produce the remedy. To whom art thou indebted, that thou art not now burning in hell? What should have become of thee, if I had not had compassion on thee, and if I had not exercised an unlimited patience towards thee, in bearing thine outrages? Have my patience and kindness only merited accumulated outrages, and aggravated insults? My love for thee has impelled me to endure a cruel death. Contemplate my dolours, my son; behold my wounds, there is not one of them which thy hand has not inflicted. This is not a figure of speech. It is thy sins which have crucified

me on Mount Calvary; they are the cause of
my death; and although I have died for the
sins of all men, it is not less true, that thy
sins have crucified me; for I died for them,
as though they alone were to be atoned for;
and it is a fact, that had there not been any
others in the world, I should in the same
manner have decended from Heaven, and
have suffered death for thee alone. But hear
me, my son! it is not once thou hast caused
my death, but every time thou hast been
guilty of mortal sin during thy life; since,
in reality, the smallest mortal sin requires
my death as an atonement, and is more re-
pelling to my Heart, than all the torments
which I have suffered,—and I should willingly descend again from Heaven, if necessary,
and suffer anew all the torments of my passion, rather than see the smallest sin committed. Thou hast renewed my passion and my
death, thou hast crucified me, every time that
thou hast consented to sin, which has caused
my death, and which is more hateful to me
than death. Raise thine eyes, and contemplate at leisure thy work; it is thou who hast
disfigured this countenance, and covered it
with filth. It is thou who hast pressed the
crown of thorns into my head. It is thou
who hast torn my body, pierced my hands
and feet, drenched me with gall and vinegar;
and who, even after my death, hast pierced

my heart with a lance. Wouldst thou have had the barbarity to treat, as I have been treated, thy greatest enemy. Oh, what evil have I done, that thou shouldst use me thus? What is there that I should have done for my vine, that I have not done for it; Nevertheless it has repaid all my cares but with bitter fruits. I have exercised towards the sinner prodigies of kindness and of love, and he has corresponded with this treatment, but by prodigies of ingratitude and cruelty.

The Sinner.—My God, this is too much; I can no longer support thy reproaches; my heart is rent with sorrow and regret. Ah! who will give water to my head, and to my eyes a fountain of tears, to weep night and day for my excess and fury, against the most tender of all friends, the most amiable of all benefactors? I have a horror of myself! Confusion and anguish overwhelm me! O Jesus, I should not dare to raise mine eyes to thee, nor to pronounce thine aborable name. O goodness outraged! O love repaid but with the blackest ingratitude! O Jesus, betrayed and crucified by a miserable wretch, on whom thou hast never ceased to shower down thy benefits, I deliver up to thee this ungrateful heart, and I give it to thee for ever. Wilt thou, even now, receive it? wilt thou forget its ingratitude? Ah! that I could expire at thy feet in penitential love.

Jesus Christ.—It is enough, my son; my heart is satisfied; it demands but a sincere return. Thy sins are forgotten, or rather they are immerged in the abyss of my blood; they are consumed in the fire with which my heart burns. Approach, that I may give thee the kiss of peace: kiss these feet and hands, pierced for the love of thee; kiss this open side. What dost thou fear, my son? Enter and remain in this asylum; it is there that thou shalt find pardon and peace, consolation and joy, thy refuge and thy assurance, thy support and thy strength, thy perseverance and eternal salvation.

REFLECTIONS

On the means of persevering in our Conversion, and advancing in Virtue.

SECOND COLLOQUY.

Between Jesus Christ crucified and the Sinner.

The Sinner.—My adorable Master, I come again to thy feet; thou art my light, my salvation, and my life: speak! thy servant attends. May thy divine instructions penetrate my soul, enliven and animate it. My heart is ready, O my God, my heart is ready; it desires only to hear thee, and faithfully to correspond with that which thou shalt teach.

Jesus Christ.—My son, it is not sufficient to detest thy sins, nor even to have obtained the pardon of them; it is necessary to preserve and entertain the spirit of compunction and repentance. If I have forgoten thy disorders, thou oughtest not thyself to forget them? and the remembrance ought to be to thee a continual source of humility, bitterness and regret. A penitent who no longer remembers his sins, after having confessed them, ought greatly to fear that he is a penitent in name only: it was not thus that

David acted; he who had been assured by a prophet, that his sin was pardoned, and who, notwithstanding, never let a night pass without watering his bed with his tears. It was not thus that Peter, the head of my church, acted; he, whose continual tears had furrowed his cheek. It was not thus that Mary Magdalene, Mary of Egypt, and so many other sinners who have become great saints, conducted themselves. A true penitent is animated by the spirit of penance, and this spirit is manifest in his exterior conduct.

The Sinner.—O my God, teach me, I beseech thee, in what doth this spirit of penance consist, with which thou desirest that my heart should be penetrated?

Jesus Christ.—My son, this spirit has divers degrees, which thou mayest learn in the lives of my saints; but attend to those which are proportioned to thy weakness. In the first place, the remembrance of thy sins ought to fill thy heart with compassion, bitterness, and regret, as I have already said; and if thou art seriously penetrated with these sentiments, thou wilt love to entertain them, and be insensible to every thing else; then thou wilt feel disgust for the amusements and pleasures of the age, and for the company of worldlings; thou wilt feel the utmost indifference and contempt for their judgments and railleries, then human respect shall not influence thee. On the contrary, thy delight will be to come often to my feet, there to renew thy sorrow and thy good resolutions, to implore mercy, and incessantly to pray that I may purify thy soul more and more, and preserve thee from relapse; that I may strengthen thee, and enable thee to advance in virtue:—such is the first effect of the spirit of penance. The second is, to fly with horror even the shadow of sin, and all that might conduct thee to it; to watch incessantly, and to use every possible precaution, in order to avoid relapsing anew into a misfortune, similar to that under which thou hadst so long groaned. And this should be an additional motive to induce thee to fly the world, its pleasures, and all other occasions of sin; and to influence thee to the practice of piety and virtue: this will secure thee against a relapse.

Finally, the third effect of the spirit of penance consists, not only in accepting with submission, and executing with fidelity, all that an enlightened confessor shall judge necessary, in order to atone for thy past sins, whether with regard to God or thy neighbour; but likewise in bearing continually in thy heart, a holy hatred towards thyself, influenced by a desire of avenging the insulted majesty of God, and satisfying his justice; in combating and subjugating the inclinations of the flesh; and, if not sufficiently animated by a spirit of fervour, to seek for sufferings, contempt, and contradictions, in receiving, at least, whatever befall thee, as coming from God, and blessing his all-powerful hand which strikes thee. Behold the narrow way which conducts to life! behold the cross which thou must carry, if thou desirest to be my disciple.

The Sinner.—O my God, what a lesson dost thou teach me. Shall I dare to acknowledge what passes within me? Thy words seem hard to me; my heart is agitated and dejected. How can I renounce my pleasures, and experience no delight but in contradiction and restraint?

Jesus Christ.—What! my son, is it then difficult to forsake the false pleasures of the world, and to abide with me? Is it so severe to receive with resignation to my will, the pains of life which thou must inevitably suffer? Behold what I require! Can I exact less from a sinner? But it is Jesus crucified who speaks to thee; raise thine eyes to me, and afterwards complain if thou canst. Is all that I require of thee to be compared to my torments? Answer me, my son. Dost thou imagine thy sufferings greater than mine? Art thou the innocent? am I the guilty?

The Sinner.—Thy words confound me, my God! and I know not what to reply. Yes, it is just that the guilty should suffer. Alas! I have deserved to suffer during an eternity the torments of hell, and I ought now to be ingulphed in that frightful abyss; but, O God of goodness, wilt thou not have compassion on my weakness?—the very name of constraint and sufferings makes me tremble.

Jesus Christ.—Have confidence my son; he who has snatched thee from eternal torments, does not design thy destruction; he who has suffered for thee such cruel pains, cannot take pleasure in rendering thee unhappy. Confide in my goodness, and allow thyself to be conducted by thy sorrow. Devote thyself earnestly to repentance; carry the cross after me, and in it thou shalt find happiness. I have said in my Gospel: 'If any man will come after me, let him deny himself, and take up his cross and follow me.'—*Matt.* xvi. Dost thou not wish to follow me? What, my son! thou beholdest me scourged, crowned with thorns, watering the way of Calvary with my blood, sinking under the weight of my cross, or rather under the weight of thy sins; and wilt thou not be moved with compassion at beholding me in this state? wilt thou not assist me in carrying my cross? Oh! blush at beholding thyself so great a sinner, and yet so delicate; blush at beholding thy God undergo for thee, so dreadful a penance; blush in beholding in his train such multitudes of persons of every age, and sex, and rank, bearing the heaviest crosses; behold these kings and queens, who place their delight in the cross; behold these decrepid old men, who, notwithstanding their age, crucify their body, behold these tender children, who have never lost their baptismal innocence, and who walk courageously in the narrow way of penance. Blush then, O sinner, at thy delicacy, and excite thyself to adopt the same course. It is my grace which has inspired so many saints: it is my grace that shall support thee. But unhappy art thou, if thou wilt attend only to thy sloth and sensuality. Have I not said in my Gospel: 'But, except you do penance, you shall all likewise perish.' Woe then, to those penitents, who are so only in name; woe to those enemies of the cross; the penance which they will not perform in this world, shall be changed into an eternal penance.

The Sinner.—O my God, thy menaces terrify me, thy reproaches confound me; but thou dost at the same time re-animate and inspire me with fortitude and courage. Yes, my Saviour, I still hope that thou wilt support me, and grant me sufficient grace to accomplish faithfully what thou requirest of me; this I implore with all my heart, and I desire to unite myself to the many pious souls, who walk after thee in the narrow way of penance. But wilt thou pardon me, divine Jesus, if I dare once more to ask thee, why dost thou not, thou whose heart is so tender and so compassionate, why dost thou not grant an entire pardon to men? Why dost thou not spare them these constraints, these contradictions, and this penance? Couldst thou not conduct them to Heaven by a way less severe, harsh, and difficult?

Jesus Christ.—O my son, how great thy ignorance! how blind art thou in the mystery of the cross! The infinite mercy of my father has sent me on earth to save sinners, by the effusion of all my blood. The smallest drop of this blood would abundantly suffice to satisfy his justice, and to purchase for men infinite happiness. without leaving any thing to be done on their part. But he has deemed it more worthy of his wisdom, that the members should participate in the sufferings of the head, in order to glorify God in a similar manner. And that the merits of my sufferings should be applied but on this condition, he has decreed that the guilty should only receive pardon, by partaking of some portion, at least, of my suffering, and by tasting of that chalice which I have drank to the dregs. He has decreed that none shall enter Heaven, or participate in that eternal bliss which my blood has purchased for them, but those who merit it themselves by their exertions and fidelity. Sinner, is this too much to exact of thee? and wilt thou imagine God deficient in goodness, for having changed eternal pains, which thou hast so often deserved, for a penance so trivial and so short; in granting an immense and an eternal weight of glory, for the labour of a few moments? But open thine eyes, my son, and learn the inestimable advantages that are contained in penance. Dost thou suppose that I have made choice of the cross, only to suffer thereon myself, to satisfy for thy offences, and procure thy happiness? Thou art grossly deceived. I have not only merited all good by my cross, but it is in it that all good is contained: my desire is, that my members may carry it, and be fastened to it with me, and that in this participation, sinners may find security and pardon; the weak, strength; the just perfection; and the Saints, perseverance and salvation.

CONTINUATION OF THE SAME COLLOQUY.

The Sinner.—I adore thee, O Eternal Wisdom, whose depth is impenetrable to human comprehension; I thank thee with all the powers of my soul, O infinite Goodness, who hast ordained that all good should be found, in that from which our blindness induces us to fly, as if containing all evil. O my divine Saviour, continue to instruct me, and dispel my darkness; discover to me the treasures that are to be found in the cross.

Jesus Christ.—Hear, then, with attention. From the moment that thou hast sinned mortally, thou art certain of having deserved hell. And how couldst thou, thus guilty, obtain the pardon of thy sins? God has promised it to penitent sinners, through my merits; but these promises suppose a true contrition, and an entire change of heart. Now canst thou search the secret recesses of thy heart, so as to develope its motives? No person can be conscious whether he is deserving of love or of hatred: and is not this uncertainty one of the bitterest ingredients of life? God has, nevertheless, instituted a means of being morally assured of having obtained the pardon of thy sins, and that is, the spirit of penance: it is of this cross I speak, and when borne with perseverance, it is a certain mark of true repentance; and when one is truly penitent, he has certainly recovered the grace of God. With what efforts shouldst thou not endeavour to obtain this sweet assurance?

But had I sent to thee a prophet, as to David, to assure thee of the pardon of thy sins; or had I given thee this assurance from my own lips, as to Magdalene; what would that avail thee, if thou shouldst relapse into thy former state? And how great danger dost thou not run of thus relapsing? O! do but observe the enemies that surround thee; the demons, like roaring lions, are ever ready to devour thee; and who can conceive the extent of their fury, their artifices, their indefatigable activity. The world fascinates and captivates thee by its pleasures and charms, by its imposing maxims, by the universal example of its admirers, by its attractions and complacencies, by its ridicule and contempt; this deceitful world reunites all that can seduce and ensnare, all that can inflame the passions, and all that can enervate reason and faith. But especially, dost thou comprehend the depth of iniquity contained in thine own heart? Suppose thou hadst no other enemy to contend with, than thine own flexibility and propensity to evil; oughtest not thou to tremble? Even those who have retained their baptismal innocence, are not divested of this fatal inclination, this sad result of the sin of their first father. But if this be true with regard to innocent souls, what must be the state of a sinner, who has delighted in vice, and who has daily augmented the influence of this unhappy propensity; whose criminal and inveterate habits have formed in him a second nature, a thousand times more inclined to evil than the first? Thou seest, then, my son, the necessity of retiring from the world, and from all that can excite the passions; thine evil inclinations must be combated, and all self-love annihilated: cherish in thy heart sentiments of piety; do violence to thyself; have continual recourse to me, since all exertions are vain without my assistance: this is that spirit of penance to which I call thee. Dost thou not see the necessity and the advantages of it?—Art thou aware of the treasures which are contained in my cross? By the cross thou canst evade the snares of thine enemies; by the cross thou art fortified and enabled to resist their attacks: the greater thy love for the cross, the more art thou strengthened in virtue, and secured against all future relapses; but experience suffices to show, that those who are not influenced by this spirit of penance, do not long continue in my grace, even though they had perfectly attained to it.

The Sinner.—O my God, I perceive that this separation from the pleasures of the world, these efforts and these continual combats, are absolutely necessary to all, and that they are much more so to sinners such as I have been. How delightful is repentance to the true penitent, in contemplating these truths. Continue, my divine Master, continue to instruct thy servant.

Jesus Christ.—It is irrevocably fixed in the decrees of God, that the sinner must do penance either in this world or in the next; with this difference, that in this world God is satisfied with a very small share of sufferings; whereas, in the other he exacts a most dreadful penance, not alone from the reprobate, who shall be eternally his enemies, but likewise from those who have died in his grace without having entirely expiated their sins. Seriously reflect on that which I require of thee; compare all that I exact,—that is to say, the relinquishing of some amusements—a momentary violence to thyself—to the torments of the other life. If thou wert condemned to be burned alive, what sacrifice wouldst thou not make, to avoid this punishment? If, in order to escape from the hands of the executioner, it was necessary for thee to fly into a desert, wouldst thou for one moment hesitate? Thou canst, my son, without flying into a desert, by entertaining in thy present state the spirit of penance, avoid the dreadful punishments of the other life; in consideration of which, those of this world might be considered as delights. The sacrifice of a dangerous amusement, the exertion over thyself for one quarter of an hour by an application of thy mind to prayer may spare thee, perhaps a month, perhaps a year, of the terrible pains of purgatory. Meditate seriously on this advantage.

But this is not all: not only by this privation, by this trifling self-denial, dost thou satisfy the justice of God, but thou wilt continually draw on thyself new graces, which are so necessary to thee in this life; and thou wilt acquire new degrees of merit and of glory in Heaven.

There is not an instant in which a penitent soul may not enrich her crown and advance in virtue. Admire the goodness of thy God, who converts to thy greatest happiness all that he exacts from thee, even the pains which are the punishment of thy sins.

The Sinner.—Be thou for ever blessed, O infinite Goodness, who art so wonderfully displayed in the exercise of thy justice, as to transform it into effects of thy mercy: but is this all, my divine Saviour? are there no other advantages to be derived from the cross.?

Jesus Christ.—My son, thou art as yet unacquainted with its most precious effect; that which crowns all the others, and without which they would be useless.

Man has not, while in this world, an absolute certainty of being in the grace of God. But, supposing that he is so, it is very uncertain if he will persevere therein. The cedars of Lebanon, have they not fallen? Have we not seen those fall, who had led the purest and holiest of lives? Have we not seen martyrs fall, after suffering the most excruciating torments, and just on the point of receiving their crown? And nevertheless, it is written: "But he that shall persevere to the end, he shall be saved."—*Matt.* xxiv. 13. Oh! what serious consideration do these truths merit! O! what vigilance should this uncertainty excite! what precaution! what prayers! Is not the least degree of assurance which could be procured thereon, of infinite value! Hear me, then, my son: the true mark of the predestinate, is their resemblance to me, who am their chief; and the grand feature of this resemblance is, love and devotion to the cross. I have passed my life on the cross; I have said to my disciples, "Ought not Christ to have suffered these things, and so to enter into his glory;" *Luke,* xxiv. 26. and my apostle has said, "They that are Christ's, have crucified their flesh, with the vices and concupiscences." *Gal.* v. 24. Thus, it is penance and the cross which are the marks of the elect; it is in them that are found the greatest assurance that one can have of final perseverance, and even the sole means of persevering.

The Sinner.—O my God! I am in admiration, in the contemplation of the advantages which thou discoverest to me in repentance! O! how true it is, that thou hast concealed in thy cross, thy most precious treasures. Amiable penance! precious cross, of my Saviour! I devote myself to thee. O how odious and contemptible are all worldly pleasures, in comparison with these maxims, when we reflect on these truths. Unhappy are you, blind worldlings! you seek in all things your gratification; you plunge into pleasures; you offer no restraint to your passions; you have no cross to carry: such are the characters of your reprobation.

Jesus Christ.—It is true, my son, the continual pursuit of pleasures, the avoiding all mortification, and of all that can put a restraint on the evil propensities of nature, are marks of reprobation; but thou art wonderfully deceived, to imagine that worldlings have no cross to carry, no violence, no opposition, no restraint to offer to their nature. They do not carry my cross; they do not walk in my train; but they carry the cross of the demon, a thousand times more oppressive than mine. Are they secured from infirmities, from sickness and pains? Are they secure from, what is termed, reverse of fortune? Do they not encounter in their domestic concerns, and even in the bosom of their families, the most cutting chagrins? These different crosses are common alike to them and to my friends, but with this essential difference, that the peace which reigns in the hearts of my followers, their love and resignation to my will, cause them to experience charms and delights in crosses the rudest and most severe; while, on the contrary, the remorse of conscience, the agitation of the passions, fury, rage, inpatience, and despair, render these same crosses insupportable to the wicked. Even supposing they should be exempt from these reverses, are not their contending passions most cruel executioners, exclusive of temporal misfortunes, which are so often the result of them? Ambition, hatred, voluptuousness, avarice, and a thousand other passions in contact with each other, rend that heart, which all cannot satisfy. But the cross which is the most insupportable is, that frightful void, the *ennui* and disgust which they find in all those objects which they have sought with so much ardour; that agitation, and the remorse of a conscience, terrified by its disorders and reproaches, and by the alarming results which it cannot refrain from apprehending. "We wearied ourselves in the way of iniquity and destruction," say the reproved, in the Book of Wisdom; "and we have walked through hard ways; but the way of the Lord we have not known,"—chap. v. 7. It is thus that the broad way which conducts to perdition, becomes harsh and painful; while the narrow way to which I invite, becomes sweet and delightful. It is thus that those who fly from the cross, are oppressed with an insupportable cross, the extreme anguish of which begins their hell, even in this world! whereas, my friends experience sweetness and delights in the cross which I impose on them, in the penance to which I call them.

The Sinner.—Yes, Lord, this life is truly a life of crosses; and when we desire to escape from thine, we encounter those which are much more oppressive. O, how deceitful are the world and the devil, in their promises of rendering us happy, by satisfying all our passions! Oh, how unhappy are those who fly the rigours of the cross, since they carry it in spite of themselves, without participatig in its inestimable advantages; but what I cannot comprehend is, that which thou hast added; that the penance and the crosses of thy friends, accompanied with sweetness and delights. Is it then so sweet to relinquish all pleasure, to oppose our inclinations, and to offer continual violence to our self-love?

Jesus Christ.—My son, that is a mystery of my bountiful providence, which can only be comprehended by experience. "O taste, and see that the Lord is sweet," (*Ps.* xxxiii. 9.) said my prophet. It is necessary to taste, in order to see; but until thou hast experience, faith ought to assure thee of it. Hast thou never read in my Gospel, these words: "Take up my yoke, and you shall find rest to your soul: for my yoke is sweet; my burthen is light."—*Matt.* xi. 29, 30. This is the peace of God, which surpasseth all understanding; this is the unction of my grace; these are the delights of my love, which render my cross so light and so sweet. And if I sometimes deem it essential to press my hand heavy on my friends, and even to deprive them of that sentiment of interior sweetness, I fortify them, I secretly support them, I carry their cross with them, and I even carry themselves, without their perceiving it. Those souls who give themselves but partially to penance, experience these delights but partially; but those generous souls who give themselves to me without reserve, discover therein, delights truly celestial. Interrogate them, my son; thou shalt not find one, who would wish to change his state with that of the happiest of worldlings. But rather make trial of it thyself; take up my yoke, carry my burthen. Enter courageously on the narrow way to which I call thee; the first steps may appear to thee rough, but scarcely shalt thou have passed them, when thou shalt find repose for thy soul, such as I have promised thee; thou wilt experience more happiness in weeping over thy sins at my feet, than thou hast ever enjoyed in the pleasures of the world, or in the satisfying of all thy passions.

APPENDIX.

―:o:―

OF INDULGENCES.

An Indulgence is a relaxation or remission of the debt of temporal punishment, which remains due to the Divine Justice for sin, after the sin itself, and the eternal punishment have been remitted by the sacrament of penance. Hence it follows, that an indulgence does not mean a pardon for sins, either mortal or venial, but supposes all mortal sins remitted by the sacrament of penance, or by perfect contrition : an indulgence, then, not only regards *the remission of the temporal punishments due to God*, but also of *the ecclesiastical penances enjoined by the Church.* The Council of Trent (1) lays down three principles concerning indulgences.—1. That the power to grant them was left by Christ in the Church. 2. That the Church made use of this power from the earliest ages. 3. That the use of them is most wholesome to christian people, and, consequently, that it should be retained.

The power of the Church to grant indulgences is grounded on the scriptures. Christ declares to his apostles : "Whatsoever you shall loose upon earth, shall be loosed in Heaven." He tells St. Peter, "I will give to thee the keys of the kingdom of Heaven, and whatsoever thou shalt loose upon earth, shall be loosed in Heaven." (2) The Church received here, in the person of the Apostles, the power to absolve penitent sinners. She received, consequently, the power to remit them the whole or a part of the punishment due to their sins. When, therefore, the Church makes use of this power, she grants indulgences. St. Paul exercised this power, though not one of the twelve apostles present when our Saviour gave them this power; for, after he excommunicated and gave over to Satan the incestuous Corinthian, (3) this sinner underwent the punishment imposed on him, with such great repentance and vehement sorrow, that the apostle granted him an indulgence, by remitting the rest of the punishment which he had enjoined him. And therefore, writing to the Corinthians, (4) he tells them; "that if he had forgiven any thing, it was for their sakes he had done it, in the person of Christ."

The bishops exercised this power from the earliest ages, as appears from Tertullian in the second, and St. Cyprian in the third century; (5) for, at the request of the martyrs and confessors, imprisoned or condemned to the mines during the persecutions, the prelates granted indulgences to sinners; in consequence of which they were dispensed from the remainder, or from a part of the canonical penance, which had been prescribed to them, according to the usage which then prevailed in the Church. The penance imposed for perjury was, to fast forty days on bread and water, and seven years' penance besides; nor were the delinquents to be ever exempted from penance. If any one swore by Heaven, or by any other creature, he was obliged to perform fifteen days penance, &c. Whoever struck his neighbour, even without hurting him, three days on bread and water. The use of indulgences is most wholesome to all the faithful, as they were instituted for the remission of the temporal punishments due to their sins, after the sins themselves, as to the guilt and eternal punishment, had been remitted by the sacrament of penance, or by perfect contrition.

The source of the benefits which the faithful receive by indulgences, proceeds from the merits and satisfactions of Christ and his Saints; these satisfactions are commonly called the *Treasure of the Church*. The merits and satisfactions of Christ are superabundant, and of infinite value; because, one drop of his blood, (much more the whole, which was shed for us on the cross,) by reason of its union with the divine nature, would have been sufficient to redeem the world. And as the merits and satisfactions of the Saints derive their value from Christ, and through him are accepted by the Father, so by the communion which all the members of Christ's mystical body have one with another, these merits and satisfactions are applicable to the faithful on earth. In consequence, then, of that communion, all those who have a lively faith, animated by charity, or who strive to obtain it by a sincere conversion, may partake of these spiritual riches.

There are two kinds of indulgences, plenary or general, and partial indulgences. A plenary indulgence is a full and entire remission of all that remains to be discharged, of the canonical penance which might have been imposed on us for our sins; and, consequently, a remission of the temporal punishment which, in the sight of God, corresponds to the canonical penance the sinner owes to God, and which he must suffer in this life, or the next, for the entire expiation of his sins. The most celebrated of all indulgences is the *Jubilee*, so called from that of the old law, which decreed every fiftieth year a general release and discharge from debts and bondage, and a reinstating of every man in his former possessions. (6) This indulgence or jubilee was established by Boniface VIII. in 1300, and he ordered it should take place every hundredth year; Clement VI. determined it to the fiftieth year; and, finally, Sixtus IV. fixed it to the twenty-fifth year, which has continued down to the present. Besides the jubilees granted at the end of every twenty-fifth year, the popes sometimes grant extraordinary ones, namely, on their exaltation to St. Peter's chair, or on some other important occasions.

By a partial indulgence is understood a limited relaxation of a certain time, as of one, seven, or more years of canonical penance, which might be, as in the early ages, imposed on us, and which should be complied with, if we followed, at present, the penitential canons of the primitive Church.

As to *indulgences* for the *dead*, they are not granted by way of *absolution*, since the pastors of the Church have not that jurisdiction over the dead; but indulgences are only available by way of *suffrage*, or spiritual succour, out of the treasure of the Church, to the souls of the faithful departed.

The authority to grant indulgences belongeth to those to whom Christ gave the power of loosing and binding, that is, to the heads of the Church, the successors of the apostles. The pope, as vicar of Christ upon earth, and head of the Catholic Church, can grant plenary or particular indulgences, or by way of jubilee, to the whole Church. The bishops have also the power to grant indulgences in their own dioceses, but indulgences of forty days only, except when they dedicate and consecrate a church; for they may, in such cases, grant a year's indulgence.

To receive the effect of indulgences, certain dispositions are requisite. The first is, that we must be in the state of grace; for the remission of the canonical punishment presupposes the pardon of sin. So the indulgence avails nothing to those who are not truly converted, and who entertain a secret attachment to sin. Besides, the Church, as being the depository of indulgences, grants them but on condition of true and sincere repentance; because, animated by the spirit of God, she cannot violate the general law, namely, that whoever has committed any mortal sin, must do penance for the same, nor can he be dispensed from it by any authority whatever.—Hence it follows, that penance is a necessary preparation for gaining indulgences.

The second disposition is, to approach the sacrament of penance with a sincere sorrow for sin, and to receive the holy communion. The third disposition is, to perform faithfully whatever the Church ordains and prescribes for gaining indulgences, as, to fast, give alms, visit the chapels, and to pray for the exaltation of the Catholic Church, the extirpation of error, the union of christian princes, and the peace and safety of their people. Such are the conditions necessary to gain indulgences, and such the harmless and pious doctrine of the Catholic Church, on these *commutations* of the ancient canonical penances, which have been imputed to her as so great a crime. They have been maliciously called new inventions by modern sectaries; but we maintain it is downright calumny to style the use of indulgences a new and mere human invention. We have proved, that this doctrine and practice are coeval with the apostolic ages, grounded on Scripture, and sanctioned by the example of St. Paul and the early fathers; nor can we conceive why, or in what respect, works of piety, charity, mortification, and penance, done through a desire to obtain pardon of sin, can be deemed superstitious. Our adversaries have often been told, but in vain, that an indulgence is a change or commutation of the ancient penances, granted in consideration of other good works, and to induce us to put these good works in practice; yet still they remain attached to their prejudice and wonted bigotry. If we told them, that their solemn fasts, commanded by supreme authority, were nothing but worldly pomp, hypocrisy, and superstition, what reply could they make? It cannot be however denied, that indulgences, or a commutation of penances, form part of the canon-law of the Church of England. "*Ecclesiastical penance* and *absolution* are also used in the discipline of the Church of England," says Godolphin, (7) "which doth affect the body of the penitent, by which he is oblige to give a public satisfaction to the *Church* for the scandal he hath given, by evil example. In the case of incontinency, the sinner is usually enjoined to do a public penance in the cathedral or some public market, barelegged and bareheaded, in a white sheet, and to make an open confession of his crime, in a prescribed form of words. Yet *these censures* may be *totally altered* by a *commutation of penance*," (or indulgence,) "*a sum of money* to be accepted in satisfaction of *public penance*. The best way for satisfaction," continues the law, "is for the ordinary or bishop to require *a sum of money* before he decrees *absolution.*"

The civil law of the British empire grants also indulgences; for how often do we not read, that through the clemency of the Sovereign, the crimes of robbery, rebellion, and sometimes of murder, are changed into transportation for life, or for a certain number of years, which, to all intents and purposes, is *an indulgence,* or *a commutation of temporal punishment.*

Luther declaimed against the abuse of indulgences, and next against the doctrine itself; yet he made no scruple to grant himself an ample indulgence, by taking up with a professed nun, notwithstanding their mutual vows of chastity and solemn engagements to God. He extended the same indulgence to his disciples, who consisted of apostate priests and monks, and, lastly, granted a famous indulgence to the Landgrave of Hesse, in 1533, to have two wives at the same time! Never did Rome, or the bishops in communion with her, grant such indulgences.

We now submit to the public, whether Luther's opinion concerning indulgences, which excluded fasting, prayer, penance, mortification, &c., be more conformable to the scriptures and fathers, than the foregoing doctrine of the Catholic Church.

INDULGENCES,

Which may be obtained by the Members of the Society of the most

SACRED HEART OF JESUS.

1st. A plenary indulgence on the day on which one is enrolled in the society.

2nd. A plenary indulgence in the feast of the most Sacred Heart, or on the Sunday following.

3rd. A plenary indulgence on Friday in the first week of every month.

4th. Another plenary indulgence once in every month, on whatever day each member shall make choice of.

5th. A plenary indulgence at the hour of death, for all members of the Society, who, being truly penitent, shall invoke, in their hearts at least, if not able to pronounce with their lips, the most holy name, 'Jesus.'

6th. An indulgence of seven years and as many days, on the four Sundays immediately preceding the feast of the most Sacred Heart.

7th. Another indulgence of sixty days, for any religious work which shall be performed on the day, in the spirit of devotion.

[*Note.*—The preceding indulgences are applicable also to the souls in Purgatory, and may be obtained by all the members of the society, without the obligation of visiting the chapel, provided the following enjoined work be performed; viz. that you say devoutly every day the Lord's Prayer, the Angelical Salutation, the Apostles' Creed in veneration of the most Sacred Heart of Jesus, and that you add the following pious aspiration:—*Sweet Heart of Jesus, Oh! make me love thee always more.*]

8th. All the members who visit the church of their society on the days for which different stations are appointed in the Roman Missal, and shall pour forth their prayers according to the intention of the Sovereign Pontiff, shall obtain the same indulgences as if they performed the stations; they are thus distributed:

LENT.

On Ash Wednesday, and on the fourth Sunday, an indulgence of fifteen years and as many forty days.

On Palm Sunday, an indulgence of twenty-five years and as many forty days.

On Holy Thursday, a plenary indulgence.

On Good Friday and Holy Saturday, an indulgence of thirty years and as many forty days.

PASCHAL TIME.

On Easter Sunday, a plenary indulgence.

On the two festivals immediately following, and during the whole octave, (till Low Sunday,) every day, an indulgence of thirty years and as many forty days.

On Ascension day, a plenary indulgence.

On Saturday before Whitsunday, an indulgence of ten years and as many forty days.

On Whitsunday, and during the whole octave, till Saturday included, every day, an indulgence of thirty years and as many forty days.

ADVENT.

On the first, second, and fourth Sundays, an indulgence of ten years and as many forty days.

On the third Sunday, an indulgence of fifteen years and as many forty days.

NATIVITY.

On the vigil, on the night, and at the Mass of the morning, an indulgence of fifteen years and as many forty days.

On the day of the Nativity, a plenary indulgence.

On the three following festivals,—the Circumcision, the Epiphany, and the Sundays, Septuagesima, Sexagesima, and Quinquagesima, an indulgence of thirty years and as many forty days.

On the three Ember days, an indulgence of ten years and as many forty days.

9th. A plenary indulgence on the feasts of the Conception, Nativity, Annunciation, Purification, and Assumption of the B. V. M. and also on the solemn feast of all Saints, and the day following. (the commemoration of All Souls,) and on the fests of St. Joseph, St. Peter, and St. Paul, and St. John the Evangelist; provided, that having confessed and received the holy Eucharist, they visit the chapel of their society.

10th. An indulgence of seven years and as many forty days on the other feasts of the Blessed Virgin and of the apostles, p ovided also, that the aforesaid chapel be visited.

[*Note.*—The above-mentioned indulgences, Nos. 8, 9, 10, in order to obtain which, the chapel should be visited, may (by special privilege) be obtained by such of the members as are prevented by sickness or otherwise from visiting the chapel, provided they perform some religious work their confessor shall appoint.]

11th. An indulgence of seven years and as many forty days, on every day of the nine days preceding the feast of the most Sacred Heart, which is celebrated on the Friday after the octave of Corpus Christi, provided, that some chapel or public oratory where the feast is celebrated be visited, and prayers be offered to God, according to the intention of the Sovereign Pontiff.

12th. A plenary indulgence on the six Sundays, or the six week-days preceding the feast of the most Sacred Heart, provided, that after having been at confession, they receive the most holy Eucharist, and on every day of the six Sundays and six week-days they piously visit some chapel or public oratory where the feast is celebrated, and offer up prayers to God according to the intention of the Sovereign Pontiff.

[*Note.*—The indulgences under 11 and 12, may also be obtained by those who are prevented from visiting the chapel, provided they perform (as above) some pious work enjoined by their confessor.]

———:o:———

The indulgences of the Sacred Heart of Jesus are to be obtained by complying with the foregoing conditions; and to become a member of the society, nothing more is required, than that the name of the individual be inscribed in the register kept open by such as have the permission from the Prior of the Congregation of the secular priests of St. Paul, of the Church of the Blessed Virgin Mary *ad Pineam*, Rome.

Form of being enrolled in the Society of the Sacred Heart.

The more to increase the glory of Jesus, pierced for us on the cross, and that of his divine Heart, burning in the most holy sacrament of the Eucharist with the utmost love for us, and, at the same time, to compensate the insults which he meets with even in this sacrament of his love, I voluntarily join those already enrolled in this holy Society; that I also may become partaker of the holy indulgences with which the Society is enriched, and every good work which is performed in it, for either the expiation of personal transgressions, or the relief of the souls of the Faithful Departed, or that yet shall have to abide the torture of expiatory flames.—Oh! sweetest Jesus, secure in the inmost recesses of thy Heart, all the members of this holy Society, that, fulfilling all the commands of thy sovereign law, and discharging faithfully the duties of their several conditions, their hearts may burn every day more fervently with the fire of thy love. *Amen.*

A Prayer to be said daily by those who carry about them an Agnus Dei.

An *Agnus Dei* (so called from the image of the Lamb of God impressed on the face of it) is made of virgin wax, balsam and chrism, blessed according to the form prescribed in the Roman Ritual. The spiritual efficacy or virtue of it, is gathered from the prayers which the church makes use of in the blessing of it. The pope consecrates the *Agnus Dei* the first year of his pontificate, and afterwards every seventh year, on the Saturday before Low Sunday, with many solemn ceremonies and devout prayers.—*Fran. Dost. Lib. 4. Christ. Instit.* c. 12]

O my Lord Jesus Christ, the true Lamb that takest away the sins of the world! by thy mercy, which is infinite, pardon my iniquities, and by thy sacred passion preserve me this day from all sin and evil, I carry about me this holy *Agnus* in thy honour, as a preservative against my own weakness, and as an incentive to the practice of that meekness, humility, and innocence, which thou hast taught. I offer myself up to thee as an entire oblation, and in memory of that sacrifice of love thou offeredst for me on the cross, and in satisfaction for my sins. Accept, O my God, the oblation I make, and may it be agreeable to thee in the odour of sweetness. Amen.

CONTENTS.

——:o:——

FIRST PART.

Chap. I.—The Origin and Progress of the Devotion to the Sacred Heart of Jesus,   1

Chap. II.—The Excellence and Solidity of this Devotion; its object and end.   4

Chap. III.—The immense Treasures contained in the Sacred Heart of Jesus.   7

Chap. IV.—Consoling and remarkable Words of the Blessed Marguerite Marie, speaking of the Devotion of the Sacred Heart, ... 10

Chap. V.—The Practice of the Devotion to the Sacred Heart,—for every Year, ... 13
Practice for every Month, ... 14
Practice for every Week, ... 14
Practice for every Day and for every Occasion, 15

Chap. VI.—Some particular Devotions in honour of the Sacred Heart, ... 25

SECOND PART.

Exercises and Prayers in honour of the most Sacred Heart of Jesus.

A Prayer for the Morning, ... 29
A Prayer for the Evening, ... 30
A Prayer to offer our Actions to the Sacred Heart, 31
An Act of Atonement to the Sacred Heart, ... 31
An Act of Consecration to the Sacred Heart, ... 33
Another Act of Consecration to the adorable Heart, 35
An Act of Consecration for Religious Persons, ... 36
An Exercise of Praise and Adoration, in honour of the Sacred Heart, ... 38
An Exercise of Love, ... 39
An Exercise of Confidence, ... 41

CONTENTS.

Aspirations to the Sacred Heart,	43
Pious Affections to the Heart of Jesus—*in Latin*,	46
Ditto, *translated in English*,	49
Invocations to the Sacred Heart for every hour of the day,	52
Beads of the Sacred Heart,	54
Affectionate Sentiments of Saint Gertrude to the Sacred Heart,	55
Extracts from passages of the Life of Saint Gertrude, being an Exercise to honour the most Holy Trinity through the Sacred Heart of Jesus	56
A Prayer to implore a change of Heart,	61
A Prayer for a happy Death,	63
A Prayer, containing short Sentiments and Ejaculations, for a happy Death,	67
Aspirations, in form of a Litany, for a happy Death,	69
A Prayer to offer our sufferings to the Sacred Heart,	71
A Prayer to obtain the Conversion of hearts,	73
A Prayer for the Confraternity of the Sacred Heart,	74
A Prayer for the Souls in Purgatory,	75

Exercises for the Feast of the Sacred Heart of Jesus.

A Novena to the Sacred Heart,	76
A Meditation for the Feast of the Sacred Heart of Jesus, divided into three points,	81
Conversation of our Lord Jesus Christ with a Disciple, on these words:—"My Son, give me thy Heart,"	97
Five Visits for the Festival of the Sacred Heart,	104
An Act of Atonement, to be repeated aloud and in common, on the Festival of the Sacred Heart,	106
Invitation to give ourselves up in spirit to the Sacred Heart of Jesus,	108

Exercises for the Holy Sacrifice of the Mass.

FIRST EXERCISE.—To unite ourselves to the Sacred Heart, during the Holy Sacrifice of the Mass,	109
SECOND EXERCISE.—	123

CONTENTS.

Exercises for Confession.

A Prayer to beg the knowledge of our Sins,	154
A Prayer to the most Holy Virgin, to our Angel-Guardian, and Patron Saints,	155
Reflections calculated to excite us to Contrition,	156
An Act of Contrition,	161
Another Act of Contrition,	166
Acts of Thanksgiving after Confession,	167
A Prayer to offer our Penance to God,	168
An invitation to make frequent Acts of Contrition,	169
Devout Aspirations of a contrite and humble heart,	170
The Prayer of a penitent soul to the Sacred Heart,	172
Sentiments of a penitent heart at the foot of the Cross,	174
Affecting Reflections on the Cross of our Lord Jesus Christ,	177

Exercises for Communion.

REMOTE PREPARATION.—For the evening preceding the day you are to communicate,	182
Affecting Sentiments extracted from the Holy Scriptures, to dispose yourself for Communion,	184
Devout Communications with our Lord, on giving himself to us in the Holy Communion,	185
Aspirations of a soul that ardently desires to communicate,	189
An Act to offer up the Communion,	191
IMMEDIATE PREPARATION.—Acts and Prayers for Mass before Communion,	193
Acts and Prayers after Communion,	202
A Prayer to the Blessed Virgin, our Angel Guardian, and Patron Saints, after Communion,	218
An Act of Reparation to the Sacred Heart of Jesus after Communion,	219
Affecting Sentiments taken from the Holy Scriptures, which may be used after Communion,	221
A Consecration of perfect Love to our Lord Jesus Christ,	222

CONTENTS.

Exercises for Visiting the most Holy Sacrament.

FIRST EXERCISE.—Divided into seven parts, ... 225
SECOND EXERCISE.—Taken from the seven petitions of the Lord's Prayer, ... 239

The Holy Exercise of the Love of God.

An Invitation to the frequent use of Acts of the Love of God, in imitation of the Sacred Heart of Jesus, 245
A Prayer to obtain the Love of God, ... 257
Considerations on the Love of God, ... 258
Acts of the Love of God, ... 266
An Abridgment of the Acts of the Love of God, 271
Aspirations by way of Prayer, to implore the Divine Love from the Holy Ghost, ... 272

———:o:———

The PROPER MASS for the FEAST of the Sacred Heart, ... 275
Acts of Adoration to the Sacred Heart to be practised during the NOVENA, and on other occasions, 308
An Act of Reparation, to the Sacred Heart, 312
The Litany of the Sacred Heart, ... 315
An Act of Dedication to the Sacred Heart, ... 317
The Daily Prayers for the Associates of the Sacred Heart, ... 318
The LITTLE OFFICE of the Sacred Heart, ... 319
Reflections, calculated to excite in the soul gratitude and love towards the Sacred Heart, in a series of colloquies between Jesus Christ and the Sinner, 329
Reflections on the means of persevering in our conversion, and advancing in virtue. 344

———:o:———

APPENDIX.—On Indulgences, ... 362
Indulgences to be obtained by Members of the Society of the Sacred Heart, ... 368
Form of being enrolled a Member, ... 371
A Prayer to be daily said by those who carry about them an *Agnus Dei*, ... 372